Great Ashes Moments

Great Ashes Moments

Ken Piesse

The Five Mile Press

The Five Mile Press Pty Ltd
1 Centre Road, Scoresby
Victoria 3179 Australia
www.fivemile.com.au

Part of the Bonnier Publishing Group
www.bonnierpublishing.com

Printed in Australia at Griffin Press.
Only wood grown from sustainable regrowth forests is used in
the manufacture of paper found in this book.

Design and typesetting by Shaun Jury

Cover illustrations (front): Len Hutton, Greg &
Ian Chappell, Shane Warne, Lindsay Hassett
Front cover image © Corbis Images
Endpapers (front): The Melbourne Cricket
Ground's scoreboard mid-match, 1894–95
(courtesy David Studham/MCC Library);
(back): A famous Don Bradman poster from the
early 1930s
All photographs from the Ken Piesse collection unless
otherwise stated

National Library of Australia Cataloguing-in-Publication entry
    Piesse, Ken, author.
    Great Ashes Moments/Ken Piesse.
    ISBN 9781743464830 (hardback)
    Includes index.
    Cricket—Australia—History.
    Cricket—England—History.
    Test matches (Cricket)—Australia—History.
    Test matches (Cricket)—England—History.
    796.35865

Contents

Foreword

June 23 and 24, 1972 remain red-letter days in my cricketing career, ones I can still recall vividly as if they happened yesterday. It was the Lord's Test and I played the innings of my life. Walking back up that little embankment into the members' and seeing them all standing and applauding was as good a feeling as I had in cricket. I made 131 and 'Ferg', Bob Massie, took 16 wickets and we rolled the Poms in four days to square the series. It was the start of something very special for us and in the years to come we were to become cricket's new world champions. Equally important in my eyes, we were to recapture the Ashes.

I can't believe 40 years have passed since that moment. Each time I walk through the gates at Lord's and sight the Pavilion and the egg-and-bacon ties I know I'm at home. Perhaps it was all those years of sitting around the radiogram listening to Alan McGilvray, John Arlott and Brian Johnston weaving their wonderful word pictures. Maybe it was my time playing at Lord's previously with Somerset. But I always felt comfortable and that I belonged at Lord's. I liked its Long Room with all the paintings of past champions and the fact that you had to actually sidestep through the drinkers to make it onto the ground. 'See you back 'ere soon,' was invariably the message.

Having just reached my hundred on that Friday night, I came back again on the Saturday and they stood as one, applauding me like I was Denis Compton or Bill Edrich.

Those moments have never left me and I'll always be grateful for their acknowledgement.

Looking back now, I'm not sure if I could have played the innings that I did without having had my years of county cricket leading into that series. I was to make more runs, more attractively in other Tests, but none were as timely or as technically satisfying.

We'd been beaten just weeks earlier in the first Test at Old Trafford and started poorly at Lord's, losing two early wickets chasing 270-odd. The wicket was doing a bit and John Snow was very menacing, hitting the seam and making it veer and bounce. At Manchester I'd made a pair of 20s, batting a reasonable time, without going on with it. This time I felt all my mental processes were working. I didn't panic. I got some good deliveries which I let go. There would have had to be a few plays and misses and inside edges. No-one can bat six hours and middle everything. But the only error I believe I truly made was to the ball from Basil D'Oliveira I got out on. Early on, Ian took them on a bit. 'Snowy' bounced him and Ian went for his shots. I was happy to play second fiddle. Once he got out just before lunch I assumed the senior role and steered the innings, having some important partnerships with Ross Edwards and Rod Marsh. We wanted to get as close as we could to their score. Any lead was a bonus.

The celebrations in those upstairs rooms on the Monday after Ferg knocked them over for a second time and we got the runs just one or two down were fantastic.

It was my stellar Ashes moment, matched by only one other time, 10 years later, when as captain, I led Australia to regain the Ashes in Sydney.

Wanting to beat England so badly had been ingrained into me from the youngest possible age, in our backyard tests at home, at No. 4 Leak Avenue in Graymore [Adelaide – ed.]. They weren't your usual friendlies. It was a war out there. Being the older brother, Ian was always 'Australia' and I had to be 'England'. That created my first conflict in life. While I didn't want to be beaten, my heart wasn't in representing England. Mind you, it didn't make me try less hard. We always played with a hard ball. Our father never believed in pads or gloves. We had a bat. What else did you need? There were tears and plenty of bumps and bruises as there was a hump in the pitch causing the ball to fly, much to Ian's delight. Once Ian hit me on the fingers with a lifter and Ian followed through to the batting end. 'I wouldn't worry about your fingers if I was you,' he said. 'It's your head next!'

The good news for me was that Ian moved on and I became 'Australia' and Trevor became 'England'. That was a much happier situation for me.

Until 1960–61 and the arrival of the West Indies, all my dreams revolved around Ashes cricket and the biggest names of the time from Freddie Trueman on. But there was something about these West Indies that you just had to like. They played such uninhibited, carefree cricket. It was exhilarating. My favourites were Garry Sobers, Rohan Kanhai and Conrad Hunte. They were all amazing strokemakers.

While my ambition always was to play Test cricket for Australia, I didn't expect it to happen — not until Ian became a regular member of the side. I'd just made South Australia's team and thought maybe I wasn't far away after all.

Cricket had been our everyday diet ever since I could remember. Our Pop, Vic Richardson, Mum's Dad, had played and captained Australia. Our Dad Martin was the keenest of players and quite a dasher, Ian tells me — not that I can recall too much of that.

There must have been a deal of frustration that his own career was severely eaten into by the Second World War. He put his energy into us playing cricket and must have driven his mates and work colleagues nuts talking about his three sons.

Sadly, he passed away before I became a coach. I would have loved to have talked coaching with him to understand what he did know. He couldn't have got so much right by accident.

I still remember the morning I came home from Sunday school, got my good gear off ready to head off and catch up with my mates in the neighbourhood when my father stopped me: 'Where are you going?'

'I'm off to see a mate.'

'No you're not ... not before you go and do half an hour's practice,' he said.

An hour and a half later into practice I was still there. Playing or training for cricket was never a great imposition for any of us.

When my time came and I was first selected for Australia, for the opening Test of the 1970−71 summer in Brisbane, I felt it was only right that we were playing England.

Some felt I should have been included earlier, maybe even as early as the 1968 Ashes tour. But I genuinely believed I hadn't done enough at that stage. It was a different feeling, though, in 1969−70 missing out on the tour to India and on to South Africa. I reckoned I'd had four good seasons. One or two who were picked had only had one or two.

Quite a few of the media had me in both touring teams. Maybe it was a lucky break for me. The team played well in India but didn't win a Test in South Africa.

The day before the start of that 1970−71 Ashes summer, we had a lunch at the Gabba on the verandah at the Cricketers' Club. I got an inkling I was going to be 12th man when Terry Jenner and I sat down next to each other. We were both starving. I wouldn't have had any breakfast that morning before training. 'T. J.' would probably have had only a fag or two. A basket of bread rolls was in front of us and just as I went to grab one, T. J. went for his with a fork and grazed the back of my hand. 'Geez mate, watch it. I've got a Test to play tomorrow,' I said. Bill Lawry (Australia's captain) was sitting opposite us: 'I wouldn't worry about it if I was you,' he said. It didn't come as a great surprise the next morning at 20 to 11 when Bill tapped me on the shoulder and said I was 12th man.

My chance came a week or so later in Perth when I made the actual XI. There was a lot of hoopla around in Perth as it was their very first Test match.

I was so fortunate to have had such a solid cricket background and such a solid grounding in everything to do with the game. I was nervous going out to bat in my first Test but I didn't feel overwhelmed by it all. Certainly it was reassuring going out there and seeing Ian Redpath at the other end. Nothing phased 'Redder'. We were able to combine in quite a stand and from being 5-107, we made 400-plus. We weren't to win this series, but the lessons were numerous. People like Red would bat as if their life depended on it. For him, the team and your mates were everything.

It was hard to win a Test and when we did, we'd celebrate like there was no tomorrow.

The satisfaction was even greater as captain, especially if you happened to knock over England.

In 1977, I lost the Ashes as captain and was quietly pissed off that England wouldn't play for the Ashes in 1979–80. There was some unfinished business there. The next chance I had to square the ledger was in 1982–83. We had the near miss in Melbourne when Allan Border and Jeff Thomson almost got us over the line. Just over a week later in Sydney we did reclaim the Ashes. That was truly a moment to savour.

You know the captains who are recognised as winners and those recognised as losers. I'm glad I'm on the credit side of the line.

Another with plenty of credits is the author of this book, Ken Piesse, who I've known for 35 years and more. Few share his passion for the game. In an email once, I jokingly referred to him as a cricket 'nuffie'. Back shot the reply: 'Nuffie ... is that a South Australian term?'

I'd meant no offence. Like me, cricket pumps through his veins each and every day. All of us are cricket nuffies. I wish Ken all the best with his latest venture, which he tells me is his 48th cricket book. I've no doubt he will reach his half century and then go on with it.

GREG CHAPPELL
Jolimont, June 2013

Introduction

The year 1964 was a very good one for me ... and the Australian cricket team. It was the year my Sunday school teacher Mr Armstrong finally agreed I was old enough to attend practice at the local cricket club. I was nine and had been pestering him for months. My first game was on a tiny school oval at Parkdale, notable for being totally bereft of grass. It was handy for a kid who had little idea which side of the wicket was square leg and which side was point. With my Kiwi-whited sandshoes, I carefully marked my position with a big 'X' in the dirt and stood there willing a ball to come my way. It took me a few games to work out the walk-in-with-the-bowler thing. I can't remember if I batted and I certainly wasn't asked to bowl. But I loved every moment. It was the start of a love affair with the game for which I have been truly blessed. When I wasn't playing or practising with my team, Beaumaris, I'd busy myself detailing player statistics, keeping newspaper stories and reading every cricket book I could find at the local library. It became taboo in our house to throw out the sports sections of the newspapers until I'd seen and cut them up. Within days the cricket clippings would be dated and neatly stuck into albums. I even learned to make my own clag, saving my pocket money for my first book, Garry Sobers' *Cricket Crusader* and subscriptions to the two overseas monthlies the *Cricketer* and *Playfair*.

Every Saturday afternoon in summer, Dad and I would watch the ABC television sports show. In between the interclub athletics and late in the season, the Melbourne District cricket finals, the scores from the interstate representative matches would be displayed. I was astonished when Peter Burge started one Sheffield

Shield year with 283 and Bobby Simpson followed a day or two later with 359. It was the first of three consecutive weekends when 'Simmo' was to make a double-century or better. I had my first cricket hero.

In that winter of '64, Australia was touring England. Simpson had inherited the captaincy from Richie Benaud. The Ashes were at stake. I had no idea what that all meant, but it sounded terribly important. I didn't want to miss a ball and lobbied for my bed to be temporarily moved into the lounge room so I could sleep next to our old Healing Radiogram and listen ball-by-ball to Arlott, McGilvray and Co. They always sounded so far away, but the descriptions and the intensity in their voices was spellbinding. Rarely, however, could I stay awake into a second session; the 40 minute luncheon interval was always a killer. But there was one notable morning late in the series at Old Trafford where I didn't miss a ball: Simpson flaying the English bowling mid-match to finish with 311. Dad reckoned Bobby had cashed in big time as he'd never before been past the 90s. Like me, he loved his stats. Simpson's epic ensured an Ashes-retaining draw and there was widespread jubilation and pride that a country like Australia, population 11 million, could not only compete against but defeat the 'mother' country — and at the very game it invented. I didn't care how old and fragile that Ashes urn may have been. Australia had won it and I wanted to see it! Just why should the trophy be permanently housed in England anyway?

Almost 50 years on and with the benefit of regular Ashes sabbaticals, I've seen the tiny urn in the Lord's museum and now know that there could not be a more appropriate home. Visitors come to Lord's 12 months of the year to pay homage, gathering respectfully in hushed groups, hands behind their backs staring seriously at the display case as if they were at the Tower of London witnessing the Crown Jewels. If there is a comment, invariably it's about the size of the urn. It *is* minute — yet no sporting symbol is as revered or as celebrated.

Ever since the first climactic 'Ashes Test' in England in 1882 when an elderly spectator was so overcome by the thrilling finish that his heart stopped, the contests between England and Australia have been followed avidly. The greatest moments and the winning of the Ashes have invariably been front-page news.

Captains have been so gripped and overpowered by the need to retain or win the Ashes that some have become prisoners-of-their-own-making, playing cautious, safety-first cricket guaranteed to drive spectators away. For all of his remarkable flair and vision, even Richie Benaud couldn't put the fizz into the 1962–63 contests. The excitement and exuberance of the unforgettable Calypso summer just 24 months earlier became but a memory. It was a giant step back for the game.

Those who have refused to be shackled or constrained by the enormity of the occasion, like Australia's fresh-faced debutants Norman O'Neill (in 1958–59) and a teenage Doug Walters (1965–66), or England expresses Frank 'Typhoon' Tyson (1954–55) and Andrew Flintoff (2005) are celebrated among the ultimate Ashes champions.

So prodigious were a young O'Neill's gifts that he was widely anointed as 'the next Bradman', having made 1000 runs in the previous Sheffield Shield season. Rushed into Australia's first Ashes Test team in Brisbane in 1958–59, he made 34 and a dashing 71 not out in under two hours of exhilarating strokeplay which fast-tracked the first of four Australian victories for the summer.

In 1965, Walters' power-packed driving at the Gabba against the off-spinning professionals Freddie Titmus and David Allen was superlative. We'd been allowed home from school early that December Friday because of the 100 degree heat (37°C) and to sit and watch Walters conduct a master-class in such a fierce forum, at the start of a new series, was spellbinding; a truly fairytale way to launch one of the great careers.

Tyson's devastating bursts in 1954–55 after being sconed by Australia's express Ray Lindwall in the Sydney Test included seven for 27 in the second innings of the controversial 'watered wicket' Test in Melbourne. On the eventful final morning with Australia comfortably placed at 2-75, chasing 240, Tyson took six for 16 in 51 balls as Australia was bowled out for little over 100 on a badly cracked pitch, which saw Tyson's thunderbolts either skid through low or take off like he was bowling a superball. It was a dramatic end to an extraordinary game. Hundreds of Melburnians returned home on trains and buses early that afternoon, their cut lunches still untouched.

In 2005, Flintoff ruled the five Tests like he was Botham-reincarnated. So stunning were his performances that it was astonishing Australia took the series into the last day at the Oval. In the summer of his life, Flintoff was a cricketing Superman, swinging the ball at express pace and smashing it with such ferocity that spectators at long-on needed crash helmets. Even Shane Warne's career-high 40 wickets for the series wasn't enough to stop England or Flintoff. It had been 16 years and 42 days since England had held the Ashes and the whole team — even one-Test batsman Paul Collingwood — received OBE's, the victory being celebrated throughout the UK like the second coming of the Beatles.

For those of us staying up late and watching every ball from this side of the equator, it felt like a death in the family. It was especially unpalatable as the Australians were undone by reverse swing and the man primarily responsible for unlocking the secrets to the English pacemen was a Tasmanian.

Flintoff never again played with the same effortless authority, but like the Western Australian Bob Massie, his career was truly defined by performing best when it counted most. Swing specialist Massie was a shooting star of the early '70s, disappearing as quickly as he'd arrived. Yet his ongoing place among cricket's Ashes immortals is assured as no-one is ever likely to equal his 16 wickets on his unforgettable debut at Lord's in 1972.

In the same game, a 23-year-old virtuoso Greg Chappell scored 131. In a career of 7000-plus Test runs, this century isn't among his highest 10 scores. Yet it is his most cherished, as it came against the Poms and at the holy of holies, Lord's. 'Every time I go through the gates at Lord's I remember walking back to the Pavilion that day with all the members standing and applauding,' Chappell said. 'It was a very special moment, one I can still vividly recall like it happened yesterday.'

Contests between England and Australia evoke amazing passion, drama and debate.

After the iconic Dr W. G. Grace mischievously ran out Australia's Sammy Jones while he was 'gardening' at the Oval in 1882, a furious Fred Spofforth called to his teammates as they re-took the field: 'C'mon, this thing can be done.' The Demon bowled unchanged to take seven for 44 to destroy the might of England.

In the opening Test of 1930, an athletic member of the Trent Bridge groundstaff, Syd Copley at wide mid-on took one of the great game-changing catches while acting as a substitute fieldsman. Running full tilt and diving at the ball with his outstretched right hand he took the ball inches from the ground. Teenage champion Stan McCabe was out and the match fortunes changed irreversibly England's way. Copley played only once for Notts but his place in Ashes annals is assured.

When Don Bradman threw the ball to Keith Miller early in the 1948 tour and told him to bowl bouncers at England's glamour batsman Bill Edrich, Miller tossed it straight back again and told the Don to get someone else to do his dirty work. Cricket was a game not a war. It was the era of rationing. Edrich was a family man. He had no intention of hurting him. Bradman's ruthlessness had been polarising opinion for years. In 1930 he pocketed 1000 pounds from an Australian UK-based businessman after his colossal 334 at Headingley. That was 400 pounds more than the entire tour fee. His teammates each received an ashtray. Bill Woodfull, Australia's touring captain that year and again in 1934, believed Bradman was too much of a soloist and said so in numerous letters home to his wife. Years later his young daughter saw him incinerate the lot. 'No-one wants to read this old junk,' he said.

Bradman remains foremost among the game's immortals for his record-breaking ways — bodyline being invented just to stop him — but many of the game's foremost, from Woodfull, the most stoic and honourable of captains through to Bill O'Reilly, Jack Fingleton and Miller, were less than enamoured by Bradman the man. In 1930, had the Don put even 50 pounds onto the bar at the tour end as a gesture of thanks to the men who had worked alongside him, it would have satisfied the rank-and-file. But it was the era of the Great Depression and Bradman was about to be married to his childhood sweetheart, Jesse. The money would assist him in the purchase of a house.

His teammates were further miffed when the young recordbreaker arrived ahead of the team to tickertape receptions in Adelaide, Melbourne and Sydney. Even Australia's manager W. L. Kelly felt it 'an insult' to the rest of the team that all the glory was going to one man rather than the touring party as a unit. Years later I asked 'Tiger' O'Reilly about his relationship with the Don. He smiled and said: 'You don't piss on statues, young Ken.'

In 1981 in mid-match at Headingley, Australian fast bowler Dennis Lillee was amazed when Ladbrokes posted on the electronic scoreboard – in use for the first time – odds of 500-1 against an English victory. He had 10 pounds on the Poms and wicketkeeper Rod Marsh five, the pair doubling their tour monies after an astonishing Botham-led revival.

In 2005, following one of the epic Ashes Tests of all which saw England win on the fifth morning by just two runs, the image of 'Freddie' Flintoff consoling a slumped Brett Lee after Australia's epic near miss remains among the game's classic photographs. There was no fiercer competitor than Flintoff and this was his mightiest triumph, yet he still had time to spend with Lee. His sportsmanship was applauded everywhere the game is played.

Unsporting happenings, however, from bodyline to doctored wickets, and even a substitute fieldsman throwing out Australia's captain at a vital moment of a Test, are all guaranteed to evoke heated responses, depending on which side of the world you come from.

We colonials would gladly have sailed Douglas Jardine into Bass Strait in a row boat without an oar, so incensed were we when Jardine dared to unleash bodyline at our darling Don. Many of us felt Jim Laker, Australia's spin nemesis in back-to-back Tests in 1956 was overrated. And as for substitute Gary Pratt who threw Ricky Ponting out at Trent Bridge in 2005 – why was he allowed to field at cover point anyway?! English supporters, however, consider Jardine to be visionary, Laker inspired and that Pratt should also have been among those to have been awarded an OBE!

INTRODUCTION

In *Great Ashes Moments,* we celebrate the heroic happenings, the greatest games and the mightiest solos, from not only my eyes, but many of the greats from now and yesteryear. I trust you will enjoy the selections.

KEN PIESSE
Mt. Eliza, May 2013

1

As It Happened

No McGrath, No Australia
Ken Piesse

England went from the hunted to the hunters after one simple accident on the opening morning of what was to become one of the immortal Ashes Tests of them all.

It was the first morning of the 2005 Edgbaston epic and just as we were heading past the Eric Hollies Stand to our vantage spots, Glenn McGrath was being ushered out, bound for hospital, his Test over before it had even started.

His pain was so intense it seemed he could be sidelined for up to a month and more. From massive outsiders, England's odds were to suddenly firm especially after their dominant opening day.

As McGrath disappeared in an ambulance bound for the local Priory Hospital – having stepped on a ball in the warm-ups – James, one of the youngest of our Events Worldwide tour party asked his mother how Australia would go without McGrath. 'Hasn't he taken almost 500 wickets?' he added.

'Think you've answered your own question,' she said.

As chief tormentor of teams around the world for a decade and more, McGrath's presence had been central to Australia's bottom line. With him, the Aussies had won 73 of 111 Tests, a 66 per cent

ROCKET ROD: Rodney Hogg burst into Test cricket like a meteor with 50 wickets in his maiden summer, including 42 in six drama-packed Tests against England in 1978–79. *Patrick Eagar*

winning rate; without him, the team's win-loss ratio was a far more moderate 48 per cent.

Significantly, too, teammates stood taller when the tormentor was around; their averages all blowing out when he happened to be missing. Take Brett Lee, for example. With McGrath sharing the new ball duties, Lee's average was 28 runs a wicket; in McGrath's absence it was 44.

All the other frontliners suffered too: Jason Gillespie (25 to 26), Michael Kasprowicz (30 to 32) and Shane Warne (24 to almost 28); the pressure McGrath was able to build from one end being crucial in wickets falling at the other.

Three weeks later at Trent Bridge, one of Australia's happiest hunting grounds, England again started with 400-plus, McGrath again an eleventh-hour withdrawal, this time with an elbow injury.

So important was the Ashes decider at the Oval that it was felt the big man with the ready smile would need to be nursed, hoping he could recapture his mastery in the showdown.

After all it had only been a few short weeks since Lord's when in one incredible turn-back-the-clock spell, he took five for 1, one of the rare times all tour where the long-time world champions were in total control.

Without the big man from the back of Bourke, however, Australia seemed rudderless and while others lifted in his absence — most notably Lee and Warne late in the game at Edgbaston — the warnings were chillingly clear. Australia was vulnerable like never before.

Ever since the mid-'80s when legendary trio Dennis Lillee, Rod Marsh and Greg Chappell retired within the same month, Australian selection committees had been in damage control, looking to blend as many younger men into the Test team as possible, knowing that one day they too would be asked to stand tall.

It was one of the reasons why Mark Waugh was pushed out and Steve Waugh denied the opportunity to captain in India, the selectors wanting to play Michael Clarke and some of the other emerging types.

So spellbinding had McGrath and Warne's influence been,

however, that it was impossible to make any meaningful bowling replacements — without a monumental backlash.

Not only did the Ashes provide a series of classic contests, it exposed the Australians as an ageing unit past its best. The 'No McGrath, No Australia' signs at Edgbaston and Trent Bridge may have been harsh — but they were chillingly realistic.

Australian Cricket Tour Guide 2005–06, Ken Piesse
(Emap Australia, Sydney, 2005)

The Loudest Cheer of All
Peter McFarline

The rise of World Series Cricket inadvertently
launched Rod Hogg from worshipper to worshipped.

Forty thousand, one hundred and fourteen people — the largest attendance of the series — had sat stunned as Australia collapsed in superb weather conditions. As England began its innings at 12.27 p.m., most of them were resigned to the thought that England was back in the match.

[Rodney] Hogg began from the outer end (at the Melbourne Cricket Ground) with a great deal of vocal encouragement — and an extraordinary field. There were three slips, [captain Graham] Yallop only a yard from the bat at silly point, extra cover, forward short leg, short backward square leg and a leg slip, as well as the conventional fine leg. The leg trap was designed to cut off [Geoff] Boycott's favourite scoring shots, nudges in an arc around square leg.

Boycott and his 'new' partner [Mike] Brearley took a single each before Hogg began the third over of the innings.

Boycott played the first two balls defensively. The third, much quicker, cut back sharply from the off stump and was through the famous defence and into the middle stump before the Boycott shuffle was complete. For a fraction of a second, there was a deadly silence — then the MCG erupted. Conservative members joined

3

with the outer in a deafening shout of acclamation for Hogg and satisfaction at the early demise of the dreaded Boycott.

In 20 football Grand Finals at this ground, all of them with crowds in excess of 100,000, I don't believe I have heard a noise to equal it. Hogg's ecstasy was infectious. He ran down the pitch, hands above his head, as his teammates ran to congratulate him. His normal grim countenance was split with an enormous grin. England, 1-2, was now engaged in a struggle it would not overcome this day.

As [Derek] Randall bounced his way to the crease, the chant began from the outer 'HOGGEE … HOGGEE … HOGGEE …'. Purely by chance, Australian cricket had discovered the successor to Lillee and Thomson. As Hogg was to admit later that evening, he had been one of those enthusiasts in the same outer four years before, chanting 'LILLEE … LILLEE …' as that great bowler wrought mayhem against England. Never had he dreamed that he would take over the mantle. A fast bowler on the fringe of the first-class game in Victoria for many years, he had never considered himself good enough to play for Australia.

But his work was not over yet. Randall took a single from the next ball, then Brearley was trapped lbw by the next to make England 2-3. The delivery cut back and kept ominously low, striking Brearley on the front pad. There was no hesitation in umpire [Max] O'Connell's decision. Hogg, two for 1 in his second over, was welcomed like the prodigal son as he took his jumper and retired to fine leg, to be inundated by the well-wishers of Bay 13, who had added him to their impressive list of idols.

Mature-age rookie Hogg took 27 wickets in his first three Ashes Tests, including 10 in the Melbourne Test, inspiring Australia's only win of the six-Test summer against a full-strength England.

A *Testing Time*, Peter McFarline (Hutchinson Group Australia, Melbourne, 1979)

TEN CAPTAINCY DECISIONS WHICH BACKFIRED

Glenn McGrath steps on the ball, Edgbaston, 2005

Having won the opening Test at Lord's and sung their victory song in England's rooms, reality bites for the cocky Australians a week later in Birmingham when Glenn McGrath is carried off on the morning of the game having badly injured his ankle. Even without his injured champion and to the consternation of at least one of his high-profile teammates back in the rooms, Australia's captain Ricky Ponting insists on bowling first and England makes 400 on a free-flowing opening day as Australia loses its hold on the Ashes in what is to become the greatest modern-day Ashes series of all.

Mark Butcher's miracle at Leeds, 2001

Looking for a 5-0 series win, stand-in Australian captain Adam Gilchrist declares on the penultimate night leaving seemingly down-and-out England 110 overs to chase down 314, a target it reaches in just 72 overs thanks to a Jessopian-like century from Mark Butcher who makes 173 not out and against a full-strength Australian attack of McGrath, Gillespie, Lee and Warne.

Graeme Hick is marooned on 98 not out, Sydney, 1994–95

Graeme Hick never was to make an Ashes 100 and hardly spoke again to Mike Atherton for the rest of the tour after Atherton's controversial declaration with Hick on 98. 'In purely cricketing terms the move was entirely justified,' Atherton was to say later, 'however, it had a

(left) **MATCHWINNER:** Glenn McGrath
(right) **DISCONSOLATE:** Graeme Hick

disheartening effect on the team ... it was not a decision I would have taken again.' Australia bats more than 120 overs to save the match.

Mike Denness bowls when he should have batted, Edgbaston, 1975
Using his lucky Canadian dollar coin, Mike Denness wins the toss and becomes the first Test captain to send in a team in Birmingham in the opening Test of 1975. Within 24 hours he has tendered his resignation after an unnamed selector publicly divulges he should have batted, Australia starting with 359 despite the heavy cloud cover. Denness makes 3 and 8, the game lasts barely three and a half days and Australia wins by an innings. Tony Greig becomes the new England leader.

Bill Lawry's change of batting order misfires, Sydney, 1970–71
Just two Tests after he'd made a career-best double-ton in Brisbane, Keith Stackpole is relegated back to the middle-order in Sydney in 1970–71. Captain Bill Lawry takes in Ian Chappell with him and Chappell makes just 14 and 0 as Australia loses by almost 300 runs. 'They [the selectors] may have thought I was playing my shots too early but this was a crazy decision,' says Stackpole.

Ted Dexter takes the second new ball, Leeds, 1964
With Australia teetering at 7-178 and his spinners Fred Titmus and Norman Gifford threatening, Ted Dexter opts to take the second new ball and Peter Burge tees off against some wayward short-pitched bowling from Freddie Trueman and Jack Flavell, making 160 to take the game away from England. 'It was the finest innings I have seen in more than 50 Tests,' Dexter says later. 'If there was a man at the ground honestly horrified at this decision [taking of the new ball], he must indeed have been a clairvoyant.' Australia's innings extends to almost 400 in a rollicking seven wicket victory, the only result of the '64 series.

Len Hutton sends Australia in, Brisbane, 1954–55
So undecided is English captain Len Hutton after calling correctly that he doesn't inform opposing captain, Australia's Ian Johnson, of his intention to send Australia in to bat until the pair are almost off the ground. Johnson can't believe his good luck. 'They've sent us in, they've sent us in!' he calls jubilantly to his players in the rooms. Australia makes 8-601 dec. and wins the opening Test by an innings. Years later Hutton says pitches are like wives: 'You never quite know how they will turn out.'

Norman Yardley bowls Len Hutton, Leeds, 1948
The turning point in Australia's remarkable chase of 400-plus on the final day at Headingley comes when England's captain Norman Yardley

SURPRISE CHOICE: Len Hutton's little-used
leg breaks proved expensive at Leeds in 1948.

calls occasional leg-spinner Len Hutton to the crease. His four overs,
punctuated by full tosses, cost 30 as Australia accelerates its run rate and
Arthur Morris and Don Bradman add a matchwinning 301 to set up one
of the great wins of all.

Don Bradman breaks his ankle, The Oval, 1938
Looking to share the workload with his exhausted frontline spinners, Don
Bradman brings himself on to bowl late on the third day with England
7-887 and early in his third over slips on a worn foothole and fractures a
bone in his ankle. He is unable to bat in either Australian innings, England
winning the decisive final Test by a record margin of an innings and 579
runs.

Johnny Douglas relegates S. F. Barnes to first change duties, Sydney, 1911–12
Stand-in English captain Johnny Douglas elects to open the bowling with
himself and Frank Foster in Sydney, the great Sydney Barnes being made
to come on at first-change. 'I can bowl with the new ball as well you
know,' says a disconsolate Barnes. Australia starts with 447 and wins the
opening Test comfortably. A fortnight later in Melbourne, Barnes is given
the new ball and produces one of the inspired Ashes spells of all, taking
four for 6 as Australia slumps to 6-38. Never again for the remainder of
the tour is 'S. F.' denied new ball status by Douglas.

Struck In the Head by Snowy
Terry Jenner

England's unprecedented walk-off in the Sydney Test of 1971
was triggered by the felling of an Australian tailender.

Bill Lawry's axing in between Tests was the biggest cricketing story for years. But he wasn't bringing out the best in the players, so it wasn't a shock to us that he lost the captaincy. But it was a surprise that he wasn't retained in the XI as an opening batsman, especially given it was the deciding Test (of 1970–71).

I had a feeling that I'd be in that final XI. Just a week earlier, against New South Wales, I'd taken four for 39 in their second innings. Sydney wasn't then regarded as a spinner's haven, but I knew tactically the selectors had to go all-out to win the game by playing their most attacking combination.

It was exciting to go to Sydney and to have a new captain in Ian Chappell. We had two first-gamers, the tall Queenslander Tony Dell and the Victorian left-hander Ken Eastwood, in for the only Test of his career. What a challenge Ian had been set. Our entire attack, Dennis Lillee, Dell, [Kerry] 'Skull' O'Keeffe and I had played just three or four Tests between all of us!

Ian won the toss and dobbed them, a rarity in Test cricket, let alone in your first Test as captain! He wanted to utilise whatever life was in the wicket.

Ian went to me first, ahead of Skull. England were barely 40 at the time. Coming into the game Les Favell (my captain at South Australia) had said to me that the selectors wanted me 'to throw them up' and that's exactly what I did after Dougie Walters had picked up an early wicket.

It was a wet deck and naturally slower. My instinct was to bowl quicker, but instead I remembered what Les had said and gave them plenty of air.

After three or four overs, Ian came up and said: 'Why are you bowling these &%#@ing donkey drops? What's brought this on?'

'Les told me that "Harv" [selector Neil Harvey] told him they were expecting me to toss them up. They felt I was a bit too defensive.'

'Right,' said Ian. 'If you were playing for South Australia today on this pitch, what would you be bowling?'

'Zooters.'

'Well bowl &%#@ing zooters.'

I dismissed three of the Poms: Ray Illingworth, John Snow and Bob Willis, all bowled. From the press box, Bill O'Reilly described my deliveries as 'magnificent wrong-uns, absolutely undetectable', when in essence they were back-spinners, or as Richie Benaud called them, when he showed me the delivery, 'sliders'.

In essence, when properly released, the ball curves in towards the batsman and continues off the pitch. This day, with the pitch damp, they scurried through, creating the illusion that they were wrong-uns.

We dismissed England for 184, O'Keeffe also taking three. There were big crowds, 29,000 and 30,000 and much anticipation for the weekend's play. We had to win to retain the Ashes.

After losing our first three wickets for 30-odd, it was 7-178 when I joined Greg Chappell. Remembering (the first Test in) Brisbane and how I'd self-destructed [making 0 and 2 — ed.], my every desire this time was to get behind the line of the ball and show I wasn't frightened of 'Snowy'. He bowled me a couple of short ones and I managed to fend them off and get off strike. We needed every run. Soon I was facing again and being bounced.

Snow had taken the new ball and, given our scoreline, the stakes could not have been higher. The field was closing in around me, looking for a catch. Snow went wide on the crease and again pitched it in short. This time, with the brand new ball, it came onto me a lot quicker. I'd stepped across to cover my stumps and in the split second saw the ball coming at my head. I had time only to turn my head and half duck. It was like a car accident. Unavoidable. The ball thudded into my skull, just above my left ear and as I fell to the ground my natural reaction was to reach for my head.

Later I was told the ball actually rebounded to cover.

It stung at first but when I saw the blood from the cut it really

DOWNED: Terry Jenner slumps to the ground after being struck by John Snow in Sydney. He'd borrowed a pair of gloves from Dennis Lillee and they were quickly saturated in blood.

hurt. I was feeling numb all over and putting the gloves I'd borrowed from Dennis Lillee to my face, covered them both with blood. I was assisted off, put on a bench and given some smelling salts as 'Doc' [Brian] Corrigan patched me up.

As all this was happening, umpire Lou Rowan, a Brisbane detective, was warning Snow for excessive short-pitched deliveries. Snow and [Ray] Illingworth (England's captain) apparently remonstrated with Rowan and at the end of Snow's over, he headed down to fine leg, waving his hands and conducting the crowd's chanting. One spectator reached out over the fence to shake his hand, but instead grabbed his shirt. It was an incredibly volatile situation. All hell broke loose. Cans were hurled onto the ground and amid volleys of boos, Illingworth led his side off in protest.

In our rooms, someone was yelling: 'We've won, we've won. They're forfeiting.'

My immediate thought was that I'd won a Test match for Australia. But what a way to do it!

However, the Poms were only off for a short time. All through the break while the cans and rubbish were being cleared, Greg Chappell and Dennis Lillee stayed in the middle. We got to stumps at 6-235 with Greg having made a gallant 50 and Dennis still not out. I'd been stitched up and was padded up ready to go out again.

After the day's play, several of the English players came into the rooms to see how I was. Colin Cowdrey was genuinely concerned and Illingworth asked if I was all right. Even Snow came in. 'You all right then?' he said. 'Let's have a look. Oh, I only grazed you.'

I was back to our hotel very early and thought I'd see the highlights on the news but went to sleep before they came on. Greg and I were rooming together and next morning we were driving to the ground when we ran into a huge traffic jam. We sat there for half an hour without hardly moving. There was only an hour to go before the game actually started.

I saw a policeman, so got out of the car and said to him: 'Greg Chappell is here. He's not out. We have to get to the ground, quick.' He immediately provided us with the escort we needed, lights flicking and all. Five minutes later, we were coming in the members' gates. It was another full house.

Doc Corrigan assessed my cut and said I'd need to wear some protection. Helmets were unheard of then, so I borrowed Keith Stackpole's cap, which was bigger than mine. I very rarely batted with a cap because I always felt I could see its peak.

Dennis was out to the very first ball of the morning and taking a few deep breaths, down the pavilion steps I went. By the time I'd walked the short distance from our rooms to the members' gate, everyone was standing and applauding. It was exhilarating. I felt like Bradman, but I was only doing what I had to do.

Surviving the first ball was important and after doing that and seeing Greg Chappell go out, I managed to hit a couple of 4s and added 22 to my original score (8) before our innings ended. Snow kept the ball up to me generally, but occasionally did what all fast bowlers had to do. I knew if I kept swinging what the consequences would be (and I'd be bounced again)! We'd extended our lead to 70 or 80. It would have been nice to have had an even bigger lead, but frankly, I didn't want to get hit in the head again!

England came from behind to win the match and the Ashes 2-0. With 30 and 4 and six wickets for the game, Jenner was one of Australia's most impressive, yet was never to command a regular place in the starting XI.

T.J. Over the Top: Cricket, Prison & Warnie, Terry Jenner with Ken Piesse (Information Australia, Melbourne, 1999)

Len Hutton's Melbourne Meltdown
Stephen Chalke

Having squared the 1954–55 series in Sydney without his
most celebrated strike bowler, Len Hutton was agonising
over the decision to again omit the great Alec Bedser
from the New Year Test in Melbourne.

'I can see Len now,' Marylebone Cricket Club tour manager Geoffrey Howard said. 'He was sitting up in his bed with a woollen vest on, staring at the wall.'

'I don't think I can play today,' Hutton told me. 'I'm not feeling too well at all.'

It was Friday, 31 December, the third Test was scheduled to start in less than two hours and the England captain had lost his will for the battle.

'He was feeling unwell,' his official biographer Gerald Howat records, 'with fibrositis [fibromyalgia] and a cold. He was white as a sheet and shivering.'

But that is not how anybody else in the room remembers it.

'He seemed to be in a very disturbed state,' Denis Compton said, 'as if suddenly things had got too much for him and he couldn't or wouldn't go on.'

'Come on, mate,' Godfrey Evans cajoled.

'Come down to the ground at any rate,' Bill Edrich suggested.

'Let's put it this way,' Howard says, 'if somebody had said, "The hotel is on fire," Len would have been out of bed and down the stairs as quick as any of us.'

The day after Christmas, with the team still recovering from their party, they had caught the train to Newcastle for a three-day country match. But their captain had not gone with them.

'He went ahead to Melbourne on his own. He wanted to think things out for himself,' said manager Howard.

TEN MORE FAMOUS ASHES 'HITS'

Steve Harmison (England) – Lord's, London, first Test, 2005

Beanpole English expressman Steve Harmison opens a much anticipated Ashes series with a searing first spell of short-pitched deliveries. Justin Langer is struck on the elbow, Ricky Ponting on the helmet grill, resulting in a cut cheek, and Matthew Hayden flush on the helmet. For the first time in many years, England are the hunters and Australia the hunted.

Brett Lee (Australia) – WACA Ground, Perth, third Test, 2002–03

Brett Lee hits English tailender Alex Tudor between the grill and helmet peak with a bouncer. Distraught, a bleeding Tudor retires hurt, never to play another Test.

Bob Willis (England) – Melbourne, the Centenary Test, 1976–77

Bob Willis breaks the jaw of Australian opener Rick McCosker as he mistimes an attempted hook at an early bouncer on the opening morning. McCosker returns to bat in the second innings jaw wired and swathed in bandages to a chorus of 'Waltzing McCosker, Waltzing McCosker ...'

Jeff Thomson (Australia) – WACA Ground, Perth, second Test, 1974–75

Few bowled as 'heavy' a ball as England's Ashes nemesis of 1974–75, Jeff Thomson. This one, delivered at close to 100 mph (160 km/h), strikes England's opener and frontline commentator-to-be David Lloyd flush in the groin, shattering his box. Film of the blow still brings tears to the eyes of fully grown men. Lloyd recovered and now laughs his way through the moment at sportsmen's nights.

Ray Lindwall (Australia) – Sydney, second Test, 1954–55

Ray Lindwall fells English fast bowler Frank Tyson with a skidding bouncer which strikes Tyson on the back of his head and knocks him out. Tyson returns, bump on head and all, to take six for 85 as England wins a classic Test by just 38 runs.

Ray Lindwall (Australia) – Old Trafford, Manchester, third Test, 1948

Having scored just 4, Denis Compton top edges a no-ball from Ray Lindwall into his forehead straight between the eyes. He goes off for treatment and plastered up, he returns at the fall of the fifth wicket and makes 145 not out in the only match of the series left drawn. Australia wins the other four.

Harold Larwood (England) – Adelaide, third Test, 1932–33

Expressman Harold Larwood, bowling to an orthodox field, fractures the skull of Australia's popular wicketkeeper Bert Oldfield after he mishooks a bouncer. Oldfield is the most tangible physical casualty of the acrimonious Bodyline series which temporarily endangers Ashes relations.

Harold Larwood (England) – Adelaide, third Test, 1932–33
Bill Woodfull was struck repeatedly by Harold Larwood and Bill Voce during the bodyline summer, the hardest hit coming in the opening half an hour in Adelaide. Having made five, Woodfull doubles up in pain having been struck a fearful blow over the heart from Larwood, operating to an orthodox field. He drops his bat and reels from the wicket in agony. Years later his widow claimed that the knock had shortened her husband's life.

Jack Gregory (Australia) – Trent Bridge, Nottingham, first Test, 1921
Having bowled Lancastrian debutant Ernest Tyldesley for a duck in the first innings, Jack Gregory raises the ire of the Trent Bridge crowd when he hits him in the face in the second innings before the ball ricochets onto the wickets, Tyldesley having made just seven from 47 high-octane deliveries. Australia wins the opening Test in two days.

George Ulyett (England) – Melbourne, inaugural Test, 1877
George Ulyett gashes the finger of Australia's opening batsman Charles Bannerman, forcing him to retire hurt on 165 in the very first 'Great Match'.

FELLED: In what was to be the turning point of the series, expressman Frank Tyson is knocked out by a Ray Lindwall bouncer late in the Test in Sydney. Returning with little more than a bump on his head, a fired-up Tyson takes six for 85 as Australia – set just 223 – is bowled out for 184, giving England fresh momentum in a series it was to win 3-1.

Peter May scored a century for the fourth successive match, Johnny Wardle and Bob Appleyard took wickets and *Wisden* records that 'MCC gave a joyous display'.

Yet all the while their captain sat in his room at the ever-so-grand Windsor Hotel in Melbourne, trying to focus his mind on the challenge of the forthcoming Test. It was Thursday afternoon before his team arrived to join him.

'Basically,' manager Howard believes, 'it all revolved around one thing: "How am I going to tell Alec [Bedser] that he's not playing?" That was the decision preying on his mind.'

The idea before the second Test had been, in the words of cricketing journalist Ian Peebles, 'to reserve Bedser for Melbourne, a favourite ground of his and let him restart at full blast'.

But, after the superb bowling of Frank Tyson and Brian Statham at Sydney, Bedser could only regain his place at the expense of spinner Wardle — and that meant disturbing the shape of a winning team.

Len Hutton grew up in Fulneck, west of Leeds, in a family steeped in Moravian Presbyterianism. He was not an active worshipper — 'I don't remember Leonard showing any signs of ever wanting to go to church,' said Howard — but he had internalised their belief in discipline, hard work and self-sufficiency and he practised the 'stillness' that for centuries had been a hallmark of the sect.

'What Moravians have said about stillness,' an early Yorkshire believer wrote, in the days when their settlements were attacked by angry mobs, 'has either been strangely misunderstood or strangely misrepresented. They mean by stillness that we should endeavour to keep our minds calm, composed and collected, free from hurry and dissipation.'

On the eve of the Melbourne Test, England captain Hutton sat drinking coffee with Appleyard and watched as Compton, Edrich and Evans skipped down the steps dressed up for a night on the town. 'Look at those three,' he said to his fellow Yorkshireman. 'They'll say they need to relax. But this is the time to be thinking about the match.'

From Sunday, when they went their separate ways at Sydney, to that Friday morning when he would not get out of bed, he had done little else but think. But what was he thinking?

'I can remember on the voyage out,' Geoffrey Howard says, 'there were times when I would retire to my cabin with a tin of toffees and a book. But I can't imagine Len doing that. He'd just have sat in his room with the radio on, staring at the wall.'

A stillness of mind and deep powers of concentration were pivotal in Hutton's batting. In 1938 he had stayed at the crease for more than 13 hours to set a new world Test record score of 364. Then after the war he had carried the fragile England batting for years, adjusting his technique to compensate for a left arm made two inches shorter by a gymnasium accident.

Compton scored sparkling runs with a carefree abandon but Hutton carried the responsibility, never more than in the Caribbean the previous winter. The first professional cricketer to lead MCC overseas, he endured a stream of attacks for his diplomatic faux pas and his inability to keep his more wayward team members under control. Yet, after losing the first two matches, he hit 169 at Georgetown, 205 at Kingston and the series was levelled.

At the start of the summer of 1954, Len Hutton had scored 6665 Test runs at an average of 61.71. 'His powers of concentration at the wicket were enormous,' Geoffrey says, 'and the statistics are wonderful. But nothing as wonderful as seeing him bat. He was such a beautiful strokemaker.'

But the Caribbean tour had taken its toll and in the summer of 1954 he was bowled for 0 in the first Test and took a month out of cricket. His replacement as England captain, David Sheppard, was an amateur, and there were many in cricket's ruling circles — not least the selector Walter Robins and the Surrey trio of Errol Holmes, H. D. G. 'Shrimp' Leveson-Gower and secretary Brian Castor — who advocated that Sheppard should take charge in Australia rather than the professional Hutton.

Apart from any other consideration, Hutton, whose official title on the tour was captain of the MCC side, was not even a member of Marylebone Cricket Club, an anomaly about which he was very sensitive. 'We were going out to a function one night,' Howard recalls, 'and I was wearing my MCC tie. "I'd rather you didn't wear that," Len said to me.'

Len Hutton could speak entertainingly at the various functions and he was always immaculately dressed. But he needed time away from the limelight, time when he did not have to be Len Hutton, MCC captain.

'I was sitting at the Windsor with him and Johnny Wardle, having a drink and this Australian sat down at our table. He was full of grog and he asked Len who he was. "My name's Joe Soap," Len said, and this chap spent the rest of the evening calling him Mister Soap.'

By the morning of the first day it had all got too much for Len and manager Howard summoned a doctor, who had been recommended back in London in case anyone needed medical help in Melbourne.

'I got him to examine Len,' said Howard.

'There's nothing really wrong with you, Mr Hutton,' he said. 'You'd better get up, have a shower and some breakfast and get down to the ground to play.'

Today there would be a sports psychologist on hand to help him through the crisis. 'He was depressed, but in those days people didn't talk about depression like they do now. You were expected to get on with your life.'

The small gathering in the room waited for the captain's reaction.

'Len didn't look overjoyed at the doctor's opinion. I think he'd made up his mind that he wasn't going to play, but he did as he was told.'

With Compton, Evans and Edrich returning to their rooms, the manager quietly offered the captain his assistance.

'If you like, I will tell Alec Bedser he's not playing.'

'No,' Len insisted. 'It's my job.'

Nearly half a century later Geoffrey Howard wonders if perhaps he should have insisted. 'The secret of captaincy lies in appreciating the feelings of the other players,' Jim Swanton had written, but it was not a lack of appreciation of Alec's feelings that was the difficulty here.

'Len knew he was going to hurt Alec and Len didn't like hurting people.'

England's record-breaker Bedser didn't play any further Tests in Australia and only one additional Test the following English home summer. In his playing farewell to Australia, Hutton successfully defended the Ashes with back-to-back wins in Melbourne and Adelaide.

At the Heart of English Cricket: The Life and Memories of Geoffrey Howard, Stephen Chalke (Fairfield Books, Bath, 2001)

Saving England at Lord's
Willie Watson

After rain had thwarted England's victory bid at Trent Bridge in the opening Test of 1953, Australia was in total command in the second Test at Lord's thanks to a fierce onslaught from pace trio Ray Lindwall, Keith Miller and Bill Johnston. Set 343 for victory, England limped to stumps on the fourth night at 3-20, teetering on the brink of defeat.

When I walked to the wicket with the England total at 12 for three and defeat staring us in the face, I felt relieved. True. That isn't boasting, it is just plain fact. I knew we were in trouble, but I knew that if I could weather the early storm and get settled,

PARTNERS: Willie Watson (left) and Trevor Bailey after they had saved England from certain defeat at Lord's in 1953.

there was no reason why I should not stay there. After all, cricket is just a game between bowler and batsman and when the batsman gets settled and starts concentrating, he sees the ball so well that all the tricks of the bowling trade are exposed.

The only snag was the break that came upon us just as Denis Compton and I were settling down. We were then faced with a complete night's rest before returning to the fray and settling in once again.

The topic of conversation that night and in the morning newspapers was, of course, the hopelessness of the England position. We had another six hours to hold on and three of our best batsmen (Don Kenyon, Len Hutton and Tom Graveney) were out. Hopes of winning, of course, were non-existent. According to most people, so were our hopes of drawing.

I kept my spirits up by wondering if we could stick it. I reasoned that if Compton and I could get our eye in again the following morning, there was no reason at all why we should not stay for a long, long time. Then we had quite a few competent batsmen to come: Trevor Bailey, Freddie Brown, Godfrey Evans, Johnny Wardle and all could be relied upon to stay there and sell their wickets dearly.

So while England moped that evening, I wondered. I knew it was a tough task, but tough tasks have been accomplished before and there was no reason at all why we shouldn't hang on. In fact the next morning I felt even more confident.

Denis Compton and I played carefully, not bothering so much about runs, for our job was to keep our wickets intact — not to score runs. The Australians tried everything they knew but still Denis and I stayed and the longer we stayed together, the more confident I became.

Then, of course, the tragedy occurred. Compton was out for 33 and we were 73 for four wickets. In all the publicity that followed the match, most people forgot completely his invaluable contribution. He had played countless fine innings for England, but I doubt whether he has ever played one of greater value than this one.

Thousands of words were written about this match in newspaper articles and in books, and most of them were about Trevor Bailey and me. Everyone said we saved England, but without hesitation I say that we could never have saved the match without Denis.

Trevor Bailey replaced Denis. Trevor was the perfect man for the crisis. He had intense concentration and no matter what the attack did, they would be unable to tempt Trevor into being rash.

As Trevor walked to the wicket, I knew that we simply must stay together for some time and I couldn't help thinking what a big part the footballing-cricketers were playing in this match. Both Compton and myself were professional footballers, although Compton had retired from the winter game by then, and Trevor was a most distinguished amateur [and in Australia's team Keith Miller, Ray Lindwall and Gil Langley had all played rugby or Australian Rules at representative level. Captain Lindsay Hassett was also an All-Australian Aussie Rules amateur. — ed.]

We were still together at lunch, when the score was 116 for four, which meant that despite the crisis we had scored 96 runs during the morning, which was comparable scoring rate wise to many innings when things were going right.

As the afternoon wore on, Bailey and I were still there and getting more confident with every over. By this time the ball looked to me as big as a football, my concentration never lapsed for a second and I felt as if I could stay there [all day]. Bailey, too, was a picture of confidence. He got his left foot out to the pitch of the ball, stuck his nose down and looked as if he would not budge for a squadron of tanks, let alone a battery of Australian bowlers!

By that time we had added another 67 runs, making the score 183 for four. I was 84 by this time and Bailey was 39 and there were only two more hours left. I felt sure we could do it.

Not one voice was raised about the slow scoring between lunch and tea, although our rate of scoring was only just over 30 runs an hour. That, to the campaigners for brighter cricket, will seem terrible, but cricket is a contest between bat and ball and in this case it was the bat's job to stay there and not score runs. It was a fascinating duel of tactics and of concentration … I was tired, but was still seeing the ball well. The one danger, of course, was that my tiredness would cause me to relax my concentration. That would be fatal.

As we walked to the wicket after tea, I told myself that I must relax, not allow my nerves to key me up so much that my concentration would snap. I took one look at Trevor and knew that nothing would shatter his concentration.

Eventually to terrific cheers, Trevor reached his half-century. It had taken him three and a half hours. I reached my century in five and a quarter hours, a rate of scoring not much faster than Trevor's, but who cared about runs?

Gradually the clock pressed on towards half-past five, but I wasn't interested in clocks. I was just interested in the Australian bowlers and getting the ball plumb in the middle of the bat. And then, just for a split second, my concentration slipped, and a ball from [Doug] Ring moved away from me, caught the edge of my bat and flew into the safe hands of [Graeme] Hole at slip. [Ring had had Watson dropped by Ray Lindwall at just two in the final over the previous night. — ed.]

I shall never forget the cheering as I walked slowly to the Pavilion. The whole of Lord's seemed to rise as one, and believe me, there was quite a crowd there. It had increased considerably as news of our fightback seeped round London and people had rushed to the ground.

As I ran up the Pavilion steps, the breath was almost knocked out of me by the people slapping my back. It was 10 minutes to six, we had scored 236 for five wickets. The game was as good as saved ...

The celebrations at Lord's after England had forced the unlikeliest of draws were joyous. It was the greatest of escapes. In his first Ashes Test, 33-year-old soccer hero Watson made 109 and Bailey, 71. On that memorable June Tuesday, they batted together from 12.42 p.m. to 5.50 p.m. to force a draw integral in England's 1-0 Coronation series victory. 'Nothing Watson had done in sport in any way paralleled this firm stand of almost six hours when England's fate seemed doomed,' wrote eyewitness, ex-Australian Test opener Jack Fingleton. Years later Colin McDonald, who was in Australia's '53 touring party, said Watson and Bailey had simply been 'unbowlable'. 'Bailey was so often a thorn in our side throughout the '50s,' he said.

Double International, Willie Watson (Stanley Paul & Co., London, 1956)

Trials and Tribulations
E. M. Wellings

Injuries to some of its most foremost, whistling
winds and chilly weather marred the start of
the MCC's much-awaited 1950–51 Ashes visit.

The team set off on the P&O ship *Stratheden* on 14 September and there was immediately bad news. Denis Compton hobbled on board, and the next day, when the ship was pitching in the Bay of Biscay, his knee was up like a balloon. [Captain] Freddie Brown called the journalists, who slightly outnumbered the team at this stage, to a conference and gloomily broke the news but asked us not to reveal it for 48 hours. At the end of that time the news was much better. The swelling had gone down under compress and massage treatment and a few days later Denis was able to start light exercise. From that time he made steady progress and fears were gradually allayed.

During the voyage Brown did a good job. He started to develop team spirit among his players. They had a regular Saturday evening session together and in one way and another Brown welded them into one body. He was starting his task well, and we who were there to follow their fortunes were encouraged in a spirit of cautious optimism.

The next setback occurred at Colombo, where the team played a Sunday match against Ceylon (Sri Lanka). The pitch was just a trifle sporting. The medium-pacers occasionally made the ball kick and [Len] Hutton received a couple on the forefinger of his right hand. Earlier in the year he had been out of action for a fortnight after being injured on the same joint during the first Test against the West Indies. This time the period of inaction was to be longer. The injury caused thickening of the joint, which was said to be permanent. That was not serious, but the pain long continued and the first joint remained pyramidal in shape. Although no bone was broken, the finger was eventually put into a splint. On arrival in Perth, Hutton had another X-ray examination. It was confirmed that there was no break, and gradually the injury mended under treatment, though Hutton was unable to play in the first three matches, in Western Australia. [Cyril] Washbrook also missed these games. For business reasons he had been given permission to travel by air long after the main party set off. That resulted in the team starting their program without two of their three main batsmen and with the third, Denis Compton, a doubtful quantity. The young learners had to be flung en bloc into the opening first-class match and there were few seniors to guide them.

In 1946 we had landed in Perth in gloriously hot, sunny weather. The Perth climate seemed perfect to us. We started with a fortnight of continuous sun. This time it was raining and chilly when we sighted land early on the morning of 9 October. By then I had packed our umbrellas and all clothing capable of keeping out rain and cold, and the bags had gone to some undisclosed part of the ship in preparation for being taken off. I was unpopular with my family and their faith in my knowledge of Australian weather was shaken. Within a month there was no faith left. For days we did not trust the signs but dressed in light clothing and shivered in the cold wind, which the locals call the Fremantle doctor. This was no doctor with cures in hand. This M.D. chilled us to the marrow and put [ex-England captain] Arthur Gilligan, who was on a broadcasting assignment, into hospital.

Disappointed in Perth, I promised hot weather in Adelaide. When the cold wind persisted there, I gave up, knowing full well that when Perth and Adelaide had failed, Melbourne could not give us an Australian summer so early. In place after place we found very different weather from what we had met four years earlier. Then we had had plenty of rain — three-quarters of the matches were interrupted by the weather — but we also had a large dose of sun. This time there was still rain in abundance but not nearly so much sun until after the first Test.

The immediate result of the indifferent weather was interference with practice plans. Indeed the practice in Perth was desultory. Before the first match Australian critics were saying that not enough hard practice was being done. It was only later that we fully agreed. It is not wise to enter into a full, hard practice program for the first few days after landing. Conditions are strange. The ball seems to travel through the air faster and to reach fielders before they are ready for it. In such circumstances it is wise to start gently.

Looking back, however, it is clear that the seeds of subsequent casualness in the matter of practice were laid in that first week in Perth.

The Western Australian is a cheery hospitable fellow. His city is beautiful and seems made for a restful life. It is not easy to ignore the attractions and distractions and get down right away to the main job of the tour. But it was up to the management to get things going as they meant them to continue. They did not. By Australian standards our practice periods were casual. Half an hour at the nets seemed to satisfy the bowlers who were apparently free to come and go as they pleased.

Those who have seen the Australians practising at Lord's at the start of a tour in England will know how they prepare for a season's play. The captain stands in a central position behind the bowlers and directs operations. He names the batsmen and the bowlers. Only two bowlers per net is usual, and they go on as long as the captain thinks and not just as they feel inclined. Those not engaged in the nets are busy at fielding practice. There is a general air of efficiency and there is obvious purpose behind the practice period. That was missing when our team practised in Australia, and the impression given was that some of the players regarded any excuse for not practising as being a good one.

On a tour of Australia the players should practise far more than during a season at home. Owing to travelling and the shorter playing day — five hours instead of six — players have much less match play than in England. Some players may go over two weeks without playing in a match of any sort, and perhaps a month or more without a first-class game.

I have no hesitation in saying that our 1950 team did not practise enough and that much of what practice they did have was not serious enough. When a player travels 12,000 miles to represent his country, it is amazing that he can be reluctant to take the necessary action to fit himself for the task. There is something wrong with the individual who allows himself to be drawn away from his main purpose. Likewise a management which does not take steps to see that each man devotes himself to the cricket. It was a bad day for English cricket when the first player was attracted by golf. Today nearly every cricketer is a spare-time golfer. On tour, [Bill] Ferguson, 'Fergie' — the scorer and baggage manager — has nearly as many golf bags as cricket bags to look after. Time which could be more profitably spent at cricket practice is devoted to golf.

I have even heard a player arranging for someone to take over his 12th man duties to free him for the golf course. That does not suggest that he has his mind on the job for which he has been sent halfway round the world.

Having been defeated 3-1 at home by the West Indies, England lost four of the five Tests in Australia, many of its batsmen falling under the spell of Australia's 'mystery' spinner Jack Iverson. The vitriolic E. M. Wellings of the *London Evening News* was one of the team's most strident critics throughout.

No Ashes for England, the Story of the Australian Tour, 1950–51, E. M. Wellings (Evans Brothers Ltd., London, 1951)

'Well, Billy, What's To Be Done? Somebody Will Have To Go!'
Smith's Weekly

Australia's 10-wicket thrashing in the opening bodyline
Test in Sydney in 1932–33 sent all Australia into a panic.

The second Test is done with. The echoes of the cheering have died away; but in their place have arisen rumblings of ominous portent for the Board of Control and its methods of team selection.

Out of the apparent calm comes a voice – the voice of the cricketers – that indicts a smashing attack against officialdom.

Bill Woodfull, whose abilities as a player, a resourceful captain and a born leader of men ... Woodfull who welded a team of youngsters into a victorious combination that won the Ashes in England ... Woodfull who kept the side together in Tests against the West Indies and South Africa (after the Africans had beaten England) ... Woodfull whose inspiring captaincy in the Melbourne Test was no small factor in Australia's success in the match – this man WOODFULL WAS ACTUALLY DROPPED FROM THE SECOND TEST TEAM and brought back into it (only) at the very last moment!

And the story of how he was brought back is here divulged by *Smith's* for the first time.

The Winning Factor

It may be accepted as an undisputed fact that teamwork wins matches rather than individual effort alone, and that the leader, who by a gifted personality can bring out the best in each of his men and turn to account the particular weaknesses of his opponents, has gone far towards success. A happy understanding between captain and players, a feeling of confidence among the players towards the captain, should be a paramount consideration in the selection of all teams.

And now *Smith's* challenges the Board of Control's selection committee on that very vital point. It conveys to the public of Australia facts that will not be denied, because they cannot be denied.

Woodfull was dropped from the second Test team by a group of selectors who should have known better. And he was dropped in an extraordinary way.

Soon after the first Test in Sydney, Woodfull was approached by a certain member of the Board's selection committee, which evidently was looking for a few scalps because of the defeat. Now, digest this brief conversation:

'Well, Billy, what's to be done? Somebody will have to go!'

'What about me?' answered Woodfull, who, as a leader, always sticks to his men and doesn't shuffle the blame of defeat on to any particular player.

Nothing more was said. But the selection committee ('Chappie' Dwyer, Charles Dolling and Bill Johnson) at once felt relieved. Yes, that's what they'd do (drop their captain, who had made 7 and 0 in Sydney) and Mr Woodfull himself had kindly suggested it. That got them out of a very unpleasant situation.

Though Woodfull's name was included in the 13 chosen, he was to all intents and purposes dropped.

And a few days later he was dropped in very fact. The decision was conveyed to Woodfull early in the week — before the Melbourne Test — and the selector who conveyed it suggested that probably if he 'regained his form in the meantime' he would be ready for the Adelaide Test a fortnight later.

But the committee's reckoning was astray.

'Oh, no,' replied Woodfull. 'I'm making no comeback!'

It then commenced to dawn upon the selectors that this strong man of cricket had placed them, not in a pleasant position, but in an extremely awkward one. He had passed them the buck. And they didn't know what to do with it! They had not bargained upon losing the services of this man for the four remaining Tests. And, after all, any other opening batsman might not do any better; nor might a new captain have the same inspiring influence on the team. What then?

Hurried consultations.

Gripped by a fear that amounted almost to panic, they somersaulted and notified the Board on the very morning that the second Test was to commence that Woodfull was in the side, and recommended his appointment as captain! And an hour or two before the start of play, the team was announced, with Woodfull's appointment as captain.

The team had to go into the game without any preconceived plan of attack or defence; each man was on pins and needles right up to the commencement of play, and probably for long afterwards. With nerves on edge, the wonder is that they were able to get the 228 runs that they did score.

Now, is that fair to the players? Is it fair to Australia? In the meantime, Woodfull had not slept for three nights, due to worry. His wife was nearly distracted by it.

Came the Friday. After Woodfull had won the toss, he returned to the Australians' dressing room. Usually the announcement of winning the toss is received by the players with a cheer. This time there was dead silence.

The game was played – and won – in spite of the bungling Board of Control; in spite of the Board's shilly-shallying selectors.

Almost immediately afterwards, the selection committee announced the names of 12 players for the third Test at Adelaide, notified the public that a 13th man – a local player – would be added and came to a quick decision that Woodfull would be captain. No wonder they didn't delay this time over Woodfull!

But they shouldn't have delayed before the Melbourne Test. Evidently these men lack confidence in themselves; so how can they expect the public, or the players, to have confidence in them?

The Board of Control, as constituted at present, is due for a scrapping, holus bolus, and the methods of the Board's selectors must be thoroughly overhauled.

Whatever our players have achieved, they have had no assistance from officialdom; rather, they have been harassed and irritated by a body of men who are out of touch with the team and yet frame ridiculous rules to restrict their liberty and undermine their morale as a matchwinning combination.

Woodfull's 'axing' in mid-summer 1932–33 went unreported in his 2011 biography *Woodfull: Gentleman and Scholar*. After his double failure to start the summer, he made 10 and 26 (in the series-squaring win in Melbourne), 22 and 73 not out (Adelaide), 67 and 19 (Brisbane) and 14 and 67 (Sydney). Australia lost the Ashes 4-1. *Smith's Weekly* was published from 1919–50.

Smith's Weekly (Saturday, 14 January 1933)

Peter Pan's Return
Sidney Rogerson

It was one of England's most famous victories, triggered
by the daring appointment of a first-time captain and the
recall of a seemingly ageless 48-year-old Yorkshireman
who took six wickets in a fairytale return.

P. F. 'Plum' Warner, more than anyone else, must have the credit for finally getting Wilfred Rhodes back into Test cricket at the Oval in 1926. He wrote:

I am not likely to forget Sunday, August 8, 1926, when the selection committee met for the last time. The prestige of English cricket seemed to depend on our decisions.

England had won only one Test match against Australia in the last 19. In the current series, four games had been played without a definite result ... we approached our task with only one object in view, the victory of England ... we had a good side, but it seemed to lack a genuine left-handed spin bowler and there was not perhaps enough concrete in the middle of the batting order (the choice of Rhodes supplied both needs). It was a difficult meeting if ever there was one.

The selection of Rhodes produced an interesting discussion ... here is the conversation that took place:

WARNER: 'We think, Wilfred, that you should play; you are still the best left-handed slow bowler in England and in a match which is to be played to a finish, it is likely that we shall have rain at some time or other. You can still spin 'em, you know.'

PERCY PERRIN: 'And your length is as good as ever.'

RHODES: 'Well, I caan keep 'em there or thereabouts.'

ARTHUR GILLIGAN: 'And you make runs for Yorkshire.'

RHODES: 'I caan get a few.'

JACK HOBBS: 'And your fielding is alright.'

RHODES: 'The further I run the slower I get.'

In his last and best-remembered Ashes Test, Rhodes took six Australian wickets for the game including four of the Aussie top seven on his way to four for 44 from 20 overs in the second innings. Set 415, Australia succumbed for 125. It was a glorious come-from-behind triumph for England and its new captain Percy Chapman.

Wilfred Rhodes, Professional and Gentleman, Sidney Rogerson (Hollis & Carter, London, 1960)

Relax ... If You Can
Bill Ponsford

Twenty-four-year-old Bill Ponsford was among
three newcomers named in Australia's first Test
team for the Christmas Test in Sydney in 1924.

To a young fellow taking part in his first Test match, the atmosphere is most trying. I shall never forget my first Test, particularly on that account.

It was the first match against Arthur Gilligan's English team on the Sydney Cricket Ground four years ago (1924–25)...30,000 or more pairs of eyes were on a young fellow walking out to combat Maurice Tate, who was bowling like a demon. There was a tenseness that could be felt — and sufficient enough to try the strongest nerves!

I had taken part in a few keenly fought interstate games, but never had I played in an atmosphere such as this.

The feeling of tenseness lasted throughout that match and has been equally pronounced in most of the other Test matches in which I have played. An old campaigner probably would not be affected by this tenseness to the same extent as his less experienced colleague and probably would revel in the grimness of the fight.

The ambition of every young cricketer is to play for Australia, but how few realise the ordeal that is in front of them!

I certainly was overjoyed when I found that I had been chosen as one of Australia's representatives, but it was not until I got into the game that I realised the grimness and the relentlessness of Test cricket.

Things that I have learnt about Test cricket are that to do himself justice, a man must be in perfect physical condition; that he must endeavour to keep his nerves under complete control; and that while the anxiety to do well is natural, the player should endeavour to avoid over anxiety as much as possible.

It is over anxiety that causes a very large percentage of the failures among new men in these keenly fought games.

One does not imagine that the keenness of the players will be any less marked in the coming games than it has been in those of the past.

Both sides are so keyed up that nothing will be given away; each will be out to do his utmost to swing the pendulum in favour of his own side. Both sides will be in deadly earnest from the call of 'Play' until the last ball is bowled.

Record-breaking Melburnian Bill Ponsford scored centuries in each of his first two Ashes Tests in 1924–25.

The Sporting Globe Cricket Book, 1928–29: Records of the Tests, International & Interstate Games and Players (Herald & Weekly Times, Melbourne, 1928)

Five Devastating Balls
Ronald Mason

The combined menace of Jack Gregory and Ted McDonald triggered unprecedented Australian success in the early 1920s, Gregory's onslaught on the opening morning at Trent Bridge seeing three of England's finest fall in five balls as Australia geared towards the sixth of eight Ashes victories in a row.

It would be pleasant to record that the Test series opened in bright sunlight. The season itself was to be one of the hottest and driest in the annals; it is inappropriate therefore, though in the upshot in fair accordance with the home side's display, that the first Test was begun in a chill wind under grey, lowering skies. [Warwick] Armstrong looked at the hard plumb wicket, a little freshened by recent drizzle but not much and left out [Arthur] Mailey, his chief spinner, who doubtless met the situation philosophically. ['Stork'] Hendry, a little surprisingly, got a place and so did ['Nip'] Pellew, as much for their supreme fielding capacities as for anything else;

FEWEST BALLS TO REACH FIVE WICKETS IN AN ASHES INNINGS, AFTER FIRST COMING ON TO BOWL

Balls bowled	Bowler (country)	Place & date of match
23	Hugh Trumble (Australia)	Melbourne, 1904
32	Bernard Bosanquet (England)	Sydney, 1904
40	M. A. 'Monty' Noble (Australia)	Melbourne, 1902
40	G. O. B. 'Gubby' Allen (England)	Brisbane, 1936

The all-time Test record holder is:

19	Ernie Toshack (Australia)	v. India, Brisbane, 1947

Table: Charles Davis

[Jack] Ryder had not struck form. ['Ernie'] Mayne had hardly started and [Bert] Oldfield was the unlucky one among the wicketkeepers. Mailey no doubt was able to keep the discarded units happy.

[Johnny] Douglas won the toss, and this was just about the last occasion during the match when England had anything to feel happy about; or at least that was how it was going to seem all too soon. [Donald] Knight and [Percy] Holmes, each playing in his first Test, coming out into the keen, harsh wind to face [Jack] Gregory and ['Ted'] McDonald, about whom they could have had no illusions, can be forgiven if they shrank within themselves. They concealed their trepidation bravely, but few Englishmen would have wished themselves [to be] Knight and Holmes at that moment.

They weathered the first blast manfully; Gregory's first fierce over was all speed and no length. Knight got a single and Holmes hit two 4s; now and then a short one shot up too high for the batsman to reach and ['Sammy'] Carter took it chest-high as it came down 20 yards [18 m] back. McDonald, all spring and silence, was less erratic; but Knight's classic straight defensive bat was well over the sharp lift that the moisture induced and Holmes, though scoring little after the first burst, seemed in no severe trouble. There was no immediate presage of disaster, though a formidable speed was worked up from the first over or two by both bowlers. Neither was any relief from the other.

The match was only four or five overs old, the score was up to 18 only, when Gregory whipped one away off the seam, Knight moved his bat but not his feet and Carter took the thick snick in triumph. Not a happy moment for Ernest Tyldesley, also in his first Test, rushed into the breach before a proper breath could be drawn. This was unkind luck enough, but his first ball was worse; it was one of Gregory's fastest and it spat savagely back from the line of the off stump. Tyldesley's defence was as good as any Number 3's in England, but though he came down hard on it, he was too late for anything but a thick inside edge and it hit his leg stump in the spasmodic smother. The next ball (of Gregory's new over) beat ['Patsy'] Hendren to the wide and having survived another, the next of Gregory's searing fourth over – testified to by all responsible spectators as the best and fastest of the whole cumulative sequence – shot his off stump yards out of the ground, a completely unplayable break-back delivered at the peak of speed. The *Cricketer* solemnly declared that this ball would have bowled the best batsman in the world at any time of an innings; no doubt Hendren would have gladly endorsed this statement with his initials and the date if in the heat and horror of the moment he could have recalled either to his memory.

England 18 for three; with that single over or two Gregory destroyed the morale of English cricket for the best part of a season … [his analysis: 3rd over 0000WW; 4th over 00W000 – *ed.*]

Destroyers Gregory and McDonald shared 46 wickets in 1921, England fielding a record 30 players including 14 debutants. Having won all five Tests in Australia, Warwick Armstrong's all-powerful tourists won 3-0 with the final two Tests drawn.

Warwick Armstrong's Australians, Ronald Mason (Epworth Press, London, 1971)

The Googly Man
P. F. 'Plum' Warner

It came before Spedegue's wondrous dropper and Benaud's
inspired flipper and initially was considered almost unfair. Just
how could an apparent leg break spin back in the opposite
direction? Was it cricket? Was it in the game's best interests?
So bewildering and masterful was Bernard James Tindal
Bosanquet's use of his reverse-spinning googly that he won a
Test and the Ashes for England in 1903–04, on a tour some
claimed he was only on because his mate happened to be captain.

The Australians were set 329 to win — a hard task against our
bowlers, but not by any means an impossible one.

Indeed, I know now that the Australians themselves thought
that they had the best of chances; and well they might, for after
the heavy roller had been on, the wicket rolled out better and faster
than ever. And had they not the inimitable [Victor] Trumper, the
brilliant [Reggie] Duff, the versatile [Clem] Hill and the determined
and skilful [Monty] Noble on their side?

But [Teddy] Arnold, [George] Hirst, [Len] Braund, [Wilfred]
Rhodes and [Bernard] Bosanquet never bowled better than they
did that afternoon of 3 March 1904, and they were backed up with
splendid fielding, [Dick] Lilley surpassing himself behind the
stumps. Finally, we were all fired with the zeal of battle and urged
on by that splendid enthusiasm which had carried us through many
long months.

There was but 10 minutes' batting before lunch, [Peter] McAlister
and Duff scoring seven runs. Immediately afterwards Hirst bowled
McAlister with a beautiful swerving ball and though Hill and Duff
made a short stand, the bowling always seemed to be on top of the
batting.

Braund was bowling very well indeed, but as the batsmen stayed
together Arnold was brought on, and in his first over clean-bowled
Duff. The ball was well pitched up and swerved from the leg stump

SPINNING THEM SQUARE: With 16 wickets in four Tests, the first great googly bowler Bernard Bosanquet was pivotal in England's series victory in 1902–03.

on to the middle and the off. Trumper made a fine stroke or two but another swinger had him palpably lbw.

The Worcestershire professional did not take another wicket; but those who know what the moral effect of the cheap dismissal of Trumper and Duff means realise how great his share was in our final triumph.

Following my almost invariable custom, I put Bosanquet on to bowl a quarter of an hour before the tea interval, and in a couple of overs he had dismissed Hill and [Syd] Gregory, so that at four o'clock five wickets were down for 76 runs.

[Bert] Hopkins, [Charlie] McLeod, [Hugh] Trumble, and [Jim] Kelly could not look at Bosanquet, who, at one time, had five wickets for 12 runs [from his first 32 balls – ed.], and though Noble and [Tibby] Cotter made one gallant effort 20 minutes before time, the match was over and England had won by 157 runs.

Beyond everything else the feature of the cricket was Bosanquet's bowling. Except when Rhodes and Arnold dismissed Victoria for 15, nothing more startling was done with the ball during the tour.

Unkind people have said that I 'ran' Bosanquet into this team because he was a friend of mine – but on this day he rivalled Hirst and Braund as an all-round cricketer and I repeat that when he gets a length on hard wickets, he is about the most difficult bowler there is. The Sydney wicket suited him better than any other, for whatever may have been the experience of former tours, we at any rate always found the Sydney wicket the fastest; and the faster the wicket the better he bowls.

Certain critics, too, suggested that we owed our success more to good fortune than to skill. I protest that this is a most unfair and ungenerous suggestion. We won the rubber fairly and squarely by superior cricket and our victory could be attributed in no way to fluke or chance. On the contrary, no match has ever been more distinctly won on sheer merit. We played over the Australians in every department of the game, except, perhaps fielding in which the honours were pretty well divided. In batting and bowling we showed to great advantage and even the most ardent Australian barracker could not deny that on the form of the five days' play, the stronger side won the match. What luck there was went to our opponents, for in their second innings the wicket was a great deal easier than at any time during the game ...

At the conclusion of the match we had a great reception from the spectators, who cheered as heartily as if it had been at Lord's or the Oval.

Next day I received between 50 and 60 telegrams from every part of the world, from the West Indies, from South Africa, from America, from New Zealand — in fact the sun did not set in the cable offices which flashed their messages of congratulations and good wishes.

And so we brought back the prize for which we had striven so hard, and won — I know I can say it — so deservedly.

The first time Bernard Bosanquet bowled his mysterious googly in a major match, it bounced four times and the opposing batsman was stumped. Bosanquet's seven Tests were all at Ashes level, his finest figures of eight for 107 coming at Trent Bridge in 1905.

How We Recovered the Ashes, P. F. 'Plum' Warner
(Chapman & Hall, London, 1904)

2

Braddles

A Miracle in Flannels
Ken Piesse

Don Bradman's prodigious scores still stagger today.
He remains a cricketing icon whose contributions to
the game on and off the field were unsurpassed.

Don Bradman was Australia's sporting colossus throughout the 1930s, the eighth wonder of the world and the ultimate idol for a nation ravaged by the Great Depression and on the verge of war.

The Don was the finest batsman of his or any era, and his freakish run of scores attracted phenomenal interest and raised spirits amid the gloom of food rationing and appalling unemployment.

So huge was the crowd during a Sydney club game at Birchgrove Oval one Saturday that instead of fighting his way through the masses to the pavilion to have a cup of tea with his St George teammates, Bradman opted to spend the interval in mid-pitch and was mobbed, with the crowd invading the ground seeking autographs and wanting to shake his hand.

'I'll be Bradman and you can be all the rest,' was the common catchcry of hundreds and thousands in backstreet and playground matches around the country.

TOSS-UP: MCC captain Gubby Allen called correctly in each of the first two 1936–37 Tests, which were won by England. Don Bradman won the last three tosses, Australia coming from 2-0 down to win the Ashes 3-2.

Bradman scored more than 50,000 runs in an unprecedented streak of staggering scores. Included were 212 centuries, 117 of them in first-class cricket and 29 in Tests. He played his first competitive match at 12 and his last at 54.

His monumental 452 not out for New South Wales at the Sydney Cricket Ground in 1929–30 remained a world record for nearly 30 years. He was chaired from the ground by the very bowlers he had battered.

In England in 1930, on the first of his four triumphant Ashes trips, his 974 runs in five Tests created a new Ashes high, eclipsing Walter Hammond's mighty 905 set just 18 months earlier in Australia. It inspired the term 'Bradmanesque'.

Small at just 5ft 7in (170 cm) and slightly built at 10st 3lb (65 kg), Bradman became Australian cricket's single most potent force. His awesome 334 in the Leeds Test of 1930 was to go unsurpassed among Australians at Test level for almost 75 years. He was all but unstoppable, relentless, focused and durable and no bowler, or captain, seemed to have a conventional answer to his devastating efficiency.

Such was his astonishing success that he was always expected to score heavily. Offices around Melbourne and Sydney would invariably empty around lunchtime if it was known the Don was 'in'.

Years ago Bradman 'Invincible', Bill Brown told the story of the Sydney Cricket Ground crowd clapping ever-so-generously one day as he was walking off. 'I thought to myself, "that's very nice" then I realised they were clapping because I was out … guess who was coming through the gate … Don!'

Another of Bradman's contemporaries, Jack Fingleton, said that it was usual to see thousands leave the ground when Bradman was dismissed. 'The atmosphere and much of the interest in the game walked back with Bradman to the pavilion. He was responsible for a great percentage of the enormous public interest in cricket between the two wars.'

Bradman's scoring was so spectacular and so consistent that 'BRADMAN FAILS' was a banner headline on Fleet Street one afternoon. He'd made 80!

After he edged Maurice Tate to George Duckworth to end his monumental 334 during his superlative 1930 tour, one London billboard simply said 'HE'S OUT'.

After being invalided out of the Army in June 1941 with fibrositis (fibromyalgia), he was reluctant to play again, but changed his mind after his wife, Jessie, said it would be a shame if their young son, John, was denied the opportunity to see him play. He wanted, too, to help cricket become established again after seven dark years of World War Two.

A MIRACLE IN FLANNELS:
The Don, everyone's favourite.

After leading the 1948 Australians undefeated in a triumphant English farewell, the Don was knighted and began his second phase in cricket as an administrator and selector; his stamina was to be just as enormous and influence vast.

In 1947, Glebe Park in Bowral, Bradman's hometown, was renamed Bradman Oval, and in 1976 a match was played as part of a rededication ceremony between local and NSW players. Fellow NSW country legend Bill O'Reilly launched the match by bowling the first ball. It was directed wide down the leg side and the Don missed it.

He'd retired as a Test selector in 1971 and stood down from his last committee responsibilities with the South Australian Cricket Association in 1985.

Bradman's death, in February 2001, aged 92, came as a genuine shock and triggered front-page tributes worldwide. If anyone was going to live to 100, we thought it was going to be Don. He was truly Australia's best-known son, a miracle in flannels.

Our Don Bradman, Ken Piesse (ABC Books, Sydney, 2008)

One Record-breaker on Another
Ken Piesse

The Don had lightning feet, exceptional balance and
an insatiable appetite for runs. Many thought he
could also 'see' the ball earlier than everyone else.

It remains two of the most compelling hours of my life. The opportunity to interview cricketing icon Bill Ponsford was simply wondrous, an unforgettable highlight.

I didn't know it at the time, but one of Ponsford's best mates, another ex-Bodyliner, Leo O'Brien, had orchestrated it all. Leo knew how keen I was on cricket and kept pestering Bill, the most reserved of champions, to break his silence and see me.

I knew Bill hadn't granted an interview in years so I did as much 'cramming' as possible, reading everything I could about him and with fresh batteries in the tape recorder and with a half a page of carefully typed questions, out I went to see him.

Weeks before I had interviewed Laurie Nash, asked one question and he was still talking an hour later. I thought every interview with a champion old player would be the same. But Ponny was rising 79 and as I soon found, far from keen at all to talk of the past.

He blocked my six expectant questions with little more than a 'yes' or a 'no'. I began to panic. We were less than 10 minutes into my much-anticipated interview and I'd all but run out of conversation. Looking around the walls of his son Geoff's lounge room, I thought it odd that there was not a hint of anything-cricket on display at all.

'Mr Ponsford,' I said. 'What did you do with all the souvenirs and mementos from your career? Your blazers? Your stumps? There's nothing here … on display.'

There was a pause and after what seemed an eternity, a smile. 'Oh,' he said. 'I used the blazers for the dogs [as kennel warmers]. As for the stumps, [they make great] tomato stakes, Ken, tomato stakes!'

We all laughed and the ice was broken. Two hours later he was still reminiscing.

He spoke about bodyline and how much he detested it — 'sorry you brought that up, it wasn't the game … just wasn't the game'. But he loved touring England and wanted to go back for one last hurrah in 1934. He had been tempted to retire altogether after the acrimonious bodyline summer. He remained silent when I asked him how many times he'd been struck, suffice to say that he and all the other leading Australians had been pilloried. [Ponsford was struck six times in three Tests, from the shoulders to the hip and the fingers and back. In the opening Test in Sydney he had his finger broken by Bill Voce and was to play only two more of the following four Tests. — ed.]

He talked wondrously of Don Bradman's talent and focus. On good wickets the Don was the best player of all. 'He had a wonderful eye, saw the ball early, quicker than most people … that was the reason for his wonderful success.'

I mentioned Bill's own flotilla of huge scores — he remains the only Australian to twice make 400 in a first-class innings — and asked how the meteoric rise of a young Bradman had affected him. Had he ever thought about going head-to-head with the Don and trying to match his huge scores? 'Oh no,' he said, 'I knew it was always hopeless to chase Bradman. He was ruthless … Bradman had the second shot at me [too]. The records were there to break … he played some wonderful knocks, especially in England.'

Ponny talked of Bradman's childhood habit of practising with a golf ball and a stump which he believed helped him develop an eagle-eye like no other. He may not have been as technically correct as some, but he trained and developed his coordination of brain, eye and muscle memory to an extraordinary level. So what if he held the bat in an unorthodox fashion and took it back towards gully. He'd been a phenomenal run machine. It had been a privilege to bat with him so often.

Before our interview ended, Ponny came outside with our *Age* newspaper photographer John Hart, a favourite old bat in hand. Seeing him settle lightly into his still-formidable side-on stance, hands-high and eyes alert made me wonder just how helpless bowlers must have felt when opposing players of his and Don Bradman's calibre. No wonder England concocted bodyline for the Don. His was the ultimate scalp, home or away. In their last Test together Ponsford had made 266 and Bradman 244. Their epic stand totalled a record 451.

My interview with the great Ponny was published over four pages in *Cricketer* magazine in October 1979. Years later at the re-opening of the W. H. Ponsford Stand at the Melbourne Cricket Ground, his sons told me how much their father had enjoyed the interview.

Cricketer (Newspress Pty. Ltd., Melbourne, October 1979)

A Law unto Himself
Cyril Washbrook

Bradman's staggering run feats saw him average
97.94 runs per innings before the war and 105.72 afterwards.
His unrelenting focus left teammates … and opponents in awe.

Bradman was a severe taskmaster. He played the hard way and gave his opponents absolutely nothing, but I think it probably true to say that, being a great player himself, he expected his men to be equally efficient in their own spheres of the game. Never have I noticed him guilty on the weak point of a number of captains, that is over-bowling a medium-fast or fast bowler who is taking wickets or looks like doing so. He was always intent upon conserving a bowler's energies.

To rank Don as one of the best captains I have seen in my comparatively short cricket career is easy, but I should hesitate to say that he was the finest. It must not be forgotten that he always had a good side under him.

As a batsman, the Don was a law unto himself. His strokes were not all contained in the instruction books and few people would declare him as enchanting to watch as Wally Hammond or Len Hutton. His strokes were utilitarian rather than graceful. His main purpose at the wicket was to make runs with the maximum of efficiency and the minimum of effort.

I feel sure Don Bradman's genius as a batsman arose from a remarkably rapid reflex action between his brain and his muscles. He seemed able to judge the length of a ball much more quickly than most batsmen and, no matter how fast the bowler against him, he was in a position to play his strokes so early that he always looked to be waiting for the ball to reach him. I seldom saw him play anything like a hurried stroke. He used all the orthodox strokes and some of his own and possessed an uncanny ability for finding holes in any field, even though it had been set purposely to prevent his scoring. His ability to concentrate for long periods was remarkable, and he had one unusual habit, which I am sure all young players would do well to copy. While the bowler was walking back to his starting point, Don would run his eye round the off-side fieldsmen, starting from gully, right to mid-off and then on to the bowler. By this method, which he appeared to employ before *every* ball, he carried in his mind a clear picture of where every off-side fieldsman was situated. I have little doubt this helped him to place his strokes with such exactitude.

There never was a better exponent of one general Australian technique in batting than Don Bradman. As long as I have known them, part of the strategy of Australian sides has always been to concentrate on not losing any wickets in the first hour or so. By this means, they hope to build a foundation on which they will be able to increase the scoring rate as the day progresses. Their aim is to be in a sound position before they start to take risks, but they are always eager to accelerate the pace as soon as practicable. In the last hour or two they are all set to give the bowling a proper caning and in 'murdering' the attack towards the end of the day nobody served the Australians better than Bradman. When the bowlers were flagging, he would generally score at a great pace.

Much play was always made about Don's supposed weakness

against fast bowling but, as I did not have the opportunity of seeing him against anybody really fast, I cannot express a view on the matter.

An outcome of our experiences in Australia in 1946–47, however, led us to hope that we had discovered a possible chink in his armour. This arose from Don's fondness for getting off the mark by taking a single wide of mid-on.

We reasoned that if an inswinger of good length could be made to do just enough to catch the inside edge of the bat, as he pushed forward trying to place the ball, a chance might go to leg slip.

This was tried against him when the Australians came to England in 1948, with Alec Bedser of Surrey the man deputed for the job. We did not catch Don napping this way at the start of his innings in the first Test and he'd scored 138 before he was out, caught by Len Hutton at leg slip off Alec. In the second he was out for a duck, Len catching him again off Alec. The same thing happened in the first innings of the next Test, at Lord's, Len again being the catcher. In every case Don was prodding forward at an inswinger, trying to place it wide of mid-on.

When Alec got him out again in the second innings of the next Test, Alec's proud distinction was that he had dismissed the great Don in six successive innings in which they had met – Alec had captured Don's wicket in the last Test innings of the 1946–47 tour and had done so earlier in the 1948 season, in the Surrey match. No other bowler can point to anything comparable with this remarkable feat against the most-celebrated rungetter of all time.

Was Alec the Master's bogey? Don soon provided the answer. I heard that a day or two after the Lord's Test, Don took special net practice and asked his bowlers to concentrate on inswingers at the middle and leg stumps – just as Alec had done against him. Whatever practice Don took, the result was that in no subsequent innings did he make the same mistake and only once again during the [1948] tour did Alec get him out [Bradman averaging 72.57 in the Tests and almost 90 overall – ed.].

For all his greatness, however, I missed the personal touch in Don's batting. Whenever I watched him, I felt that I should not suffer any terrific loss if I missed seeing him play any one ball. Not so with Wally Hammond in his prime. An innings by him was always something to savour ...

Cyril Washbrook played in 25 of England's first 27 Tests after World War Two and averaged 40-plus in his 37 Tests, his two Ashes centuries coming at Melbourne in 1946–47 and at Leeds in 1948.

Cricket: the Silver Lining, Cyril Washbrook
(Sportsguide Publications, London, 1950)

The Greatest Knock of All
A. G. 'Johnnie' Moyes

Numerically it wasn't the highest of all, but it
remained Don Bradman's all-time favourite ...

Don Bradman rates his 254 for Australia against England at Lord's in 1930 as the finest innings he ever played.

You will notice that he has passed by his world record of 452 not out, his 334 and 304, both at Leeds in Test matches. In fact, his 254 ranks only 12th as far as runs are concerned, but he places it first in point of technical skill.

Well, he should know and perhaps his verdict will help to settle the discussions which so often arise on this point. It still leaves us another point for debate, however ... just which of his innings has been the most useful?

Why did Bradman choose his 254? I asked him one day to tell me his finest innings and why he selected it as the best.

'Throughout my 254,' he said, 'I do not remember a single stroke which did not go exactly where it was intended. Even the one from which I got out went in the right place, but was slightly lofted and [Percy] Chapman took a remarkable catch.'

Days like that come to every batsman, days when everything

is perfectly attuned to the task. The only difference is that the Bradman has many more such days than the ordinary player.

England's attack in that Lord's Test comprised 'Gubby' Allen, Maurice Tate, Jack White, Walter Robins, Wally Hammond and Frank Woolley.

Bill Woodfull and Bill Ponsford opened with a partnership of 162 and then Bradman hit 155 in 160 minutes. Next morning he added another 99 in 180 minutes.

Wisden said this: 'The famous Australian gave nothing approaching a chance. He nearly played on at 111 and when 191 in trying to turn the ball to leg he edged it deep to the slips, but apart from those trifling errors no real fault could be found with his display.'

In this match Australia closed at 6-729 and won by seven wickets.

Bradman ranked his double-century higher than, for example, his 334 at Leeds, when he scored 102 out of 127 in 95 minutes before lunch, after Archie Jackson had gone for a duck. This century before lunch and the new ball led by Harold Larwood and Maurice Tate was dazzling enough as was the aftermath, because at the end of the day Bradman was 309 not out.

Yet in point of technique he ranks the 254 higher and so does *Wisden* which said: 'It did not quite approach his 254 at Lord's in freedom from fault, but as to its extraordinary merit there could be no two opinions.'

Putting aside the question of technical excellence, which of his centuries has been of greatest value to the team? That is not easy to answer.

Back in the 'bodyline' summer (1932–33), his 103 not out at Melbourne helped materially to win a Test match. In 1938 at Headingley, his 103 made in the dark, was, with [Bill] O'Reilly's masterly bowling, the major factor in Australia's win, while his 144 not out at Trent Bridge in the same season was a masterpiece of defence which brought the leaking ship back to port after [Stan] McCabe's dazzling 232 in the first innings had kept it from being wrecked.

Bradman has played so many superb innings that selecting the most valuable is not as simple as it looks. His 187 in Brisbane this season (1946—47) was particularly opportune after [Arthur] Morris had gone for 2 and [Sid] Barnes had also departed with only 46 on the board. Had Bradman been of lesser clay he might have succumbed during that uneasy pre-lunch period and Australia, not England, would have had to have batted first on the wet wicket.

Some of those scores in 1936—37 season when he made a double hundred in each of the third and fourth Tests and a century in the fifth were pretty good cricket.

In the season during which the South Africans visited us (1931—32), his form was amazing and he hit four centuries in the Test matches (he batted only five times) but somehow or other when looking for the best we always go to England versus Australia matches to find it. They are above all others, the real Test matches — the aristocracy of cricket.

The 452 not out against Queensland [playing for NSW] was a great display, not only for runs scored but for the speed at which he made them.

It is all a matter of opinion, no doubt. Bradman has chosen his 254 as his high-water mark of batting excellence, an innings cut short only because he lofted one ball and the amazing Chapman who was left-handed, snared the catch with his right hand — it was one of those efforts which can win a match.

From the point of view of values, however, one would be inclined to plump for one of the modest 103s, either that in Melbourne in 1932—33, or that at Leeds in 1938, an innings which prompted Neville Cardus to say that Bradman 'could get a century in Piccadilly by candlelight'.

Cricketer, journalist, commentator, author and Bradman-confidant Johnnie Moyes was part of the New South Wales selection panel which first promoted Don Bradman from club into Sheffield Shield ranks. He wrote the first definitive Bradman biography, in 1948.

Sporting Life (Associated Newspapers, Sydney, April 1947)

The Unchallenged Champion
Harry Altham

Don Bradman was still a headliner even in war-time.

When the first contingent of the Australian Expeditionary Force joined their comrades in the field, I have little doubt that one of the first and most frequent questions addressed to them will be: 'Is Don Bradman as good as ever?'

Even in the middle of Armageddon, the little man has retained 'headline value' and 'Bradman O' is still more sensational news than the usual 'Bradman Again!' to the tune of a double century.

How is it that amidst all the stresses and distortions of our distracted world, we still can feel not merely interest but a pulse of happiness and reassurance when we read of a man playing a game 13,000 miles away?

I will court the sneers of 'our brittle intellectuals' and say that it is mainly, I conceive, because we believe in that game as a cement of good fellowship, sanity and fair dealing between men and peoples, as embodying within its code and its traditions much of what we are fighting for.

Moreover, the bare legend of a day's play in Adelaide or Sydney revives for so many countless happy memories of our own: it may be of that evening in the 'St George and the Dragon' when we and our friends of the rival and vanquished village, over tankards of immortal vintage, tired the sun with talking and sent him down the sky; or of a sunbaked day at Lord's, when in shirtsleeves with a paper over our heads we watched Walter Hammond in all the majesty of his power and grace; or, more distant but no less precious, of the moment when, in the new and slightly embarrassing glory of a pair of batting gloves, we opened the innings for the Under 11 team of our preparatory school.

And of this game, with its happy associations and its reflection of so much that we hold worthwhile, Don Bradman is the unchallenged champion.

It is idle, if alluring, to compare the champions of different epochs: we may wonder indefinitely how H. L. Doherty would have fared with Budge; or Harry Vardon with Henry Cotton; whether Alex James in his prime would have bewildered the brothers Walters in theirs; whether Ronnie Poulton's swerve would have been checkmated by the closer defensive tactics of a modern international. Would 'W. G.' have been really bothered by the googly and the leg-side field? And how would Hammond have fared on the old fiery wickets of Lord's in the '70s?

Such questions cannot be answered, but we may with a feeling of absolute security assert that in no age and at no game has any man more dominated his contemporaries than has Don Bradman in the dozen years — and they are no more — of his first-class career. How many runs on a good wicket would England barter for the surety of seeing Bradman's back twice disappearing into the pavilion? What odds would any man lay, when he reaches a century, against that hundred being turned into two?

How much of Test match history in those dozen years can be assigned to him and him alone? Figures can lie, but in cricket, taken in the large, they tell the truth and in his case defy all argument. In that period 23 matches have been finished, England winning 13 and Australia 10; in nine out of those 10 times Bradman has made more than 100, in six of the 10 more than 200. It has been the same in all his cricket from Test match to grade. No-one in the game has approached him for consistency over anything like the same period. He has already far outstripped in aggregate all other Australian batsmen, from Victor Trumper and Charlie Macartney, through to Clem Hill and Joe Darling and Syd Gregory and Warren Bardsley.

To total 1000 runs in a domestic season 10 times in the Dominion is a tremendous achievement: only Bill Ponsford and Alan Kippax have done it more than once; in each case twice. Bradman has done it every season except one when he first appeared.

What, then, is the secret of this astonishing phenomenon? Let us consider first the physical equipment. Bradman is a small man and were a stranger to meet him standing still in ordinary clothes he would notice nothing remarkable about him except a pair of exceptionally high shoulders, an unusually resolute jaw and a keen pair of eyes. But see the same figure in flannels and in action and the first secret is not far to seek. For here is obviously a perfectly coordinated body, balanced on feet as neat, and at the same time as strong, as any professional dancer's, which ensure maximum speed and accuracy of movement; add to this that flexibility of hip which is a hallmark of nearly all great games players, great power of forearm, wrist and (often forgotten) hand, and you have some idea of the machine that turns out the runs. Machines need looking after and Bradman has always known how to keep his not merely, it would seem, in good running, but in racing trim. But greatest of all his assets is a speed of reaction which, I believe, scientific tests have proved to be quite abnormal; perhaps only with 'Ranji' was there so small a time-lag between conception and execution, and this is the secret of his strokeplay whether in defence or attack. He sees the ball sooner, watches it longer and can play the stroke later than anyone else. Remember, too, that in his case each stroke decision is regulated by a singularly acute cricket brain and by now immense, batting experience.

POWER-PACKED:
Walter Hammond's driving
was incomparable.

It would be illogical to expect in a man of his build the effortless ease of stroke play which one associated with Frank Woolley or the power of Walter Hammond's driving, though in all conscience there is power enough; nor can he rival one of the greatest of English batsmen George Gunn in giving the impression that he has 'all day' to play his shot. The tempo of his batting is staccato. But the power and versatility of his stroke play is astonishing. Unlike the vast majority of his contemporaries he can fight a war on two fronts, for he seems equally at home with an off-side or leg-side attack: he can hit the ball through the covers with equal facility off the front or back leg, and he is a brilliant cutter, both square and late; but it is on the other side of the wicket that his mastery is most impressive.

He is the finest hooker in the world and can direct this stroke at will anywhere from wide mid-on to fine leg with the vital, and very rare, security of hardly ever lifting the ball, whilst to bowl even a fairly accurate length on the line of his leg stump or legs is to ask for punishment; here, perhaps, his peculiar genius is most pronounced in his ability to force the ball through any inviting gap, generally off the back foot, meeting it very near his body, and with a combined thrust of the forearms and flick of the wrists played with a perfection of timing that makes a utilitarian stroke into a work of art.

Allied with this great variety of stroke play there goes an extraordinary facility for placing the ball, and only very accurate bowling and the most skilfully adjusted placing of the field has any chance of keeping him even moderately quiet on a good wicket.

In his earlier years — and even now when the whim takes him — he could and can go the pace of a pure hitter, and for a time in the early part of the 1934 tour he seemed practically to have selected that role for himself. Then, I believe, an almost stern remonstrance from [captain Bill] Woodfull sobered him, with the monumental result that we all remember, and since then, though his strokeplay could never be anything but remarkable, runs rather than strokes appear to have become his main objective. For the extraordinary consistency with which he pursues that aim we must look beyond the mere technique of a superlative defence coupled with outstanding physical fitness and a stamina that sustains him through the longest day. If I may borrow terms from another sphere, Bradman is not a romantic but a realist: he finds his satisfaction in achievement rather than in method; he is not tempted, as Jack Hobbs often was, to try dangerous strokes simply because the mere making of runs by ordinarily secure means had begun to pall, or to regard a mere century as the signal for 'chancing his arm', either as a concession to his physical nature or from the feeling that made

Michelangelo want to give up painting in favour of sculpture, because it was 'too easy'.

He will always play to the clock and the state of the game and very rarely fails to take drastic toll of a tiring attack during the last 90 minutes of a day's play; but, other things being equal, he is content to go on his way from his first century to his second and from his second to his third with the same deliberate speed, unwearied, unexcited and, above all, undiverted.

It is sometimes said that Bradman cannot play on a 'sticky' wicket. What nonsense! With his natural gifts he could not help being good under those conditions, when the ability to move the feet quickly and play a delayed stroke accurately mean so much.

In the Leeds Test match of 1938 the ball was consistently on top of the bat, but he made his century as usual and that century settled the match, whilst in that absorbing game, in which all Yorkshire to this day believe they were robbed of victory by rain, he played [Hedley] Verity, on Verity's own admission, as well as he ever remembers being played.

Another statement that I have sometimes heard made, in a sort of vague disparagement, against Bradman is that he is 'inhuman'. If this means that he is uniquely immune from the ordinary frailties of the cricketing flesh, he certainly stands condemned, for he does not tire, he does not relax, and even on the days when he is, for him, palpably out of form, a long stay is more probable that a short one. But if it implies that he lacks personality or the capacity to enjoy himself and make others enjoy it, then that is ludicrously false. His immense vitality, for one thing, gives it the lie: one cannot be bored with a man who is so tremendously alive every moment he is on the field. But it was finally and utterly disproved by his captaincy of the Australians in 1938. No-one can have been surprised at his tactical shrewdness on that tour, but I doubt whether anyone was quite prepared for the personal ascendancy which he established over his team. I do not think I have ever admired anything on the cricket field so much as his leadership through those heartbreaking days at the Oval in August [in 1938, when Len Hutton broke Bradman's Test match solo record − ed.]. His own fielding was an inspiration in itself, and as hour succeeded hour with nothing going right and the prospect of the rubber receding over a hopeless horizon, it was, one felt, his courage and gaiety that alone sustained his side. And when the tragic accident came [Bradman twisting his ankle when relief bowling], the game was over, the balloon was pricked and his team was a team no more.

I have written much more than I meant; much more, indeed, than my friend the editor asked me; more perhaps than he will see fit to publish, and I have caught myself wondering whether a sense of proportion in time as well as space has not been left out in a schoolmaster's 'arrested development'. But if Falstaff in a tavern in Eastcheap babbled o' green fields, may we not find comfort in remembering our own Arcadia?

I am the happier now for having seen 'W. G.' bat and [Charles] Kortright bowl, for having fielded to 'Ranji' and Archie MacLaren and for having been comprehensively bowled by Colin Blythe. But in the many pictures that I have stored in my mind from the 'burnt-out Junes' of 40 years, there is none more dramatic or compelling than that Bradman's small, serenely moving figure in its big-peaked green cap coming out of the pavilion shadows into the sunshine, with the concentration, ardour and apprehension of surrounding thousands centred upon him, and the destiny of a Test match in his hands.

Harry Altham stands tall in a pantheon of English cricket lovers and writers whose history of the game, first published in 1926, remains a seminal work. His own first-class career spanned four decades and his passion and off-field contributions once prompted Walter Robins to declare: 'We have the Grace Gates, the Harris Gardens and the Warner Stand, but in my humble opinion Harry very quietly did more for cricket than any of them.'

The Cricketer Spring Annual 1940 (W. H. Hillman & Co., London, 1940)

Bowling the Don ... First Ball
George Tribe

It was the only time he ever bowled against the Don.

W e were in the nets in Brisbane on the morning of Don's comeback Test (in 1946) and I actually knocked him over with my very first ball. I couldn't believe it. Keith Miller and I went out and Don, too, followed by all the photographers.

Don walked into the nets and straightened the stumps up and first ball I bowled, over they went. He just turned around, threw the ball back to me, straightened the stumps up and then looking at them, took his (new) guard right out on the off stump. He wanted to make certain if he missed it was going to hit his legs. He wasn't going to be bowled out again. I did learn something that day. If you are in trouble, always bat off stump.

I never did get to bowl at him again in the nets. Normally we would bowl only against our own (state) players. New South Wales bowlers wouldn't bowl to our blokes in the nets. It didn't matter that you were playing for Australia. If you were a Victorian we would only bowl against each other. Guys like Ray Lindwall (from NSW) wouldn't bowl to you. It just wasn't done.

George Tribe's only three Tests came in the 1946–47 Ashes summer before he began a professional career in England.

Pavilion (Australian Cricket Society, Melbourne, 2009)

HE BOWLED THE DON: George Tribe at the height of his professional career in England.

He Was Ruthless
Jack Hobbs

Jack Hobbs' last Ashes summer was Don Bradman's first in
England. The Master was amazed by what he saw.

B ut what a wonderful thing it was all the same, to bat as Don did
on English turf for the first time.

I would not compare Bradman to George Gunn, Archie MacLaren,
Reggie Spooner, Frank Woolley or one of our great classic batsmen.
He is more of a rungetting machine; first kinsman to Phil Mead
of 20 years ago. Bradman never hit the ball in the air. He had an
exceptionally accurate sense of timing. He had marvellous sight.
The pace he got on his hits on the leg-side was astounding. He
seemed to only place his bat against the ball and yet it flew with
the force of a full-blooded drive.

As for Bradman the man, we had heard a lot about him and
particularly in relation to his alleged aloofness. It is the easiest
thing in the world for any action of a successful man to be construed
into 'swollen-headedness'. I know this is my own experience.
Personally I always found Bradman an attractive, simple-hearted
lad ... although he has surely done enough to be excused a certain
amount of swollen-headedness which, let me add, I have never
observed in him.

I must say, however, that it would have pleased me better had
he been more demonstrative. He ought to have shown more *joie de
vie* (joy of life) especially after he got his third 100 (of the innings)
at Headingley. But he acted much like an old-stager instead of the
boy of 21 or so that he is.

When Charlie Macartney used to reach his hundred he would
begin hitting out through the sheer delight at his achievement.
But Bradman never batted an eyelid and just kept on going. He was
ruthless.

Bradman's superlative displays in England in 1930 saw him amass an extraordinary 974 runs at 139.14 in five Ashes Tests, a run feast still unsurpassed more than 80 years later.

The Sporting Globe Cricket Book: Records of the Tests,
International & Interstate Games and Players (Herald &
Weekly Times, Melbourne, 1932)

Toscanini and the Cricket
Neville Cardus

After two consecutive losses, Don Bradman's right to the
Australian captaincy was being questioned, especially by
South Australians loyal to their own Vic Richardson who had
led with such outstanding results in South Africa the previous
season. With Australia 2-0 down in the fight for the Ashes,
Melbourne's New Year Test set new attendance records and
was in the balance on the fourth morning when Bradman
resumed on 56 in Australia's second innings.

On a rich couch stuffed with runs, Australia made victory only a matter of time. [Don] Bradman and [Jack] Fingleton seized a ripe chance. In the happiest conditions for batsmen, rare skill is required to sustain a stand of nearly a day's duration. And England's attack was as good as heart-breaking turf could allow any attack to be that did not contain a Barnes or a Larwood.

[Hedley] Verity was magnificent; in his absence Bradman might have scored another hundred runs. Up to a point, Bradman played at his second best. Nonetheless his greatness was beyond argument. I never believed in his poor scores and I was not prophetic but merely deductive when I wrote that Bradman's day was coming back and was almost on us.

Bradman and Fingleton scored 343 together in 364 minutes and [wrist spinner Jim] Sims broke the partnership. He was scarcely used enough in a state of affairs which called for some humorous bowling now and then. Australia was so far ahead and Bradman and Fingleton so thoroughly set, that a few extra runs to the growing pile would not have mattered. Sims is always likely to fool a confident player into a blunder.

It was a lovely morning for the fourth day, soft sunshine and sailing white clouds, like any summer day at Old Trafford. And again a fine crowd to see Bradman; work and all forms of manual labour are rightly dismissed from the mind by Melbourne whenever Test cricket is shaking the continent. On this morning as I left my hotel, I saw a group of little girls setting forth — armed with wickets and bats ready for action at the first signs of failure in Australian manhood, and no doubt qualified already to join the women in the crowd and scream for Australia at the top of their voices.

Bradman and Fingleton came to the wicket, to strengthen further a strong position which nobody foresaw on Friday. The rain was the villain of the piece for England. Fortune, as I say, snatched away from [England captain 'Gubby'] Allen quite as much as she gave him at Brisbane and Sydney, where the wickets never became half as sinful as Melbourne's. But the scurviest trick served by luck to England was the drizzle which on the third afternoon reduced a confident attack to greasy impotence. A sticky wicket one day is, so to say, part of the game, to be accepted philosophically. But a slippery ball the next day …!

To mention these matters is not to detract from the keen, skilful way Australia seized the chances. Here at last was much of the old hostility, the swift pounce on the broken enemy. The wicket was as easy for Bradman and Fingleton as middle-age, or vintage port. [Bill] Voce could scarcely make the new ball rise knee-high and Bradman pulled his deliveries with the familiar dynamic movement. The conditions were his ally.

Allen bowled with so great an effort that after a single ball his hair became tousled; he actually sent a ball flying past Fingleton's breastbone to the off, but this miracle was, as miracles should be: exceptional.

Voce then forced Bradman back in a superb over of perfect length and rhythm. Bradman was glad to edge a fine outswinger for a single and the next ball, a masterpiece of accurate swerve, went through the slips, also behind Fingleton's back, while Fingleton was probably wondering in a flash of apprehension whether anybody had held a catch while he wasn't looking. It was easy to feel the sense of strain in the efforts of England's fast bowlers to take a wicket. Allen troubled Bradman, who was guilty of a dangerous stroke to point. The batting and the turf frustrated the onslaught and [Walter] Hammond came to the relief of Voce. It is always good captaincy to give Hammond the ball while it is still new.

Fingleton again played perpendicularly, not obviously thinking of runs, which came to him by a sort of interest on the time accumulated during his stay at the wicket. And Bradman could not unleash himself; his batting was tied to the kennel for a long time. Nonetheless, Australia was attending to the right job, grimly digging the deep hole for England's funeral.

The English attack was admirably steady and Voce worked heroically on a wicket sent by heaven to Australia's batsman, so soon after the shambles. The runs continued to come slowly, a by-product of the general war of attrition. Bradman's cricket was, in the term of Karl Marx, congealed labour. The gigantic crowd sunned itself in placid contentment: men, women, children; sitting, standing, craning their necks, squatting on steps, even hanging on to rails. I suppose that a number of the population of Melbourne was actually not present, but working at home, or in offices, with all their excuses worn out for the time being. In England we do not know what a Test match is, as an expression of the national consciousness.

At lunch, Bradman and Fingleton were still not out, and apparently beyond serious error. After lunch (which by the way consisted of oysters, turkey, asparagus, jelly and trifle), Verity proceeded with his precise bowling, which before the interval cost England only seven runs in 56 balls. His length dropped with the persistence of water on a rock. I began to look for stalactites hanging down to the earth.

The wicket was now the best and most cosy and comfortable seen in the Test matches during the season. Bradman cut Voce brilliantly, and reached his 100, a State Occasion effort, related to his cricket in England of six years ago as the honest mason's productions are related to architecture. But as I say, I expected him to begin at any moment and shed his armour.

The dazzling returns of [Walter] Robins produced further hysterics among the women. Bradman drove Sims with a grand running drive and pulled voraciously to leg. The banked fires of his innings appeared at last to have been struck into a blaze. But Sims had the honour of beating him at least once. This was the only sign of mortality in

THE DON: Bradman worked as a stockbroker in Adelaide from the mid-1930s.

Bradman that the England attack had witnessed for many, many persevering overs, during which the really encouraging influence to Allen was Robins' attempts to run somebody out. He seemed to cover acres of space and cover or back up all the other fieldsmen, himself included. He was a joy to see and you had to be quick to see him, as he flashed and swooped here, there and everywhere.

Verity put another shovel of damp coal on Bradman's play; he worried the great man, who, even against a long-hop from Sims now and again pulled prodigiously and got only a single. The old genius shot out once more as soon as Allen came on at 323 — a fierce off-drive from the back foot. So was England's pit deepened and Fingleton went his ways, a good second gravedigger, who might have said that he had been on this job at this cemetery, man and boy, these many years. He does his job diligently with a straight bat seldom lifted up higher than his knee and he is always ready, for the cause, to contribute his share modestly, even anonymously. He deserves his sojourn on today's heavenly wicket, for he played a brave and lonely hand at Brisbane and at Sydney he was also dependable, in difficult straits.

When Fingleton reached his 100 he was given roars of applause, the generous like of which I have seldom heard at a cricket match; they were prolonged, and culminated in three rousing cheers. It was the sort of ovation that the foreigners give to Toscanini after he has conducted an opera. The English team accepted the situation now with commendable philosophy, and Robins, having sought in vain to run the batsmen out, came on to bowl, also apparently for run-outs.

After tea, Verity continued his artistic bowling, and twice in one over he beat Bradman. The duel between Bradman and Verity was the vital interest of the afternoon and Verity did not emerge second best on points, as they say. Nothing but consummate length and flight could have checked Bradman, in circumstances made for Bradman. Nowadays, all the applause is for the batsman, but the Melbourne crowd appreciated Verity's skill and recognised it warmly after an over which Bradman needed all his wits to counter. Verity's accuracy made the position of 'silly' point as safe as it was necessary, technically and psychologically, all day. Every run scored from Verity had to be earned. It was beautiful bowling, delightful to the eye and to the intellect.

In the hour between five and six, Bradman was helping himself, for now the attack failed from sheer weariness. Allen endeavoured to transform himself into a slow-to-medium-paced bowler; he expressed a noble disgust.

Following England's victories in the two first weather-affected Tests of the 'Goodwill Series', Australia won the third comfortably in Melbourne after Fingleton in at No. 6, made 136 and Bradman, in at No. 7, made 270. It was Bradman's first win as captain and was the first of three victories in a row as Australia defended the Ashes 3-2. Bradman's right to lead was never again questioned. Neville Cardus was knighted for his contributions to cricket writing.

Australian Summer, Neville Cardus (Jonathan Cape, London, 1937)

What They Said About the Don

'There was such a huge human interest in him as a player and as a man. The Bradman Museum feel some sense of guilt that it was through our energies that he allowed himself to become much more of a public figure in 1990s than he was prepared to do so in 1940s. The more he allowed himself to become part of public domain the more the public wanted to know about him.' – Richard Mulvaney, long-time curator of the Bradman Museum, 2004

'Don Bradman was Mary MacKillop with pads on.' – Garry Linnell, the *Bulletin*, 2001

'The message of Bradman's career is that a boy from the country without any advantages of a wealthy background and without much education, can achieve greatness through sheer talent and hard work.' – Bruce Collins, Bradman Trust chairman on the launching of the Bradman Museum in Bowral in 1989

'When he hooked the ball he could almost choose the picket it was going to hit along the boundary. He controlled his hook shot as I have never seen any other batsman control it.' – Keith Miller, 1955

'More than anyone else Bradman took the initiative away from bowlers. In the glory of his youth and strength, he was the most relentless rungetter of all time. Some challenged, like Trumper; some charmed, like Ranjitsinhji; Bradman devastated – deliberately, coldly, ruthlessly. His power was his delight and his use of it the greatest single attraction in the cricket of his age. Wherever cricket lives, he will be discussed, dissected.' — Jim Kilburn, 1975

'How to get Bradman out is developing into a pastime for rainy days.' — Arthur Mailey, 1934

'He just belts the hell out of every ball he can reach.' — Jack Ryder, 1930

'On and on he seemed to go, batting into eternity.' — Jack Fingleton, 1948

'So deep was his concentration that at the wicket he rarely uttered a word and a century to him appeared to be just a signal post on the way to a double or a treble hundred.' — Denis Compton, 1950

'Don was to batting almost what Walter Lindrum was to billiards. Applying the precision Lindrum employed, he used to score threes from the last balls of overs, not singles, to retain the strike.' — umpire George Hele, 1975

'If Don breaks any more records I don't know how I will manage to get through the clerical work involved in answering congratulations.' — Emily Bradman, Don's mother, 1930

'It didn't matter what side Don was in, he had a huge influence. He was an outstanding player and a very great tactician. I used to discuss things with him about attacking certain batsmen. We didn't have computers to help us in those days. It was all done with your brain.' — Bill Johnston, 1993

'Even as recently as 1938 I heard the remark in a bitter voice, "Here comes the boy wonder." It surprised me, for the speaker had never had cause to dislike Bradman. It was the expression, in an unguarded moment, of resentment against one who had climbed higher than his fellows. Some of them just couldn't take it.' — Jack Fingleton, 1946

'Bradman knew our weaknesses and went for them with the greatest skill.' — Denis Compton, 1950

'He sat and talked with me for three-quarters of an hour because he didn't want me to be alone on the morning of my first Test. It was, I think, the must human thing I have encountered in sport.' — Ian Johnson, 1992

'All they wanted to write about was the Don. No need for him to chase publicity. It chased him.' — Sid Barnes, 1953

'The highlight of that Test was the last appearance of Don Bradman. As he walked out to the wicket, I shall never forget the thunder of cheering that went up.' — Godfrey Evans, 1957

'No-one taught me to play cricket. I was not coached. I found out for myself; and perhaps it was the best way.' — Don Bradman, 1959

3
Giants of the Game

Living His Dreams
Ken Piesse

Bright-eyed country boy Adam Gilchrist soon
became one of the most celebrated stars in
Australia's champion teams of the 2000s.

Spend any time with Adam Gilchrist and it's like you're his next door neighbour, so comfortable does he make you feel and so easygoing is the rapport.

Not only is he the world's No. 1 ranked batsman, he's also the heartbeat of Australian cricket, warm and obliging; a country kid still with stars in his eyes.

We're seated on a lounge at the Quay West, the new trendy home for the Australian players when they're in Melbourne. Gilchrist is in jeans and shirt and the latest casual shoes from lifestyle company Oakley.

'Got some new gear?' asks Shane Watson, the youngest member of the team. 'Yeah mate, backed the truck up!' says Gilchrist with a grin.

The players are organising tickets for the football that night.

It's a cold and wet Friday afternoon, but most are going.

MAIDEN TOUR: Miffed at missing selection on Australia's extended tour of Ceylon (Sri Lanka), India and South Africa in 1969–70, Greg Chappell was pivotal in Australia's rejuvenation in England in 1972 when on his maiden Test appearance at Lord's he made the finest of his nine Ashes centuries.

Opportunities to truly relax are rare for the elite players, especially with Australia's ever-widening program, home and away.

No-one is busier than Gilchrist. He has just filmed an advertisement for Orange, the new sponsors of Australian cricket. Puma report vibrant sales of its Adam Gilchrist 'signature' bats. He's in demand, just like a Shane Warne at the zenith of his popularity in the mid-'90s.

Like every cricket-mad young kid, he'd always wanted to play for Australia. Now he is living his dreams, travelling the world and loving every moment.

Never before has he felt more comfortable with his surroundings. The wintertime break, interrupted only by a week's out-of-season cricket against the visiting Pakistanis, allowed him and his wife Melinda some quality time together with their young son, Harrison.

The pre-tour training camp in Brisbane in late August saw him catch up with his family, one of the proudest of all bush cricketing clans.

His grandfather Bill, a trapper, kangaroo shooter and farmer, once took 18 wickets in a match. His father, Mungindi-born Stan Gilchrist bowled leggies and like Adam, batted in the top-order. In a schoolteaching career which took him from Sydney to Deniliquin and on to Lismore, Stan played with and against some outstanding players, including 'the Tamworth Twister' John Gleeson and famed West Indian expressman Wes Hall. Gilchrist's brothers Dean and Glenn also played high level cricket, Dean coaching Gordon in senior Sydney grade ranks for more than 10 years. His sister Jacki, who is the eldest and like Adam, left-handed, was the first woman to play cricket with the men at 'A' grade level in Deniliquin.

As much as Stan has revelled in Adam's doings in Australian colours, he says his all-time proudest moment in cricket came at Deniliquin one day when the 'A' graders were several short and Jacki, Adam and Glenn were enlisted to field.

Cricket has always been pivotal in Gilchrist's life. He remembers his Dad walking out to bat one day and asking someone 'to keep an eye on me'.

POWERHOUSES: Adam Gilchrist (left) and Matthew Hayden were among the most dominant Australians during an unprecedented run of 16 Test wins in a row from 1999 to 2001.

'I can't remember anyone having to babysit me for too long, mind you — but Dad could bowl a bit and his wrong-un was right up there with Warnie's.'

Gilchrist says he was fast-tracked playing against cricketers older and more mature than him. 'Maybe that held me in good stead for the future.'

As a 14-year-old, he still can recall taking a catch and a stumping from his father's bowling during a grand final in Lismore.

Like all country kids, Gilchrist tried virtually every sport, including Aussie Rules and tennis and for a stage, was just as keen on soccer as cricket. He still has an ambition now to play a season when things become a little less hectic.

But cricket took precedence from the time of his first representative honour when chosen for the Riverina Primary School team for a carnival in Kempsey.

'It was the first time I'd been away from home and while I got billeted out to some lovely people I was as homesick as. I think it was one reason why I played so well. I'm thinking, "I'm here, I just have to play well."

'I didn't have any of my [usual] teammates around me — it was just me. Once the cricket stopped I wasn't sure what to do next.'

He still fondly remembers the test matches out on the street with the next door neighbours, Tony and Peter Jefferies who went on to represent Geelong CC.

But it was in Lismore from the ages of 12 to 17 where his talent truly blossomed.

Stan and his wife June say Adam's appetite for cricket was insatiable. He'd walk around the house with his green and white wicketkeeping gloves on — even wear them to the dinner table.

He remained just as keen even when he had his nose broken the first time he ever kept wickets in a game, for Deniliquin South Primary School.

'It was one of those cement slabs with the malthoid laid on top. The sides were an inch and a half higher. The ball deflected off one of the edges and it hit me straight between the eyes!' Adam says.

Stan adds, 'He wasn't too happy until I told him how many times Rod Marsh had also been hit in the head and how it was part and parcel of keeping wickets. He bucked up after that.'

Gilchrist says he learnt to love the team element of cricket from these formative days and having to switch cities from Sydney to Perth in the mid-'90s was part of his apprenticeship which now sees him ranked the world's No. 1 batsman and a 'keeper of renown'.

Just being a part of the Australian XI and knowing the stories of those who have come before him is a thrill.

'It's just magic,' he says. 'We all know the rivalry and amazing moments in every series which pop up. The stand-out moments: [Dennis] Lillee and Marsh, [Ian] Botham, Steve Waugh in '89 ... to be a small part of that is great.'

He says this summer's series [2002–03] is likely to be closer than many in the last decade.

'While a 4-1 result (against England in 2001) may look like a

STEVE WAUGH ON GILCHRIST

What an asset to the side Adam Gilchrist is, coming in at five down and regularly taking the game away from the opposition in the space of an hour. It's a perfect role for him. He often comes in around the time of the second new ball, with no limitations or designated rules to stick to, which allows his natural, unaffected style to take the game by the scruff of the neck. I've never seen a guy block a ball harder. 'Gilly' has steel-infused wrists and refuses to defend meekly. Every shot is played with the intent of scoring runs, and the extra arc he creates by holding the bat high in his grip translates into extra speed on the down-swing and more pace for the ball off the face of the bat. He must have an eye like a bald eagle, because he never seems to mistime or leave any balls; each delivery is an offering to be dispatched to his liking. Instead of backing down after an onslaught, he ups the tempo to a new level and demolishes bowlers like the tornado did Dorothy's house. He is the modern-day batting prototype, tackling each assignment with the bravado of an Indiana Jones.

Out of my Comfort Zone: The Autobiography,
Steve Waugh (Viking, Melbourne, 2005)

GILLY: Steve Waugh says Adam Gilchrist has an eye like a bald eagle.
Patrick Eagar

comprehensive thumping, there were moments where England had their chances,' he says.

'The playing field was very level. It was just that we were always able to step up and grab the momentum or the opportunity which arose. Hopefully we can do that again. I don't want to be part of a team which loses the Ashes!'

Gilchrist was to play 96 Tests in a row for Australia, becoming the first wicket-keeper to also be ranked as the No. 1 batsman in the world. He averaged 45 and five dismissals in his 20 Ashes Tests, home and away. His only losing Ashes campaign came in 2005, the greatest modern-day series of all, when England won 2-1.

Australian Cricket Tour Guide 2002–03, Ken Piesse
(Emap Australia, Sydney)

One Hell of a Delivery
Graham Gooch

Fast-tracked into Australia's best XI way before his time, Shane Warne made a stunning entry into Ashes Tests at Old Trafford.

The (1993) series started really well at Manchester when we bowled Australia out for 289 in their first innings. My premonitions and fears began to dissolve, and as Mike Atherton and I comfortably reached 71 for the first wicket in reply, I thought to myself, 'We're okay. This is going to be a competitive series after all.'

Then Merv Hughes had Atherton caught behind. Mike Gatting, our acknowledged champion against spin, strode in — and, give him his due, (Australia's captain) Allan Border immediately threw down the gauntlet and summoned up the young leg spinner Shane Warne, whom the Australians had been keeping comparatively under wraps during their build-up matches to the Tests.

First ball from Warne — would it be a loosener? No chance!

Warne flicked it out of his hand on the line of Gatting's pads and then it hung and dipped in the air even further towards the leg side. If Mike had been set and not just arrived at the crease, most days of the week he would have treated it like a full-toss leg-side cheese-roll, put his left leg down the pitch and whacked it unceremoniously over mid wicket, one bounce and over the ropes for 4. But quite correctly, in a Test with a new bowler, he wanted a good look and was happy just to push out, cover up and either block it or let it continue floating down the leg side. Then the ball pitched. It turned a good foot, almost at right angles; in a blur it ripped across Gatt's body and whisked away the off-bail.

Gatt could scarcely believe it and stood there transfixed. I was at the other end, poking and prodding and pretending nothing extraordinary had happened. But in my mind I was thinking it was one hell of a delivery. The Australians went potty with glee and more so immediately afterwards, when Warne had Robin Smith caught at slip groping vaguely. From 70 for no wicket, we collapsed and were eventually all out for 210, Warne having taken four for 51 in 21 overs.

That game was the first I'd ever faced Shane in a game. I got to 60 before he bowled me a high full toss. He had just one man (Brendon Julian) in front of the wicket on the leg side at mid-on and I hit it straight to him.

I had a very good relationship with Shane on and off the field. There was a good rivalry. I got a few runs against him and he got me out quite a few times too.

In Brisbane during the following tour (in 1994–95), he was rolling through us in the second innings. I was batting pretty well and was 50 not out or so. I said to him: 'You're getting all the others but you're not going to have me.'

It was a good wicket and I was playing him okay only to suddenly play this horrendous slog across the line. I don't know why. Ian Healy took a great catch off the bottom edge … it was my major disappointment of that series.

Shane Warne amassed 34 wickets during his extraordinary first tour of England during which be proposed to his girlfriend Simone on a dinghy in-between Tests and bamboozled the might of England's finest in Australia's emphatic 4-1 Ashes victory. Despite turning 40 in mid-series, Gooch was clearly England's outstanding batsman with 673 runs in six Tests.

Gooch: My Autobiography, Graham Gooch with
Frank Keating (CollinsWillow, London, 1995)

Cricket's Incomparable Artist
Ken Piesse

His grandfather was Australian Test captain
Vic Richardson. Many felt him born to rule.

Australian cricket's incomparable artist, a batsman of infinite skill, charm and polish,

Greg Chappell was the outstanding Australian batsman of his generation, whose contribution on and off the field was Bradmanlike. He had his moments of controversy and regret, but few argue with his elite standing alongside Ricky Ponting as Australia's finest batsman since the Don.

From the time Chappell made a classic century on his Ashes debut in Perth, he thrilled cricket crowds like few before or since and stimulated his ever-competitive big brother Ian to perform with fresh consistency. Chappell's sublime century on a green wicket at Lord's in 1972 was pivotal in Australia squaring the series and stands tall alongside three centuries for World Series Cricket (WSC) Australia in the West Indies in 1978 as the finest of his illustrious career.

Few played with his upright majesty or with as classically a straight bat. His on-driving on his Test debut against John Snow and Co. was superlative. Later after a grip change at the recommendation of Bradman, he hit the ball through mid-off with equal flair. He averaged 73 against India, 66 Sri Lanka, 63 Pakistan, 56 West Indies and New Zealand and 45 England. In World Series Cricket his Supertest average was 56, in seven seasons with his native South Australia 45 and in a decade with Queensland almost 70.

Like Ian Chappell, his eagle-eyed catching in the slips was stunning, right up in Mark Waugh's class and his bouncy medium pacers were once responsible for a 'five-for' in an international against England. His on-and-off captaincy reign included the 5-1 defeat of the West Indies in 1975–76. He will always be haunted by his insistence that brother Trevor finish an ODI (One Day International) in Melbourne with an underarm. It was within the rules at the time – but totally alien to the spirit of cricket. Selector and Bradman disciple Sam Loxton ventured down the stairs to the dressing room in tears. 'Helluva way to win a cricket match,' he said. Chappell would have loved to have had those few minutes of madness back.

Along with contemporaries Dennis Lillee and Rodney Marsh, Chappell was a giant of Australian cricket and remained intrinsically involved as selector, coach, advisor and mentor. He also coached India's Test team.

From Australia's most famous cricket family, Chappell attended one of the country's most illustrious cricket schools, Prince Alfred College. He first played for SA at 18 years and for Australia at 22.

Encyclopaedia of Australian Cricket Players, Ken Piesse & Charles Davis (New Holland Publishing, Sydney, 2012)

A MOMENT OF MADNESS: Cricket was the loser when Greg Chappell ordered brother Trevor to bowl an underarm to finish a one-dayer in Melbourne in February, 1981. *Peter Bull*

Ode to Peter May
Christopher Martin-Jenkins

*The arrival of Peter Barker Howard May at the wicket was always
a joyous occasion, unless you were in the bowling team …*

The precision of Peter May's batting was like one of those
sunny winter mornings when a sharp frost has frozen away all
muddiness, leaving trees and buildings etched in clean lines against
the blueness of the sky.

Bare-headed except when hot weather demanded a cap, he kept
his hair short and always immaculate above sharp features and
broad shoulders. His kit, too, was always pristine white. A carefully
cared-for Stuart Surridge bat moved in straight lines through the
path of the ball, sending it skimming past mid-off or mid-on, not
with a Pietersen whip of the wrists but with the full face extended
until the ball hit the boundary. He was the most professional of all
amateurs, although firmness of purpose was never confused with
anything underhand or unsporting.

Like his predecessor Len Hutton, as England captain, the man
known respectfully by every colleague and opponent as 'P. B. H.'
was uncomfortable with the public esteem and attention that his
eminence attracted. He never lacked inner steel or confidence but
he was shy, perhaps from being a prodigy adulated even in his
schooldays at Charterhouse, always courteous and modest to a fault.
He could enjoy team camaraderie as much as anyone, but he was
happier with his wife and four daughters at home than he was in a
bar talking cricket.

Against an unclear background he never saw the first ball bowled
to him in a Test match (from Athol Rowan), against South Africa at
Leeds, but he pushed out in hope [and hit it for 4 — ed.] and went
on to make 100 at the age of 21. He had not yet had his third year at
Cambridge, but quite soon he was the best batsman in England.

The responsibilities that entailed, together with the captaincy
and the close attentions of a press that he would rather have kept

PROLIFIC: With a record five consecutive half-centuries against the Australians, Peter May was the outstanding batsman in the world in the mid-1950s. At Headingley in 1956 he made a heroic 101 after England had slumped to 3-17 against the pace of robust Queenslander seamer Ron Archer.

at a greater distance, shortened his career. He still made more than 1000 runs in 14 seasons and more than 2000 in five of them. He captained Surrey from 1957 to 1962 and England 41 times.

His 285 at Edgbaston in 1957, when his partnership with Colin Cowdrey added 411 for the fourth wicket, drew the sting from Sonny Ramadhin's mysterious spin. He averaged 97.80 in the series. In 21 Tests against Australia he scored 1566 runs at 46, sharing in the home triumphs of 1953 and 1956 when he had the pleasure of leading one of the strongest bowling sides England have ever had.

The short-lived period of English supremacy was abruptly ended in Australia in 1958–59; yet he played one of his most majestic innings on that tour, against an Australian XI at Sydney, scoring his second hundred of the match between lunch and tea on the third day.

Illness in the West Indies in 1959–60 forced him home early and he played only four more Tests, at home to Australia in 1961, before retiring to an insurance job in the city. His strong sense of duty to cricket remained, however. Both locally and nationally he took on several roles as president and chairman and he was chairman of England's selectors from 1982 to 1988.

The Top 100 Cricketers of All Time, Christopher Martin-Jenkins (Corinthian Books, London, 2009)

ARISTOCRAT: 'P. B. H.' tosses with Ian Craig in the NSW international in Sydney in 1958–59.

Ashes Greats: Position by Position
Ken Piesse

The top 11 Ashes batsmen of them all, for England and Australia.

Who would you want to bat for your life? And in what slot? You have the choice of the best players from any era, the only proviso being that only Ashes battles count.

Other than Don Bradman at No. 3 and Steve Waugh somewhere in the middle-order, few picked themselves.

The early champions such as Victor Trumper were disadvantaged given the uncovered wickets of their era and the resultant lower scores.

It was tough, too, to truly rate the overall contribution of the modern-day icons, such as Matthew Hayden, for example, when his runs were being scored on shortened boundaries with bats as wide as wood splitters.

Ricky Ponting, Australia's modern-day Bradman, averaged 56 from No. 3, well below the Don's 93.

The most prolific openers are shown as follows.

Most prolific Ashes openers

Player	Country	Runs	Ashes average
Jack Hobbs	England	3483	53
Geoff Boycott	England	2945	47
Herbert Sutcliffe	England	2708	67
Mark Taylor	Australia	2496	41
Len Hutton	England	2306	56

Others with 1000 runs plus included tough-as-teak John Edrich (1692 at 48) and pioneering pair Archie MacLaren (1717 at 37) and Dr W. G. Grace (1089 at 32).

Among Australian openers, Trumper averaged 28 in an era of low scores and challenging wickets, Bill Lawry 48 and Arthur Morris 50.

After the Don at No. 3, those with the highest average were Englishmen Walter Hammond (70) and David Gower (60).

Hammond's high rating was built around his extraordinary 1928–29 summer when he amassed 905 runs, an incredibly prolific summer featured by two double centuries, in Sydney in mid-December and in Melbourne in the New Year. In Adelaide, too, he notched twin 100s on his way to 1553 first-class runs, a record by a visiting player and one likely to go unsurpassed with abridged modern-day tour schedules.

Ironically, 1928–29 was the season in which a young Don Bradman made a century in his second Test and showed signs of what was to come with 340 not out against Victoria. Amazingly as he was applauded from the Sydney Cricket Ground, he looked fresh and ready for more, despite batting for eight hours and tweaking a groin in the process!

The debate over the best Ashes all-rounder is always spirited, Keith Miller having a host of old-time admirers, as does Ian Botham. Many feel Adam Gilchrist simply has to be the best No. 7 of them all, but former Test captain Warwick Armstrong and more recently Brad Haddin have the most imposing average of all: more than 50 runs per innings.

Coming to the best No. 11s, the most 'prolific' five are shown as follows.

Most prolific Ashes No. 11 players

Player	Country	Runs	Ashes average
Bob Willis	England	186	10
Brian Statham	England	152	25
Arthur Mailey	Australia	151	13
Tom Richardson	England	149	10
Jeff Thomson	Australia	146	16

The most prolific Ashes batsmen of all time: position by position

AUSTRALIA

Position	Batsman	Innings	Runs	Average
1 & 2	Sid Barnes	11	771	77
1 & 2	Bobby Simpson	22	1244	62
3	Don Bradman	41	3349	93
4	Allan Border	32	1542	59
5	Steve Waugh	32	1559	62
6	Steve Waugh	33	1389	60
7	Brad Haddin	13	602	50
8	Alan Davidson	14	364	30
9	Bert Oldfield	11	311	51
10	Dennis Lillee	13	210	30
11	Jeff Thomson	17	146	16

ENGLAND

Position	Batsman	Innings	Runs	Average
1 & 2	Herbert Sutcliffe	45	2708	67
1 & 2	Michael Vaughan	10	663	63
3	Walter Hammond	26	1695	70
4	Ken Barrington	14	872	67
5	Denis Compton	11	608	76
6	Tony Greig	25	948	39
7	Ian Botham	16	653	46
8	John Emburey	12	389	43
9	Maurice Tate	10	276	30
10	Alec Bedser	14	136	17
11	Bob Willis	21	186	10

Table: Charles Davis

Pavilion (Australian Cricket Society, Melbourne, 2007)
Story and statistics updated 2013.

Move Over Don
John King

Just who played Australia's greatest-ever Ashes innings?
Was it Don Bradman, whose 334 remains a statistical
high, or is there a more worthy innings?

S tatistical comparisons can sometimes deceive, but Neil Harvey has a good case for having played the greatest Australian Test innings of all.

His 167 against England in Melbourne in 1958—59 could be declared superior to Don Bradman's 334 against England at Leeds in 1930.

A system of adjusting Test batting performances for the match conditions and the quality of the opposition calculates the 'equivalent score' in an 'average' match against 'average' opposition.

Scores in low-scoring matches and against strong teams are increased. High-scoring matches and weak opponents result in negative adjustments.

Harvey's 167 against England at the MCG in 1958—59 came in a very low-scoring match against the reigning world champions. This was equivalent to 424 runs in an 'average' match. Bradman's 334 at Leeds in 1930 in a match close to 'average' status is equivalent to 314. It's still in the top 10 among Australia's Ashes centurions, but his 304 at Leeds four years later takes precedence as his most important mega-score against the most-rated opposition. When Bradman scored his 304, Bill Ponsford's 181 was the only other score in excess of 50. England had won by an innings at Lord's just three weeks earlier.

Charles Bannerman's 165 retired hurt in the inaugural Test in 1876—77, which Australia won by just 45 runs, was an exceptional score in an era when centuries were very rare. His score was 67.3 per cent of Australia's score — still a world record. No other Australian exceeded 20.

Arthur Morris' 196 at the Oval in 1948 was a great innings over-

NEIL HARVEY ON HIS 1958–59 INNINGS

It was the highest I have ever played against England and one of the best of my 20 Test centuries. Right from the start everything went according to schedule. The scoring rate was quite brisk, although Peter May employed Tony Lock in a negative capacity, allowing him to bowl down the leg side with six fieldsmen on the on side. Lock was at his most negative when Norman O'Neill and I were associated in a century stand for the third wicket in which we added 118 in two hours and 20 minutes. Despite Lock's 'go slow' tactics, O'Neill and I managed to prove that even when bowling is at its most negative, Test batsmen should still be able to keep pace with the clock. We taught the Englishmen that day a lesson in enterprise.

My World of Cricket, Neil Harvey (Hodder & Stoughton, London, 1963)

shadowed by the most famous duck in cricket history, from the Don.

Percy McDonnell scored 147 in a low-scoring game in 1881–82. Harry Graham's 105 at Sydney in 1894–85 was also in the lowest-scoring match.

Australia's top six Ashes innings – by the statistics

Player	Score	Equivalent score	Venue, date
Neil Harvey	167	424	Melbourne, 1958–59
Don Bradman	304	418	Leeds, 1934
Charles Bannerman	165 rh	407 rh	Melbourne, 1876–77
Arthur Morris	196	381	The Oval, London, 1948
Percy McDonnell	147	327	Sydney, 1881–82
Harry Graham	105	323	Sydney, 1894–95

rh = retired hurt

Australian Cricket, John King (Mason Stewart Publishing, Sydney, February 1996)

Stepping On a Legend
The Cricketer

When W. G. Grace's old house at Downend, Bristol, was pulled down, the doorstep was saved and has now been placed at the foot of the steps of the Wellingborough School's cricket pavilion. The step was placed in position by the old England and Lancashire cricketer A. C. MacLaren during the match between the school and the Forty Club.

The Cricketer (W. H. Hillman & Co., London, 20 July 1940)

The Biggest Feet of All
Jack Fingleton

With 36 in the five Tests in his maiden trip Down Under in 1924–25, Maurice Tate won immediate acclaim as one of the finest of all England's medium-fast bowlers.

Maurice Tate has two outstanding characteristics, apart from his sunny nature. He has the biggest feet I've seen (apart from Tiny, the cheery deckhand of the *Strathaird,* who had his size 15s specially made for him in Belfast) ... and he has the smallest voice. He barely whispers. Maurice was three pounds when he was born and was minus fingernails and toenails. For every cricket season for 25 years he shed the nail of his big toes, so hard did he pound the turf in delivery. A room attendant said to him one day in Adelaide (when Tate was in terrible agony) that he could fix things for him. The attendant left for town with Tate's boot. He returned with the toe of the boot opened up and the stiffener removed. Tate played with his boots like that until the end of his cricketing days.

The first ball he ever bowled in Australia, in Perth, threw him back. The hard pitch, unlike the soft English ones, would not take his weight. He was very worried and told [Herbert] Strudwick so, but 'Struddy' told him not to worry, that he would get used to it. He did.

Maurice was undoubtedly one of the great bowlers of all time.

In his first of three visits Down Under in 1924–25, Tate took 20 wickets in the opening two Tests. On debut, earlier that calendar year, he helped Arthur Gilligan bowl South Africa out for 30.

Brightly Fades the Don, Jack Fingleton (Collins, London, 1949)

A Hero Always
Philip Opas

Few visiting English cricketers were as popular as between-the-wars fast bowler Maurice Tate.

I was just eight years old at the time. It was an Ashes summer (in 1924–25) and I was at the MCG, already a home away from home, foxing balls for the Englishmen at the nets.

Maurice Tate was batting and I stopped one of the balls he'd hit and he waved his bat in thanks and asked if I wanted to come and have a bowl. He had this big infectious grin and thrust out his hand to me. I had a new hero. He introduced me to the MCC's captain Arthur Gilligan who asked if I was going to the match tomorrow — and would I like to be his guest at the Test!

'Would I!' I said.

'All right, wait for me at the gates at 9.30 a.m. at the members' entrance tomorrow.'

It was a miracle if I slept at all that night. I was so excited and was at the ground by 8.30 a.m. — just in case I'd got the time wrong. Gilligan saw me, took me inside and I watched the entire game from the dressing rooms.

I found it difficult to fathom why the Englishmen assembled on the ground via two gates and someone pointed out to me that the

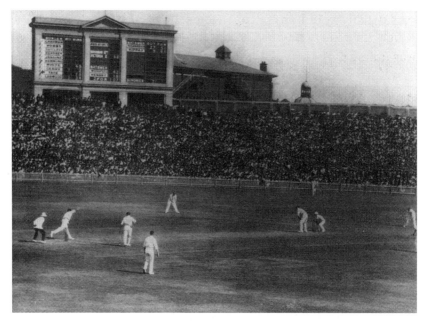

BIG-HEARTED: Maurice Tate opposes tall Australian 'Stork' Hendry on the opening day of the 1928–29 Sydney Test. He conceded just 29 runs from his 21 overs in the Australian first innings and bowled 46 more overs in the second, returning figures of four for 99.

amateurs in the team went on together and the professionals would walk on from a separate gate. It did look strange.

During the game I asked Maurice home for dinner and he said he couldn't while the Test was on — but he would when the team came back for the game against the Victorians in a few weeks' time.

When they arrived back from Adelaide I was waiting at the Spencer St rail station and he said: 'I haven't forgotten,' and he came out and had tea with us all. In the backyard he showed us how to hold the ball for swing.

Back then we'd collect the old cigarette cards with biographies on the back and I wrote a letter to him for his birthday, addressing it as: 'Mr. M. Tate, the best bowler in the world, England' and it got there!

He came out again with [Percy] Chapman's team four years later and was there during the Bodyline tour, too — not that he got a look-in.

I scored every ball of that famous Melbourne Test, the one in which Bradman got a duck first ball and a century in the second. It was unforgettable.

Pocket-sized Philip Opas, QC, was the author of seven books and one of cricket's most passionate, known for keeping wickets for the Australian Cricket Society's Wandering XI into his 70s.

Pavilion 2006 (Australian Cricket Society, Melbourne, 2005)

Time of the Terror
Ric Sissons

Lord's has been a long-time stronghold for Australian teams ever since 1888 when Percy McDonnell's XI, inspired by a 10-wicket haul by C. T. B. 'Terror' Turner, upset all-England.

The scene was now set for the opening international at Lord's from Monday, 16 July. Heavy rain on the Sunday had a significant impact on the result. The Australians, weakened by the illness to Sammy Jones, gave the 21-year-old Cambridge University student Sammy Woods the opportunity to make his Test debut. Although born in NSW, Woods had never played first class cricket in the colony, having gone 'home' to complete his schooling. On the England side, *Cricket: A Weekly Record of the Game* was unusually frank in its criticism of the selectors, on this occasion a sub-committee of the Marylebone Cricket Club. The weekly magazine wrote, 'the selection ... had given, it must be stated, anything but satisfaction.' The contentious issue was the lack of a hitter amongst the batsmen, the merits of George Bonnor foremost in their minds.

The wet weather delayed the start from noon until 3 p.m. Australia won the toss, batted and collapsed. Coming together at 9-82, John Edwards and Jack Ferris put on 34 valuable runs

THE TERROR: C. T. B. Charlie Turner took eight wickets on his Test debut in 1887 and helped himself to nine more a month later, both Tests in Sydney *Michael Saunders*

for the last wicket and the total reached 116. Before a crowd of 9500, England stumbled to 3-18 at the close. Certain of a low scoring, yet exciting day's play, more than 16,000 paid the sixpence admission on Tuesday. And they were not disappointed. Between 11.30 a.m. and 4.25 p.m., 27 wickets fell and only 157 runs were scored. Charlie Turner took five for 27 as England were bowled out for 53. Johnny Briggs, in at 10, top-scored with 17. In their second innings the Australians fared little better as George Lohmann and Bobby Peel dismissed them for 60. The only players to reach double figures were Turner with 12 and Ferris, batting last, with a decisive, albeit lucky, 20 not out. The Australian batsmen realised that the only hope for making runs was by hitting out, whereas the defensive approach adopted by England was summarily unsuccessful.

England began their second innings after lunch needing 124 to win but only made half the target, Turner with five for 36 and Ferris five for 26 bowling unchanged in poor light as the game reached its inevitable conclusion. The Australians had won their first Test in England since the initial historic victory at the Oval in 1882 — and achieved their first win at Lord's, the 'home of cricket'.

The *Morning Post,* while recognising the talent and 'world-wide reputation' of Turner and Ferris, claimed that the wicket was a 'mudheap' and 'never fit for serious cricket'. The London daily continued, criticising the England batsmen for 'a lack of energy' and lamenting their poor fielding. They concluded that on this wicket the game was 'a mere accumulation of uncertainties'. The conditions were ideal for Charlie, and the *Morning Post* recognised his brilliant performance 'bowling from the Pavilion end all through the two innings of England ... the young Sydney cricketer had the greatest share in the colonial triumph'.

The victory was greeted with acclaim in Australia. According to the *Hobart Mercury*'s correspondent, 'at the conclusion of the match, the immense crowd at Lord's cheered the Australian team over and over again. The heroes of the day came out and bowed their acknowledgments ... there was nothing but admiration for the men who had fairly and squarely beaten the picked champions of England.'

More than 25,700 spectators had seen the opening Test, the Australians receiving more than £500 for two days work; £128 was handed over to the Cricketers Fund.

While Australia won the first Test, it lost the second and third to forfeit the Ashes 2-1. Charlie Turner amassed a record 314 wickets on the tour. Originally from Bathurst, he bowled fastish off breaks and made a habit of hitting the stumps. He was the first Australian to take 100 Ashes wickets, at a strike rate of six per match, superior to even Glenn McGrath and Shane Warne. Controversially he was dropped for the deciding Test of the 1894–95 home series and never played Tests again.

The Terror, Charlie Turner, Australia's Greatest Bowler,
Ric Sissons (www.cricketbooks.com.au, Melbourne, 2012)

4
Heroes & Villains

'Oh God, Nass, What Have You Done?'
Nasser Hussain

It was like a horror movie for England after captain Nasser
Hussain agonised over who should bat first in Brisbane …

On the morning of the first (2002–03) Test I walked over to the nets and had a conversation with Marcus Trescothick which I laugh about to this day. He wasn't officially my vice-captain but he was very much my second-in-command and at that stage was being lined up to take over from me when I eventually packed up the captaincy. Marcus said to me, 'I've just had a net and it did a bit. The wicket looks just the same as the nets to me. I think we should bowl first.'

I took that on board, but then I made my big mistake. I should have gone to the middle, had a good look at the wicket and then had a chat with Duncan [Fletcher], as I usually do. Instead, I went and had some throw-downs and then got embroiled in peripheral Ashes-type matters, like what coin should we use for the toss and other weighty concerns like that. I must confess I was looking for things that weren't there while trying to convince myself that we should bowl first. It was like we were in a crisis situation and I was

NO-BAALLL: Umpire 'Dickie' Bird calls expressman Jeff Thomson for overstepping during the opening Test of the 1975 series at Edgbaston. Four Tests were played immediately after the 1975 World Cup which was also staged in England. *Patrick Eagar* trying to move the goalposts, do anything that could help us in our predicament against such a strong side ...

Before the toss I managed to grab a quick word with Duncan, who admitted he was in two minds and probably would bowl first and I found out later that Steve Waugh would have inserted us, so I didn't exactly make the most surprising decision in the world. But when I won the toss I said we would bowl and it has since been labelled the biggest mistake I made as England captain.

I went into the dressing room and I could see Andrew Caddick's face drop straight away at the prospect of being (immediately) thrust into the spotlight. The ball swung a bit at first and I thought, 'Maybe this is going to work out,' but by the fifth or sixth over nothing was happening and I could feel the world closing in on me. I thought to myself, 'Oh God, Nass, what have you done?' and I was clever enough to realise, even in that first season, that the next 25 days of Test cricket were going to be absolute hell. The only consolation I had in my mind was that I hadn't taken the easy option. There are captains out there who never try anything unusual and always take the easy option, knowing that if it doesn't work it won't rebound so horribly on themselves. In my defence I was always looking to try things that might have won us a game even if it wasn't in the textbook way and I was always prepared to put my head on the block.

I threw the ball to Simon Jones, who had been missing since that encouraging Test debut at Lord's in our win against India. He immediately bowled well and I thought, 'Well, at least there is a silver lining to this dark cloud that has descended on me.' Then it happened. I was at mid-off; Jones was at mid-on, someone hit a ball past him and, as he chased it and slid to stop it, I heard the crack and the noise straight away. I'm terribly weak-stomached about things like that so I didn't even want to go over and have a look. I knew it was bad. It was the Brisbane outfield that was to blame. They play other sports on it and it was too soft underfoot.

Simon was in agony with what turned out to be a serious knee injury. He was writhing in pain and we all knew straight away that it was serious. I felt terrible; I couldn't believe what was happening

TEN MORE ASHES BOO-BOOS

Kevin Pietersen's sledge on Andrew Symonds, Melbourne, 2006–07

As Birmingham-born Andrew Symonds, Test average 19, walks in to bat in the Christmas Test in Melbourne, Kevin Pietersen accuses Symonds of being little more than 'a specialist fieldsman'. Symonds makes a career-revitalising 156.

Steve Waugh calls for an extra half-hour's play, Melbourne, 1998–99

With just over a dozen more runs needed for victory, Australia opts to play extra time deep into the fourth day of the Christmas Test only to lose three wickets for 1 to Dean Headley and Darren Gough as England clinch one of its finest away-from-home victories. Set 175, Australia is bowled out for 162 with Steve Waugh, in at No. 5, marooned on 30. England had wanted to go off, but Waugh insisted on continuing. 'I believed we were on the verge of winning,' he says later. The last session goes for three and a half hours, the game finishing at 7.33 p.m., a record late finish for a Down Under Ashes Test.

Australia fails to recall its Packer rebels, 1977

Three weeks before the first Ashes Test, news breaks at Hove of Kerry Packer's plans to stage a rival cricket circuit, thrusting Australian cricket into its biggest controversy since bodyline. All but four of Australia's 1977 touring team in England are implicated, including captain Greg Chappell, but

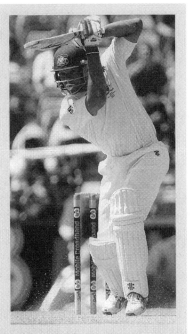

DEFINING: Andrew Symonds's MCG century in 2006–07 was pivotal in his career fortunes.

REALISTIC: Youngest of the '77 team, David Hookes said the rebels should have been sent home.

instead of recalling those with Packer contracts in their pockets and sending replacements, the Australian Cricket Board allows them to stay in England and they are thrashed. David Hookes, one of the rebels, says later the Aussie teams lacked focus amidst the controversy invoked by Packer taking on establishment. 'We shouldn't have been there,' he said. Tour manager Len Maddocks says all but the first week of the 15-week tour was a shambles.

Australia gambles and loses with a broken-down debutant, Melbourne, 1970–71

Thrilled to be selected for Australia for the first time in mid-series in 1970–71, Queensland-born Ross Duncan complains of a heel injury during practice on the eve of the match. Doctors administer painkilling injections and assure the sole selector at the ground Sam Loxton that Duncan will be okay. He bowls just 14 less-than-brisk overs in the first innings and is so sore by mid-match that he's unable to bowl in the second and is never selected again. With a pop-gun, injury-ravaged attack, Australia can only draw the game, despite starting with almost 500.

Keith Stackpole's run out reprieve, Brisbane, first Test, 1970–71

Geoff Boycott's direct hit from mid-on catches Keith Stackpole 12–18 inches (30–46 cm) short of his crease, but umpire Lou Rowan adjudges him not out. The next day's Brisbane *Courier-Mail* publishes a side-on photo of the heavyweight opener failing to make his ground. He was 18 at the time and goes on to score a Test-best 207. One UK writer calls it 'one of the worst decisions in cricket history'.

Frank Chester gets it wrong, Leeds, 1953

In his last Test match, an unwell Frank Chester – one of the great umpires at his best – gives frontline Englishman Reg Simpson not out at Headingley when Simpson, looking to farm the strike, takes off for an unlikely third run on Lindsay Hassett's arm. Keith Miller, normally the most affable of sportsmen, throws the ball into the pitch in disgust, believing Simpson has been caught a yard short of his crease at his, the non-striker's end. It costs Australia only a dozen runs and 15 or so minutes but it proves vital as chasing at 70 runs an hour on the final day, the Aussies finish at 4-147 having been set 177 in 115 minutes. They lose the deciding Test a fortnight later at the Oval.

Cricket interrupts Cabinet as McIntyre's run out costs England, Brisbane, 1950–51

So exciting is the cricket that Prime Minister Robert Menzies defers Cabinet matters and flanked by key staff adjourns to an ante-room to listen to the radio description from the Gabba. 'Get back you fool,' says one of his staffers as England's first-gamer Arthur McIntyre attempts a fourth run, only to be run out within minutes of stumps on the penultimate night, reducing the tourists to 6-30. England only needed someone to stay with an in-form Hutton on the final day to win the rain-affected Test, but Hutton is marooned on 62 (out of 122) as the Englishmen lose the opening Test by 70.

Don Bradman dropped, Sydney, 1928–29

Australia is beaten by a record margin in the opening Ashes Test of 1928–29 and 20-year-old Sydney prodigy Don Bradman is among the casualties, serving as 12th man in the second Test a week and a half later. In what was to become a selection blunder of monumental proportions, Bradman is to average 102 in 51 future Tests.

Charlie Turner dumped from the deciding Test, 1894–85

Despite being a selector, Charlie 'the Terror' Turner is overruled by (co-selectors) Jack Blackham and George Giffen and dropped from the XI for the fifth Test of the greatest Ashes series of the 19th century. Turner had taken seven wickets in the previous Test nine days later. His replacement, Tom McKibbin, from Turner's old hometown of Bathurst, is unsuccessful, taking only two expensive wickets as England wins the final Test – and the Ashes – by six wickets. Turner never plays Test cricket again.

Kenny Burn's selection as 'wicketkeeper', 1890 Ashes tour

Tasmanian Kenny Burn is chosen as a reserve wicketkeeper behind Jack Blackham for the 1890 tour of England, despite never having kept wickets in his life. During the tour, all players, except for Burn have a turn behind the stumps to spell Blackham!

to us. And it carried on in similar vein. Simon was carried off, we carried on misfielding, Matt Hayden provided some catching practice for [Michael] Vaughan and he dropped it, and by now the Aussie crowd were laughing at us. Actually laughing at us. And I couldn't blame them. It was our worst day's cricket in at least five years.

We were very quiet that evening in the dressing room. Somebody asked: 'Is it still doing a bit, skip?' but nobody laughed. I was embarrassed about what we had done.

Having been inserted on a belter of a wicket on the opening day of the new Ashes summer – shades of 1954–55 – Australia made a whopping 2-364, local hero Matthew Hayden going to stumps on 186. Australia won in four days by almost 400 runs on its way to a 4-1 drubbing.

Playing with Fire: The Autobiography, Nasser Hussain
(Michael Joseph, an imprint of Penguin Group, London, 2004)

The Wild Ones
Ken Piesse

The most celebrated fast bowlers tend to have split
personalities – amiable off the field and positively lethal on it.

Jeff Thomson was a wild one. Brutal, callous and with an infamous mean streak, he bowled faster than any of the speed kings of the '70s. He was responsible, too, for one of cricket's immortal quotes when he told my *Cricketer* magazine colleague Phil Wilkins: 'It doesn't worry me in the least to see a batsman hurt, rolling around screaming and blood on the pitch.'

The ultimate batsman-hater incurred a life-long ban from soccer for smashing a referee. When it came to cricket, the angrier he was, the faster he'd bowl.

Wild-eyed teammate Rodney Hogg would stomp around a

dressing room slapping his face, trying to fire himself up. For him, white line fever meant the difference between bowling medium pace and express. 'You'd try and go berserk within yourself,' he said. 'Fast bowling was a way of getting rid of frustration and getting rid of all your anger.'

No-one lived and breathed the scent of battle, though, quite like Dennis Lillee. 'I was always prepared to fight it out,' Lillee said. 'I was quite happy to die on the pitch. I'd never save myself.'

Hitting a batsman was a vital part of the intimidation process. Lillee would aim his bouncers directly at a batsman's throat, as they were harder to avoid.

Not only did Lillee become the most motivated, record-breaking bowler in Australian Test history, he was involved in one of cricket's most unsavoury incidents in Perth when he got physical with provocative Pakistani Javed Miandad.

Contemporary Australian pacemen Glenn McGrath and Jason Gillespie are just as tunnel visioned and, occasionally, equally testy. Quietly spoken and amiable off the field, their personalities change dramatically once armed with a new ball. So angry was McGrath in the deciding Test with the West Indies in Antigua in April (1999) that he kicked the fence in his fury at a dropped catch and so badly ricked his ankle that he needed around-the-clock treatment before he could bowl the next day. Few are as affable as McGrath off the field, but opinion is coloured when it comes to his on-field behaviour.

So incensed was Brian Lara at McGrath's spitting in the direction of young West Indian Adrian Griffith on the penultimate day at St John's that he made a very public complaint to match referee Raman Subba Row, resulting in the Australian being handed a $2000 fine.

Unapologetic and vowing to be just as nasty next time Lara and any of the other West Indians are in his precinct, McGrath believes the ability to intimidate is a key element in his arsenal; the day he retreats will be the day he retires.

'A fast bowler who lacks a bit of mongrel in his mental make-up isn't going to last in the big time very long,' he said. 'If he isn't prepared to do whatever it takes to bag a batsman's wicket, then they're going to chew him up and spit him out.'

Gillespie, returning to cricket soon after a broken leg, says there's no room in cricket for a fast bowler to sit back and admire a batsman's cover-driven 4. 'I like getting back to my mark as quickly as I can,' he says. 'I want to let the batsmen know through my body language just how keen I am to steam back in and knock them over. Certain batsmen I may have a bit of a [verbal] dip at. If I believe I can get an edge and soften someone up, I'll do that. I'm there to win cricket games whatever way I can do it … I'm certainly not going to be crying if I try to hit someone and hit him. If there's blood on the pitch so what?'

The motivation to bowl faster can come in an instant, from a crowd remark, an umpire's no-ball call or a simple snick which fails to go to hand.

In Trinidad in 1984, Hogg was so fired up after a wicket that he threw a punch that almost connected with his captain Kim Hughes, who had rushed in to offer his congratulations. 'I went ape shit,' Hogg said. 'I'd been snicked for two 4s in row … the punch all but landed. When a batsman hits a 4 against me, it's like sticking a little knife into you. Fast bowling is like running a hot and cold tap. I remember going to Victorian practice and they'd say, "Aren't you going to bowl quicker than that?"

'But there has to be something that takes you from just going through the motions to bowling quick. Someone may yell out something from the crowd, a batsman might irritate you. There has to be something in your personality which makes you go mad.'

Given the lack of head protection and the lethal speed of fast bowlers from Harold Larwood and Ray Lindwall through to Lillee, Thomson and the never-ending array of West Indians who bowled bouncers at a blink of an eye, it's surprising more batsmen haven't been seriously hurt.

Australia's popular Bodyline wicketkeeper Bert Oldfield deflected an attempted hook shot against Larwood into his skull and was carried off the Adelaide Oval. The crowd acted like a lynch mob, counting out Larwood and his captain Douglas Jardine. Had even one jumped the fence, there could have been an international incident.

Former Australian captain Ian Craig retired from all forms of cricket after first encountering the frightening pace of a young Jeff Thomson at Sydney grade level in the early '70s.

Veteran West Indian Lance Gibbs approached Australian captain Greg Chappell before play in one 1975–76 Test and pleaded that Thommo not bowl any bouncers to him. He was a family man and wanted to return to the Caribbean in one piece.

Australian Cricket Tour Guide 2000–01 (Emap Australia, Sydney, 2000)

Kipper to the Rescue
Ashley Mallett with Jeff Thomson

Reinforcing England's tour party from the Perth Test
of 1974–75 was one of its grandest post-war warriors,
Colin Cowdrey on his sixth trip and keen to meet
Australia's new expressman Jeff Thomson …

After the physical and psychological battering they received in Brisbane, England's batting line-up looked decidedly vulnerable [for the second Test in Perth]. David Lloyd and Brian Luckhurst put on a creditable 44 for the first wicket, Luckhurst cutting a ball from Max Walker straight to me in the gully. This brought the man of the hour, Colin Cowdrey, to the crease.

> JEFF THOMSON: I had just taken my cap from the umpire when up comes the roly-poly England batsman we call 'Kipper'. And he thrusts out his hand and introduces himself. I must admit it was a bit bizarre. This bloke has just turned up in Australia, Dennis Lillee and I had just dismantled his team in Brisbane and we were about to do the same here, and Colin Cowdrey arrives at the crease all smiles and looking for a nice chat in the middle.

Cowdrey batted with grace and great skill. He moved back and across, usually before 'Thommo' or Lillee let the ball go, and there was often a delivery which got past his broad bat and thudded heavily into his chest.

After one particularly savage Thommo over, in which he copped at least four painful blows to the chest area, Cowdrey waltzed down the wicket to his partner, David Lloyd, and told him how much fun he was having, back in the Test arena and batting against the pace of Thommo. Cowdrey was so heavily padded in the chest area that Lillee jokingly referred to him as England's latest knight, 'all ready for a joust'.

With Thommo and Lillee bowling in tandem, fielding in the gully was something else. I had to very smartly develop a method to see the edges and slashed shots which were bound to come my way. With all the other fast bowlers — even Lillee — you could watch their delivery all the way from the time they let the ball go to the time it was about halfway down the track, then quickly focus your attention on the edge of the bat. With Thommo there was no time for that strategy. I found that I watched him until his load-up at delivery and a split second before he was about to release the ball, I directed all my attention to the edge of the bat. It gave me a split second more time to see the ball. I decided to get as close to the bat as possible and worked out that seven paces was the go. The closer you get to the bat, the tighter the angle and there are lots more catching opportunities. Gully specialists in later years, the likes of Geoff Marsh, Steve Waugh and Matthew Hayden, stood so deep you felt there was more a chance of batsmen running 2 rather than a chance in the offing.

At lunch England had lost only Luckhurst, with Lloyd surviving on 25 and Cowdrey 9. At drinks the score had sneaked along to 1-99. Seemingly, there were no gremlins in the pitch, but then Thommo floored Lloyd with a brute of a ball which hit him squarely in the nether region. Lloyd collapsed in a screaming heap. Thommo's fireball had split Lloyd's protector and one of Lloyd's testicles was flopping out of the protector and the other contained within, thus contributing to his immense pain.

Soon after, Lloyd, who had batted bravely for 49, followed a Thommo delivery which had moved across him, succeeding only in edging the ball to Greg Chappell at second slip. When Lloyd staggered painfully back to the pavilion, Mike Denness was padding up nearby and he said, 'Well played, David.'

'Bluddy 'ell, captain, ya never get any balls in yer own 'alf,' said Lloyd.

Having swapped a winter at home trying to keep warm, Colin Cowdrey, on the verge of his 42nd birthday, made 22 and 41 in his return to Test cricket and played in each of the four remaining Tests in a high-powered, one-sided summer dominated by Lillee and Thomson.

Thommo Speaks Out: The Authorised Biography of Jeff Thomson, Ashley Mallett (Allen & Unwin, Sydney, 2009)

The Day the Wicket Was Watered
Frank Tyson

The 1954–55 Ashes series was balanced at one-all
coming to Melbourne, a low-scoring affair in which the
game's laws were ignored amid searing temperatures
to help the match extend beyond a third day.

Monday, 3 January 1955 — We arrived at the ground expecting the worst: we fully anticipated that yesterday's 'scorcher' would have reduced the Melbourne wicket to a state of total fragility. The cracks in the pitch must have widened. Batting will be like threading one's way through a minefield! Before play, I went up into the members' stand to speak to a 'Pommie' radio commentator. Imagine my surprise when, looking down from the broadcasting position on the third balcony of the stand, I saw that the colour of the Merri Creek soil on the square was not the dried, baked grey I had expected — but black, as though it were damp!

It fell to [Brian] 'George' Statham to bowl the first ball of the day. On Saturday he had slipped several times in his run-up on the glass-like approaches — his spikes unable to provide the necessary purchase. Today he moved back to his bowling mark and glided into his smooth run-up, accelerating ready to leap into his delivery stride. As was his habit, he grounded the side of his right boot and stepped forward to deliver the ball. The spikes on his rear boot sank into soft turf and skidded slightly. The ground was wet! How could this be? The pitch had been exposed to the tropical sun and hot northerly wind for the whole of Sunday. It should have been bone-hard and crumbly. Close inspection revealed that Saturday's mosaic of a wicket was now whole once again. The cracks had mysteriously closed and the holes where pieces of the surface had crumbled had been filled. Rumours abounded. One incredible explanation was that there was a subterranean spring under the MCG wicket. The verdict of the official MCC committee appointed to investigate the 'mystery' was that the wickets had sweated under its tarpaulin covers.

The most credible and probable reason given, however, was that of Percy Beames, the Melbourne *Age*'s chief cricket writer who stated quite bluntly that the pitch had been watered during the wee hours. He had seen it with his own eyes when walking past the ground. [Beames was actually told the pitch had been watered via a phone call to his Collins St office from an old footballing friend, Bill Vanthoff, who worked on the groundstaff. Beames delayed writing the story for 24 hours. — *ed.*]

Apparently, after the pitch broke up during the MCC versus Victoria game, the Melbourne club recruited the services of the best curator in Victoria, Jack House, to prevent a recurrence of the problem in the Test. Faced with a dual disaster of a disintegrating pitch and an air temperature of 105 degrees (40.5 °C) on the rest day, House chose to turn on his sprinklers rather than risk not having a wicket at all on the third day.

The result of House's initiative was obvious from the first delivery bowled on Monday morning. The bounce was even and slow. [Len] Maddocks, [Ian] Johnson and [Bill] Johnston helped themselves to 43 additional runs, hoisting the Australian total to 231 and establishing a useful 43 run lead.

When the Melbourne *Age* published Beames' (scoop) story on Tuesday morning, the Victorian Cricket Association and the Melbourne Cricket Club issued a joint communiqué denying the story and saying that the pitch had *not* been watered since the commencement of the game on New Year's Eve … the men in the middle, however, knew the truth.

By an ironic twist of fate, the actions of an Australian groundsman spelt defeat for his own team. The much improved pitch enabled our batsmen to give a far better account of themselves in our second innings. We had all but wiped off our arrears before a Johnston delivery turned sharply from leg to clip the top of Bill Edrich's off-stump. Our vice-captain and captain then dug in, playing some scintillating drives to add 56 for the second wicket. Then the gremlins in the pitch began to re-appear as it dried out and cracks in its surface widened. After a dogged 42, Len [Hutton] got a [Ron] Archer off-cutter which crept, hitting him on the ankle in front of middle stump. He slouched back in the dressing room, slumped in a corner, burying his head in his hands and did not even bother to take off his pads for another hour. He was not a well man. In the interim, 'Kipper' [Colin Cowdrey] was dismissed in a most unfortunate manner. Playing defensively at a [Richie] Benaud leggie, he dropped the ball at his feet where it behaved as if it had a life of its own, curling like a spinning top around his pads. P. B. H.'s warning shout came too late. The ball clipped his stumps, toppling a bail. With steely determination, [Peter 'P. B. H.'] May played the role of Horatio, helping [Denis] Compton to hold the bridge against all attacks. Stumps found them still together with England's score at 3-159: 119 runs to the good and with seven wickets in reserve. When we joined the press for a beer in the Snake Pit bar at the Western end of the Grey Smith Stand, the consensus of opinion was that England had had the better of the day. The wicket was bound to deteriorate and if we could put together a half-decent total, we were in with a chance of winning the Test.

The Aussie press seemed a decent bunch and treated the story quite impartially. John Priestley of the Melbourne *Herald* and Rex Pullen of the *Sun* respected our requests for confidentiality on our opinions of the watered pitch. With the Test having run three-fifths of its course, this was not the time for high jinks. We ate a quiet meal in the Windsor dining room. I had beer with (friends) Alan and Rita Jenkins in the mahogany surrounds of the hotel lounge — and then to bed, tired but ready for the last supreme effort.

In the match of his life, expressman Tyson was to take seven for 27 on the final morning as Australia slumped to a 128 run defeat. He was dubbed the 'Typhoon' and with 28 wickets in the series of his life was pivotal in England retaining the Ashes.

In the Eye of the Typhoon, Recollections of the Marylebone Cricket Club Tour of Australia, 1954−55, Frank Tyson (The Parrs Wood Press, Manchester, 2004)

Ernie McCormick Remembers
Bob Coleman

He was Australia's fastest bowler of the 1930s
and one of the game's great characters who made
a stunning Ashes debut in Brisbane.

BOB COLEMAN: How did you go in your first Ashes Test series? 1936−37 wasn't it?

ERNIE MCCORMICK: Yes, I played in the first Test in Brisbane and took a wicket with my first ball, having their opener Stan Worthington caught behind. Then I got Arthur Fagg [for 4 at the start of his fourth over] and in came Walter Hammond and I got him, too, first ball. One jumped on him and he jabbed it straight into Ray Robinson's hands. Don Bradman said [after five overs] I'd better have a rest before I got into them again and I was to bowl only another three overs as my back tightened right up and I couldn't move freely at all. I hardly took part in the game after that first morning.

BC: What happened?
EM: Unfortunately I'd picked up a chill in the back going up on the train [to Brisbane]. Arthur Chipperfield also got it. It had been warm and we didn't bother with any sheet or blanket and we rode into a change of weather during the night and we arrived up north pretty stiff. But I got some treatment and everything seemed to be right. Anyway after my second spell my back was playing up and then I had an attack of lumbago [more severe back pain] and it was off to hospital for me.

[McCormick batted in the first innings at No. 11, making 1 not out, but didn't bat or bowl in the second innings of the match, Australia being bowled out on a sticky wicket for 58 to lose the first Test by an embarrassing 300 run margin. – ed.]

NO-BALL PROBLEMS: Ernie McCormick's 30 yard run-up often saw him overstep, most famously at the tour start in England in 1938.

It was rather humorous, when I was at the hospital and [Bill] Voce and ['Gubby']Allen were going through us. The physiotherapist looking after me said he'd turn on the wireless. In those days they took a while to 'warm-up' and by the time we got a score we were already four-down. So I got him to cut it short [the treatment] so I could get down to the ground. On the way all of the various shops had the scores up in their windows and suddenly we are five and then six down. By the time I got there we were all out (having batted only 10 men). I met Arthur Mailey coming around to the press box and asked, 'What happened Arthur?' and he said, 'I don't know. I was putting my head under the seat and …'

BC: How did you go for the rest of that first Ashes campaign?

EM: I played in the second Test [in Sydney] but I really shouldn't have. I don't think I was quite fit enough and I didn't perform very well after that. [McCormick took eight wickets in three Tests, having missed the Melbourne epic, highlighted by the world record crowds and Don Bradman's 270. − ed.].

BC: Your next Test series would have been England in 1938?
EM: Yes, that's right, Bradman was captain.

BC: You had a little bit of trouble with your run-up didn't you? Had no-ball problems been a worry in Australia for you too?
EM: No, not really. I couldn't practise properly at Lord's because they had a big net behind us, just 10−11 yards [9−10 m] from the bowling crease to stop the balls from going back to the nursery end and I couldn't practise my normal, long run-in. However, I did try a few overs away from the nets.

BC: How long a run did you take Ernie?
EM: Thirty, sometimes 31 yards [27−28 m]. I'd carefully step it out. If I bowled my first ball and I was just over, I'd take the mark back six inches [15 cm], sometimes more. It was all trial and error. In the first proper game at Worcester I just couldn't get my stride right and I lost my rhythm completely.

BC: How many paces is 30 yards?
EM: Thirty-six, maybe 37.

BC: You'd be pacing a lot longer than a yard.
EM: Yes, and what happens of course, when you start bowling no-balls, you start watching the bowling crease which is no good. We even took slow motion photographs on films with a Cine-camera. I was rooming with Bill Brown and we'd be watching all this tape. Not that it did much good. Once you got called a lot the other umpires at the other counties would be waiting for you. [After an incident-free first over in the following match at Oxford, where McCormick was filmed, he was called four times in three overs

by umpire Hendren, Patsy's brother and in the following game at Leicester he was called 15 times. − *ed.*]

BC: How did Bradman feel about all these early tour problems?
EM: He was upset because he had great plans, as I did. I had bowled extremely well in Australia when I had the opportunity − my back had been playing up though, so while I played all the games [in 1937−38], I couldn't always bowl as much as I wanted to. [On arrival in England, Bradman declared McCormick to be the world's fastest bowler. − *ed.*]

BC: So how many no-balls did you actually bowl at Worcester?
EM: Thirty, maybe 35! I know four of the first five balls were called. My run-up was all over the place. [Umpire Baldwin called him 19 times in his first three overs, his first over going 14 balls and his second 15. The first three overs of Worcester's innings took 26 minutes. − ed.]

BC: Is that when you said, 'Don't worry boys. The umpire can't call me anymore. He's hoarse!'
EM: Yes. And he was too.

BC: Did you take any wickets in that first game?
EM: None in the first innings anyway [and only one in the second]. But on that first morning one of their boys [opener Charlie Bull] tried to hook a bouncer and he edged it straight onto his jaw. They carted him off to hospital and when he came back he had this terrific shiner. On the Sunday [rest day] we went to an air pageant and I met Charlie's wife and apologised to her and said I was very sorry about her husband. 'Don't worry Mr McCormick,' she said, 'I've been trying to do that for 20 years!'

Seven of Ernie McCormick's 12 Tests were against England, his best match figures of seven for 173 coming at Lord's in 1938, including the first three in the opening half-hour of the match: Len Hutton (4), Bill Edrich (0) and Charles Barnett (18) in McCormick's hostile opening blitz. A jeweller by trade,

McCormick later crafted the original Frank Worrell Trophy for Tests between Australia and the West Indies.

Unpublished word-for-word 1990 interview with journalist and author Bob Coleman, author of *Seasons in the Sun* (Hargreen Publishing, Melbourne, 1993)

A Nervous Wreck
R. E. S. 'Bob' Wyatt

Warwickshire's Bob Wyatt captained England on his Ashes debut, scoring 64 and 7 against Bill Woodfull's 1930 Australians.

My introduction into England v. Australian cricket in the final Test of 1930 made me the recipient of the highest honour an England cricketer can have — captaining England in a Test match against Australia. At the same time, however, I became the centre of a sensational outburst by the press, who decried the dropping of Percy Chapman. He had proved himself to be a very successful and popular captain, and they fairly went to town on it. In order to strengthen their case they did not hesitate to disparage my ability both as captain and player, which was not likely to improve my morale.

These adverse comments in the press continued for a week before the match and were undoubtedly the reason why I received one of the greatest receptions ever accorded a cricketer when I went in to bat.

The sporting and sympathetic public did not cease their applause until I reached the wicket, leaving me almost a nervous wreck as I took guard to face the remaining five balls before the tea interval from [Clarrie] Grimmett. Those five balls are seared into my memory! The first ball was a leg break to which I played forward. The second was also a leg break, pitching outside the off stump, which I let go. The third, an obvious googly, I played with ease.

To the fourth, a leg break short of a good length, I played back. The fifth, to which I started to play forward thinking it was a leg break, dipped and was pitching outside the off stump so I stopped my shot, allowing the ball to pass. To my horror it was a googly and only just missed the off stump — leaving me wondering, during the tea interval, if I would be able to spot Grimmett's googly. The wily bowler had shown me the obvious googly in order to deceive me with the more disguised one.

Grimmett was a great artist of flight with a wonderful control of length and direction. He was at his best in this country where the heavier atmosphere and viscosity assisted his curious flight. He and [Bill] O'Reilly were considered by knowledgeable critics to be the best combination of leg spin and googly exponents of all time. They were very largely instrumental in winning the Ashes on the easy-paced wickets of 1934, when the pair captured 53 wickets out of the 71 which fell.

O'Reilly was every bit as accurate as Grimmett. He varied his pace cleverly without any perceptive change of action and spun the ball just enough to beat the bat. Added to this he had the ability to make the ball lift.

Fortunately I survived after tea and helped [Herbert] Sutcliffe to put on 170 runs for the sixth wicket. But I never cease to wonder what the cricket writers would have written had that last ball before tea just flicked the off stump!

We reached the respectable score of 405 but Australia replied with 695. [Don] Bradman, [Bill] Ponsford and [Bill] Woodfull played fine innings but were all missed early on behind the wicket by [George] Duckworth, usually the most reliable of wicketkeepers. England, batting on a rain-affected pitch, were beaten by an innings and 39 runs.

It was in this Test that I first saw Bradman and Ponsford in action. Bradman had by then established himself as a phenomenal rungetter and emphasised this fact by scoring 232. The finest batting in this match at the Oval, however, was that by Ponsford who played beautifully, scoring 110 out of 159 for the first wicket in two hours and 40 minutes.

MATCHSAVER: Walter Hammond's 240 in 1938 was one of the great innings at Lord's.

These two batsmen were to prove themselves a tower of strength against England in 1934, both averaging over 90 and with the assistance of [Stan] McCabe they scored most of the runs.

Bradman first dominated the Test matches in 1930 and it was not until 1932–33, when he met the fast leg theory attack that he was curbed in his scoring. Even then he had a Test average of 56 in spite of having been out for 0 in his first innings of the series.

In this match at Melbourne I was fielding in the outfield at the start, and each time I returned to the boundary I was greeted with the words, 'Wait until our Don comes in!'

At the fall of the second wicket Don Bradman came in and was promptly bowled out by [Bill] Bowes. There was silence when I returned to the boundary. I made no comment until two more wickets fell, after which I enquired when was 'Our Don' coming in?

This remark was greeted with much laughter and an explanation that they were referring to the second innings. In this he made a magnificent not out century out of a total of 191.

It has often been said that Bradman was not a good player on a turning wicket. He failed twice at Lord's in 1934 on a pitch which wasn't really sticky when [Hedley] Verity bowled Australia out twice, taking 15 wickets, but when I was left in charge at Sydney in a New South Wales match and there had been rain overnight, I took Verity out to look at the pitch. After sticking his thumb into the turf, his only comment was, 'Poor Don.' Don made a brilliant 71 out of a total of 128 – and a large proportion of his runs came off Verity! Hedley was never allowed to forget this but took it all in good part.

This 1932–33 tour, known as the 'Bodyline' tour, resulted in bitter controversy owing to the employment of the fast leg theory attack with a close leg-side field – a form of attack which bred ill-feeling, which must be bad for any game.

It was [Harold] Larwood's amazing speed and accuracy that made it possible to apply this line of attack economically. He would still have been a great force bowling in the normal manner, as was shown by 'Gubby' Allen, who, never resorting to leg theory, bowled really fast with great success, taking 21 wickets in the series.

The fast leg theory shook the morale of the Australian batsmen, but although batting was fraught with danger it was not unplayable, as was demonstrated by Stan McCabe in the first Test match when he played a glorious innings of 187 not out. This was a magnificent exhibition of batting and his hooking of Larwood, bowling at a furious pace, was superb. This and his innings at Nottingham in 1938 were two of the finest I have ever witnessed. His 232 at Trent Bridge, made in four hours out of 300 scored while he was at the wicket, stands out in my memory as the best. He played all the strokes, his driving being particularly good. Anything short of a length was hooked with power. He took complete control when he was keeping the tailenders away from the bowling.

Another great innings of the 1938 series was that played by [Walter] Hammond at Lord's in the second Test match. After three wickets had fallen for 31 he saved his side by scoring a magnificent 240. He played every bowler with complete mastery. It was a great display of the art of batsmanship, executed with such ease and grace and with tremendous power. Those who saw it will never forget that innings. Hammond was always in perfect poise before and after the stroke — one of the signs of a really great batsman.

Test matches on the whole between the wars were played with the keenest rivalry, but were enjoyable. The crowds were appreciative but not too vociferous in showing their appreciation or disapproval except at times in Australia. Many are the stories told about the comments emanating from the Hill at Sydney. One of the best was directed at me. Sutcliffe and I had put on 140 for the first wicket. Sitting on the Hill was a man who I presume was waiting to see the famous Hammond bat. Presently he yelled, 'Come on, Wyatt — get out! We've seen all your strokes. You've got 'em all but one, and it will be a bloody good job when you get that ... and that's sunstroke!' I took this as a compliment!

Wyatt was deputy-captain to Douglas Jardine on the 1932–33 Bodyline tour and led England in four of the five Tests of 1934.

Cricket '77 (Test & County Board, London, 1977)

Trent Bridge Fairytale
Percy Fender

It was a catch which changed a match and remains one of
the most famous ever made by a substitute fieldsman.

At lunch (at Trent Bridge in 1930) the score was 198 for three
and Australia wanted 231 more to win and though this seemed
still a colossal task, they had four full hours left for play and so did
not need to press for runs.

With only [Maurice] Tate, [Dick] Tyldesley, [Walter] Robins and
[Walter] Hammond to bowl, it was not nearly so impossible a task
that the figures would seem to show.

Tate bowled like a Trojan for one and a half hours, without a
rest directly after lunch, and though a wicket was credited to him
towards the end of that period, I feel sure that he himself would
be the very first to concede that someone other than himself was
mainly responsible for getting it. Tate took the new ball almost
directly after the re-start, and Hammond bowled at the other end.
No impression was made on [Don] Bradman, who went on stolidly
with his task of taking everything that he could that Tate bowled
and attempting to do no more than stop him. He kept [young
Stan] McCabe away from Tate, especially with the new ball, as
much as he possibly could, and only made one false stroke to him,
which flew clear through the slips between [Percy] Chapman and
Hammond.

It may well be mentioned here, as an indication of the caution
and methods of Bradman, that it was 2.45 p.m. and he had been at
the wicket for three hours that day before he hit his first boundary.
He had made a couple overnight, but not one on the Tuesday and
it was only when Hammond was bowling with the new ball at 200
that he made a fine square cut to the ropes off that bowler.

McCabe was not quite as happy and made three uppish shots
behind the wicket on the off side off Tate and one off Hammond,
but they were all out of possible reach and, as the shine began to

HE TURNED A TEST:
Syd Copley, the
substitute fieldsman who
took the catch of the
match at Trent Bridge in
1930. *David Frith Collection*

wear off the ball and the youngster began to play more confidently, one gradually began to feel the game slipping away from England.

It was three o'clock, and neither the new ball nor the interval had brought the wicket to break the partnership, when the score was 229, still for three wickets, and one was just beginning to wonder whether Tate could keep going, or would crack under the pressure.

He had plenty of fire in the first few overs after lunch, but now that seemed to be fading away and he was not getting many balls past the bat, nor was he bowling quite the pace. In what must have been very nearly his last over, he bowled his slower one to McCabe; the batsman made what looked to be a very good drive off it, just wide of mid-on's right hand. Everyone thought it was 4, but there was a scurry of feet, an outstretched hand, a fall and a rollover, and one saw the young Notts substitute (Syd Copley) rise holding the ball firmly in his right hand. He had literally picked it off his toes in falling and he made a catch upon which, in my opinion, the result of the game may well be said to have rested.

Perhaps Chapman, or [Patsy] Hendren – had either been at mid-on – might have held that catch, but to any other fielder on the English side that day, I think that, despite all efforts, that hit would have been 4 runs, so that perhaps Dame Fortune, after seeming to have turned her back, at the last moment had been moved by the grit and courage which Tate had shown, striving against adversity in a terrible fix and had provided such a fielder to help him out of a hole, just when he must have been at the breaking-point.

It was a grand catch, and if others think, as I do, that it was the turning point of that innings, I feel that it was a worthy one, and a credit not only to the game, but to all concerned. At the time, however, when we had recovered from the enthusiasm inspired by the effort, it was somewhat of a shock to many of us to realise that Bradman was still there. There was plenty of time, Vic Richardson was the new batsman, and the game was by no means won yet, although 200 runs were still wanted. Three hours and a quarter remained – and so did Bradman. But that catch had really only put us back in the fight ...

The dismissal of 19-year-old Stan McCabe on his first of three Ashes tours turned the match, England winning by 93 runs despite a century from Don Bradman. Sydney Herbert Copley was to play just one county game a fortnight later for Nottinghamshire but remains a celebrated name at Trent Bridge for his miraculous, matchwinning one-hander. The only other instance of a non-first-class player taking a Test match catch in an Ashes Test occurred at Lord's in 1989 when Robin Sims from the Lord's groundstaff caught Allan Border in Australia's second innings.

The Tests of 1930, 17th Australian team to England,
P. G. H. Fender (Faber & Faber, London, 1930)

Dropping the Captaincy
Arthur Carr

A century in a session from the 'Governor-General' Charlie Macartney proved critical in England's decision to sack its captain, especially after he'd dropped Macartney when he'd made just 2.

From Lord's to Leeds for the third Test (of 1926) and there the greatest catastrophe of all. The weather had been wet and when I won the toss the question was which side should bat first? [Selectors] 'Plum' Warner, Arthur Gilligan, Jack Hobbs and I went solemnly out to have a look at the wicket and tried to make up our minds. Wilfred Rhodes, the very man we most wanted just then because, as a Yorkshire player he must have known more about the tricks of the ground than any of the rest of us, was not there – he

TEN MORE 'SUPER SUBS'

Gary Pratt (England) – Trent Bridge, fourth Test, 2005

A modestly performed county player, Durham's Gary Pratt ensures his place in Ashes annals when, from cover at a crucial stage of a most combative Test, he runs out Australia's captain Ricky Ponting with a rocket-propelled direct hit. On his return to the pavilion, an angry Ponting criticises English management about fielding a 'specialist' as a substitute.

Brad Hodge (Australia) – Old Trafford, third Test, 2005

One of the unluckiest not to play an Ashes Test, Brad Hodge is a regular 12th man throughout the 2005 tour, most notably taking two catches in an innings in the Manchester Test, including England's captain Michael Vaughan from a skied pull shot which sees Hodge dash 30 metres around the Stretford End boundary to complete a fine catch from Brett Lee's bowling. It is one of the feature catches of the series.

STRETFORD SUB: Brad Hodge's boundary-riding catch at Manchester was one of the best of 2005.

Matthew Hayden (Australia) – Lord's, second Test, 1993

Twenty-two-year-old tour rookie Matthew Hayden, still years away from establishing a regular place at the head of the Australian top-order, is fielding as a substitute at short leg and catches Robin Smith from the bowling of off-spinner Tim May in a juggling, reflex effort which sees him dive and catch the ball with his outstretched right hand.

Peter Cantrell (Australia) – Brisbane, first Test, 1990–91

Fielding in the gully for an incapacitated David Boon, ahead of selected 12th man Carl Rackemann, in hometown Brisbane, Peter Cantrell holds two catches from the bowling of Terry Alderman. The first one from a full-blooded Alec Stewart cut shot is extraordinary.

EAGLE-EYE: Peter Cantrell's gully catch to dismiss Alec Stewart was one of the highlights of the opening Ashes Test in 1990–91.

Ian Gould (England) – Melbourne, fourth Test, 1982–83

England's reserve wicketkeeper, used in the ring, catches the masterly Greg Chappell diving low at cover in the Australian second innings on the penultimate day in a classic match, which is won by England by just three runs.

Graham Yallop (Australia) – Sydney, fourth Test, 1978–79

Substituting for injured wicketkeeper John Maclean, Australian captain Graham Yallop catches England's topscorer Ian Botham high above his head from a Rodney Hogg bouncer which Botham top edged. Yallop had kept wickets previously at Carey Grammar and in one club season in England with Walsall.

MCG CLASSIC: Ian Gould, enjoying a run in the ring, dismissed Greg Chappell in Melbourne in 1982–83.

Sam Loxton (Australia) – Adelaide, fourth Test, 1950–51

Australia's 12th man Sam Loxton catches Denis Compton for a duck low down at short leg and Len Hutton left-handed over his head jumping high at mid-wicket. Eyewitness Jack Fingleton calls the Hutton catch 'a beauty'. Both of Loxton's catches are taken from the bowling of fellow Victorian 'Big Bill' Johnston.

Don Bradman (Australia) – Sydney, second Test, 1928–29

Named 12th man for the only time of his almighty career, Don Bradman fielded throughout the match after Bill Ponsford had his finger broken by Harold Larwood on the opening morning. In the last minutes of the match he caught Maurice Tate at mid-off from the bowling of 'Stork' Hendry shortly before England completed an eight wicket victory.

Herbert Strudwick (England) – Melbourne, second Test, 1903–04

England's reserve wicketkeeper, fielding as a substitute for A. A. Lilley, catches 'Monty' Noble, Hugh Trumble and Bert Hopkins in Australia's first innings.

Billy Murdoch (Australia) – Lord's, second Test, 1884

The Australian captain fields as 'sub' for England – a not uncommon practice which continues for years – and catches his teammate Henry 'Tup' Scott! [This was to occur four times in Ashes Tests. The last was Joe Vine who caught a skier at mid-on from English teammate 'Tiger' Smith in the third Test in Adelaide 1911–12. – *ed.*]

was, if you please, engaged in a comparatively small match for his county, at Northampton.

Well, we all looked hard at the wicket, prodded it with our thumbs, looked at the sun which was shining brightly and learnedly discussed what was the best thing to be done. I believe that Leyland (Maurice Leyland's father), who was then the Leeds groundsman had expressed the opinion that the Australians should be put in and certainly Warner was determined in that opinion.

And so, not at all certain in my own mind that I was doing the right thing, I went back to the pavilion and said to Warren Bardsley, Australia's acting captain: 'You bat.'

I know that it was a tremendously difficult thing to decide, and that quite likely, if [Warren] Bardsley had won the toss, he would have put us in first. But, looking back, I now wonder if I was quite old enough for all the responsibilities and worries which a Test captain has to face [he *was* 33 − *ed.*]. I know that if I had been two or three years older I should have insisted upon having my own way more and would not have listened to so much advice from other people.

In the XI finally chosen for the match, Charlie Parker, the Gloucestershire left-hand bowler, for whom the wicket looked made, was left out for George Macaulay. A very great deal of criticism arose over this, but, in my opinion, it did not matter; as it turned out the pitch let us completely down. The sun went in and the ball did not turn. What seemed as if it might be a paradise for bowlers was in fact a fairly happy hunting ground for batsmen.

We got rid of the dangerous Bardsley quickly, but then came Charlie Macartney …

What a marvellous innings batting genius Macartney played that morning. However, confession being good for the soul, I must make an awful admission: I should have caught Macartney when his score was 2.

In whispered confab with 'Patsy' Hendren I had laid a trap for him. We banked upon Macartney giving an early chance in the slips off Tate and the manoeuvre was for me to move quietly out of the gully into the slips. Macartney slipped me a catch that I could have caught 99 times in a hundred and I put it on the floor.

I must be forgiven if I do not go into the painful details of how, after this let-off, Macartney put our bowling in his pocket and proceeded to dazzle up just about the most wonderful century I've ever seen. The whole memory of that missed catch is almost more than I can bear.

I think I spent the most dreadful luncheon interval in all my experience of cricket. Every blessed thing had gone wrong for me, and you can imagine how awful it was to have to sit next to some bigwig and not be able to think of a thing to say, or to eat a mouthful. I forget the bigwig's name, but he must have thought me the dumbest person he had ever had the misfortune to sit next to at lunch.

To add to my miseries, P. F. Warner sat at the table a few places away with a face like nothing on earth.

I took the whole thing most terribly to heart and spent about the most miserable weekend I have ever spent in my life ...

After his fourth ball let-off, Macartney made an imperious 151, including a century before lunch as Australia reached 494. Weeks later, on the eve of the deciding Test, Arthur Carr was sacked.

Cricket with the Lid Off, A. W. Carr (Hutchinson & Co., London, 1935)

TEN MORE EXPENSIVE LET-OFFS

Ricky Ponting (Australia) – Adelaide, second Test, 2006–07

Chasing a mammoth 551, Australia is 3-78 with Justin Langer, Matthew Hayden and Damien Martyn all back in the Bradman Stand when captain Ricky Ponting, on 35, is dropped by Ashley Giles. The unlucky bowler Matthew Hoggard gets his man with the second new ball but not until Ponting has made 142. Australia reach 513 and clinch an extraordinary last day victory thanks to a mesmerising, extended spell from Shane Warne.

Steve Waugh (Australia) – Melbourne, fourth Test, 2002–03

With Australia collapsing on the drama-packed final morning, having been set just 105 to win, a far-from-well Steve Waugh feathers a catch behind from Steve Harmison but no-one appeals and he survives to make an important 14 as Australia only just gets home by five wickets. Afterwards at a packed press conference, Waugh just smiles and says, 'What do you reckon?' when asked if he'd touched the ball.

Kevin Pietersen (England) – The Oval, fifth Test, 2005

Dropped at first slip by Shane Warne from the bowling of Brett Lee in early afternoon after he'd made just 15, Pietersen makes 158 to help clinch the Ashes for his adopted country.

LET-OFF: Missed early, Matthew Elliott made 199 at Leeds in 1997.

Matthew Elliott (Australia) – Leeds, fourth Test, 1997

Before he makes 30, Matthew Elliott is dropped at slip by Graham Thorpe and accelerates to a Test-best 199, lifting Australia from a precarious 4-50 chasing 172 to a matchwinning 500-plus. Australia win their second Test in three as England again forfeits the Ashes.

John Dyson (Australia) – Sydney, fifth Test, 1982–83

Clearly run out by England's captain Bob Willis in the first over of the game without a run having been scored, John Dyson is reprieved by umpire Mel Johnson and makes 79 in a drawn encounter which enables Australia to hold the Ashes. Film of the incident shows he is 18 inches (46 cm) short of his crease, but no Decision Review System was in place back then.

Geoff Boycott (England) – Trent Bridge, third Test, 1977
Having taken three hours to make 20 in his comeback Test, Geoff Boycott gives Rick McCosker at second slip a regulation catch from the bowling of Len Pascoe, only for the chance to be grassed. After 30 Tests in exile, Boycott goes on to 107, his 98th first-class century as England wins by seven wickets.

Willie Watson (England) – Lord's, second Test, 1953
Dropped at short-leg by Ray Lindwall from the bowling of leg-spinner Doug Ring in the final over of the penultimate night when he'd scored just 2, Ashes debutant Watson bats most of the final day to score 109 and force a draw. It remains one of the most classic Ashes rearguard actions of all.

Don Bradman (Australia) – Headingley, fourth Test, 1948
Early in the epic, matchwinning stand with fellow centurion Arthur Morris, Bradman, on 22, is dropped by Jack Crapp, a comparatively easy chest-high chance, from the wrist spin of Denis Compton. The Don goes on to make 173 as Australia chases down 400 on the final day in the mightiest win of Bradman's career.

Len Hutton (England) – The Oval, fifth Test, 1938
Missed being stumped at 40 by wicketkeeper Ben Barnett from the bowling of 'Chuck' Fleetwood-Smith, Len Hutton makes a new world record score of 364.

Bill Ponsford (Australia) – The Oval, fifth Test, 1934
'Ponny' is dropped six times in making his 266, the first time at 57. Batting partner Don Bradman's 244 is chanceless. Together the pair add a record 451 in just over five hours.

PONNY: A mega stand before farewelling Test cricket

5
History in the Making

'He Looked Like He'd Been in Test Cricket for Years'
Angus Fraser

Having taken just three Tests to retain the Ashes,
Allan Border's 1990–91 Australians unleashed one of
the great players in the fourth Test in Adelaide.

Fourth Test, Adelaide Oval, 25–29 January 1991: Day one – Our first morning warm-up at the Adelaide Oval had been accompanied by the theme from *The Dam Busters* being played over the Tannoy – someone clearly had a sense of humour – but my mind was on my hip. I'd got through the one-day games and didn't know what to do. The hip didn't feel very good and I wrote in my diary that I didn't think I should play – but it was just about passable at the start of the day.

I wasn't going to go for it until I spoke with [coach] Micky [Stewart], who really wanted me to play; so for the first time in a Test, we left Jack [Russell] out of the side and asked Alec Stewart to keep wicket so that an extra bowler could play as cover for me. This, of course, has been a policy followed often since, as England's selectors have desperately searched for an all-rounder to give our side the balance it requires. It has always been a great shame for Jack, who was one of the last people who deserved to be dropped

CONQUEROR: Ian Botham's audacious century at Leeds in 1981 set up an astonishing English revival, one of the best in Test history. *Patrick Eagar* then and, more often than not, since then, too, he has been a victim of other people's poor form.

Australia won the toss and batted and my hip soon felt bad in the field, particularly after tea. I wondered even then if I was buggering my body up because it felt so sore, but at least we were doing quite well — until Mark Waugh got going. After tea, Waugh, on his debut, really took it away from us with a brilliant innings.

Adelaide has a reputation for being flat, but there is usually something in it early on and so it proved on this occasion, until after tea. Mark was so composed it looked as though he'd been in Test cricket for years. He didn't look nervous at all, just went out and did the business and looked bloody good, scoring 100 off just 124 balls. Australia, after being in a bit of trouble, was 269 for five at the close (and in command).

Since my injury, I have always thrown myself at my cricket with the attitude that I would see how my body shapes up at the end of it. If I have to have a hip replacement when I'm older, then so be it. I just hope the process is so far advanced that it will be, by then, a relatively easy operation. But I didn't feel that way in Adelaide in early 1991. Then, I was worried that it might be something serious and was concerned that it wasn't going to go away.

That didn't stop me giving my all in the fourth Test and I bowled quite well, beating the bat quite a bit, but I failed to take a wicket in 23 overs in Australia's first innings. I also went over on my ankle, coming round the wicket to a left-hander for the second time that winter, and twisted it so badly that I couldn't bowl on the second day. I was desperate to be fit because I thought it was my kind of wicket, one that if you put something in you'd get something out of it — but (this day) I wasn't getting as much out of it as the others.

Lionhearted Angus Fraser took 11 wickets in his three 1990–91 Ashes Tests and bowled almost 50 overs in a drawn result in Adelaide, featured by Australian first-gamer Mark Waugh's majestic 138.

My Tour Diaries, the Real Story of Life on Tour with England,
Angus Fraser (Headline Book Publishing, London, 1999)

The Miracle at Headingley
Mike Brearley

England's Ashes dreams were in tatters as Graham Dilley
joined Ian Botham at the wicket, with Ladbrokes
rating England's chances of victory at 500-1.

[I an] Botham was not the only one to have booked out of the hotel that (1981) morning. I would have done so too, except that since Middlesex was due to play at Old Trafford on Wednesday, I would be staying in the north. It was a pleasure for him to book back into the hotel on Monday night, and for me to unpack my bag again for the 10.30 start on [that late July] Tuesday. So, how did it happen?

Botham started relatively quietly, scoring 39 in 87 minutes before tea. He said afterwards, tongue in cheek, that he was playing for a not out! It was [Graham] Dilley who at first played more aggressively. His method was to plant his front foot somewhere near middle stump, and swing the bat hard at anything to the off side of where he stood. He hit — and missed — very hard.

After tea, Ian hit even harder. I remember some outrageous strokes, a wind-up aimed at mid wicket that sent the ball way over the slips and another that went off the inside edge behind square leg for 4. (He was using Graham Gooch's bat; Gooch claims the patent for the off-drive that the Duncan Fearnley inside edge speeds away to square leg. 'He hadn't used it much during the match,' said Ian later, 'and I thought there were a few runs left in it.')

Overall, Ian played wonderfully. He was particularly severe on [Terry] Alderman, who was kept on until he was exhausted. Botham drove him over mid-off, through extra cover and past gully. He went down the pitch and hit him splendidly straight for 6. In the dressing room, we started to think of making Australia bat again — this target, 227, we reached while Dilley was still in — and of lasting out until the next day. It might easily rain on Tuesday, after all.

Gradually, our hopes became more ambitious. If Dilley could stay with Botham until the close ... At a quarter to five, however, he was out for 56, playing on to Alderman who was by then bowling round the wicket to give the batsmen less room for their shots. This was his first Test 50; the stand was worth 117 in 80 minutes. Since tea, the pair had added 76 in 44 minutes.

Despite this exhilarating stand, we were in effect only 25 for eight; our elation was, realistically, for two magnificent individual innings. Bob Willis said, fiercely, to me, 'Make Chilli *play!*' We sent [Chris] 'Chilli' Old on his way with a mixture of pleas, exhortations and threats, the latter largely from [Peter] Willey. Chris is a talented striker of the ball, but one of those batsmen whose initial movement against quick bowlers is back towards square leg. However strenuously he orders that left foot to stay its ground, it always rebels. On the television screen, inside the pavilion, Willey wedged a bat handle against Old's bottom, trying to keep it in place. Chilli did his best, and so did his back foot. Together they accompanied Botham as he reached his hundred – off only 87 balls – and added 67 runs against an increasingly desperate side reduced by this fierce onslaught from magnificence to mediocrity. The desperation was highlighted by two beamers in an over from [Geoff] Lawson to Botham after which umpire Evans spoke to [Australian captain Kim] Hughes. The beamer has been universally condemned by cricketers as an unfair delivery since the best batsmen have been unable to pick it up even in bright sunshine when well set.

What could Australia have done? I know well the feeling of impotence that Botham can engender; we have felt it often enough at the hands of Viv Richards. However, I did feel the Australian seamers went on too long bowling their orthodox line just outside off stump. Admittedly, Botham, Dilley and Old were all liable, even at times likely, to be caught off the outside edge. But they were often hitting the ball hard, or missing altogether; and the edges cleared the rapidly diminishing number of slips. And despite my reluctance to bowl Willey (earlier in the match), I was surprised that [Ray] Bright did not come on at all until the score reached 309-8. I should have wanted to try him much sooner, though with a defensive field. When he did bowl, he came within a hair's breadth of hitting Botham's off stump.

The dismissal of Old was not the end, either, for Botham protected Willis so well that he had to face only five balls in the last 20 minutes, and we added another 31 crucial runs. At the close we were 351-9, 124 runs ahead. Another 60 or 70 runs, we felt and we would actually be favourites!

Afterwards, I made the mistake of going into the Australian dressing room. I had been there on Saturday evening, when they were cock-a-hoop. Perhaps I went too soon, for in the few seconds that I stood there I sensed thunderous silence, like the moment of Doom, everyone frozen in postures of dejection. Not even Rodney Hogg responded to my arrival. At last someone, I think Peter Philpott, the team coach, asked me if I was looking for anyone in particular. I went out again. Certainly the last thing I wanted to do was crow or appear to gloat.

Ian was keen to avoid the reporters. He asked me to tell them that he didn't want to talk. We escorted him through the crowds with a towel gagging his mouth. One newspaper made the best of a bad job with the caption: 'Actions speak louder than words'.

Half a dozen of us went to Bryan's Fish and Chippery up the road from the ground. We got a round of applause — a rare thing, I imagine, for the friendly but staid clientele of this splendid eating-house. Like a group of John the Baptists we were preparing a path for one greater than ourselves, for Ian and his family came in soon after. Poor Liam Botham, probably overwhelmed and excited by his long stay at the cricket, got a bone stuck in his throat and his day ended in tears.

Ian Botham's monumental 149 not out allowed England to recover miraculously from 7-135 to 358, and a lead of 129. Bob Willis' eight for 43 completed the fairytale as Australia was bowled out for just 111 in one of the great reverses of them all. This was the game in which Dennis Lillee and Rod Marsh backed against Australia ... and won a small fortune.

Phoenix from the Ashes: The Story of the England—Australia Series 1981, Mike Brearley (Hodder and Stoughton, London, 1982)

Getting the Buggers at Old Trafford
Alan Davidson

It was Richie Benaud's sweetest moment as Australian
captain: the retention of the Ashes after one of the
great comebacks led by his two fast bowlers, one on
his last tour of England and the other on his first.

I walked out for the start of the last day's play with my roommate
[Ken] 'Slasher' Mackay, who was munching away on his customary
four packets of PK chewing gum. My back had been giving me a hell
of a lot of trouble and I spent an hour on the massage table before
taking the field. David Allen, the off spinner, came on immediately
to bowl around the wicket into the rough footmarks and Slasher
pushed his second ball straight to slip.

Richie Benaud was next. He pushed the first couple of balls up
the wicket and then went back to one that straightened and was
plumb leg-before. Wally Grout
tried to win the match with one
hit and holed out to deep mid-
off. We'd lost three wickets for
three runs to have a lead of just
157 with one wicket left.

Graham McKenzie walked
through the gate. He had just
turned 20 and was playing in only
his third Test, so I walked across
for a fatherly chat. I needn't
have bothered. Here was Garth
whistling away as if he was taking
his dog for a walk on the beach at
Cottesloe. The kid didn't have a
worry in the world.

OUT EARLY: Ken Mackay, pushed
one straight to slip.

'Well, mate,' I said, 'it's up to
us now. Just play straight.'

Garth could play well, provided he played straight. To keep him away from the spin, I played six maidens in a row from Allen and left him to play straight to [the medium pace of] Ted Dexter.

Soon the adrenalin was pumping [however], so I decided to go after Allen, who was bowling into the rough and turning it away from me. First ball I went down the track and pinged him over mid-off for 6. I hit the third ball first bounce into the crowd just wide of the sightscreen. Ten off three balls. Not surprisingly, Allen threw the following ball a bit wider and I tried to smash him through the covers, but a bloke dived full length and stopped it. I had them sprawling everywhere, and off the fifth ball I went bang and pierced the cover field for 4 more.

What would Allen do now? Would he bowl one wide? No, he won't, I thought. He'll bowl it straight and bowl it in tight. I read it perfectly, danced into the ball and hoisted it over mid-off. It was a massive 6er, one of the sweetest I've hit in my life. If it hadn't hit the outer brick wall, it would have finished in the railway yards.

Garth and I got rid of Freddie Trueman and Brian Statham with the new ball and had put on 98 when they brought back Jack Flavell, who was pedestrian compared with the other two. Up he came, and would you believe it, he ducked one in towards Garth's pads, the ball ricocheted off one pad onto the other and rolled onto the stumps. I was left with 77 not out. When we got back to the room everybody was very excited, so I said: 'Let's go out and knock the buggers over.' And we did ...

The epic Davidson–McKenzie stand increased Australia's overall lead from a modest 157 to 255 before England was bowled out a second time for 201, Richie Benaud going around the wicket to take six for 70 in his most celebrated spell. Davidson's form in the calendar years of 1960 and 1961 entitled him to be ranked only just behind Garry Sobers as world cricket's most outstanding all-rounder.

Bedside Book of Cricket Centuries, Terry Smith
(Angus & Robertson, Sydney, 1991)

It Was Like Batting at Bondi Beach
Colin McDonald

Having won at Lord's on a greentop, Ian Johnson's 1956
Australians headed north for the decisive Tests in the series.

O n to Headingley and disaster. Our victory at Lord's was not part of England officialdom's plan for retaining the Ashes and there was plenty of innuendo doing the rounds of cricketing circles concerning the unlikelihood of us winning a Test match 'up north', at either Leeds or Manchester. The reasoning became apparent when we previewed the Leeds Test match pitch. Although there had been a copious amount of rain some days earlier, it was almost bone dry, totally devoid of grass, and crumbly. It was quite unlike previous Headingley strips any of us had seen. Perhaps the fact that Surrey had beaten us at the Oval earlier in the season, largely due to the spin of Jim Laker, had something to do with it? And after all, Laker and Tony Lock were superior orthodox spin bowlers than our own captain (Ian Johnson) and had a great deal more experience in the art under English conditions.

Richie Benaud, of course, was a very fine spin bowler under any conditions, especially on harder, bouncier Australian surfaces. A new word was also entering our consciousness – marl. I had heard of the word but had no idea of what it really was or for that matter, why it was so significant. We were to learn that it is, as described in my copy of Webster's *New World,* 'a mixture of clay, sand and limestone in varying proportions, that is soft and crumbly and usually contains shell fragments'.

We were also to learn that it was quite normal to distribute marl over cricket pitches in England during winter. It would soak into the pitch and have both a beneficial soil-binding and grass-growing effect. However, if mixed with water and poured onto a pitch a few days before a match, it would be, precisely as stated in my dictionary, soft and crumbly. I believe that the latter use of marl is precisely what was intended at Headingley and in the following

Test, too, at Old Trafford. We were thrashed by an innings in both, due totally to the masterly spin bowling of Laker and Lock. If that was officialdom's plan, it was brilliantly successful. The fact that it was aided in its purpose by fortuitous weather conditions was an incidental.

The England players, of course, had to play their part, and after going down at Lord's, they lifted magnificently.

At Headingley, I was the only player to be dismissed by Freddie Trueman — twice — as Laker and Lock took the other 18 wickets between them. England did have the decided advantage of winning the toss and batting first on undamaged dry pitches at both locations.

At Headingley, Peter May and a recalled Cyril Washbrook performed admirably, making 101 and 98 respectively — enough to see us off twice. Only Neil Harvey and, to a lesser extent, Keith Miller did much with the bat.

Life was tough and about to become even tougher when we arrived at Old Trafford [a week later] for the fourth Test. The strip prepared for the match was similar in every respect to the one encountered at Headingley. If anything it was even yellower, resembling Bondi beach. I doubt if Old Trafford before or since has ever had a similar hue. The England batsmen rather liked a benign first day slow wicket, so much so that both Peter Richardson and the Reverend David Sheppard scored centuries. What was to come was clear, however, as Richie and 'Johnno' bowled 94 overs between them; pace was of little consequence in such conditions. By the time we batted, the surface of the dry pitch was not much more than rolled dust and, despite Jim Burke and I having a 48 run opening partnership while the 'rolled dust' held together, we were all out for 84 of which I somehow contributed 32. For some unaccountable reason Laker took nine wickets while Lock, bowling at the other end, could claim only one, the very first to fall, my opening partner Jimmy Burke. From there, Laker famously took the next 19 wickets, one by one by one. In that first innings, after our opening partnership, the next highest score was Ian Craig's 8!

We were asked to follow-on, batting on what was left of the

re-rolled dust, after much of it had been rendered airborne by 'whisk brooms'. With the total at 28, I was forced to retire, my very troublesome left knee misbehaving. 'Harv' replaced me and was out first ball to a full toss. He didn't know whether to hit it for 4 or 6 and achieved neither. A four-ball duck in the first innings followed by one of the golden variety in the second — hardly a highlight in an illustrious career.

Early on the next morning, after Burke was dismissed, I returned to a very wet and sticky pitch. Ian Craig and I survived a rain-restricted Saturday. Sunday, as usual then, was a rest day and on the Monday play was further restricted to one hour in all, in dreadful weather conditions. We lasted that hour, too, during which heavy bails were required in order that play not be continually interrupted. Play was again delayed for a short time on the Tuesday, the last scheduled day. The wicket was sodden and with the sun appearing occasionally, very sticky. It was ideal for Jim Laker — but not for us. Craig and I, however, survived pre-lunch before well into the period before tea he was dismissed for 38 after batting for a total of four hours and 23 minutes. It was a very fine innings, not the highest but certainly the best he ever played for his country. I was to lose four more partners before tea on that final day. Runs were of absolutely no importance. Time was of the essence and with six out at tea and the pitch at its most treacherous, we were uplifted by Johnson's rev-up remarks to the effect that we could save the match. 'I'll give you six to four [we don't],' chirped 'Nugget' [Miller] from the back stalls. It was a realistic and intentionally cynical remark. Johnson finished not out 0 at the finish. My innings ended two balls after tea, Laker finally forcing me into error with a ball which spun nearly at right angles, found the edge of the bat and ended up in the hands of Alan Oakman at very short square leg. I had batted for a total of five hours and 41 minutes for a score of a largely irrelevant 89 and had occupied the batting crease on four separate days. My fellow players and I had batted on a modified version of Bondi beach in the first innings and a sticky, uncovered mud heap in the second. Even though my innings did not save the match or the Ashes, it was certainly my best ever for Australia.

IAN CRAIG ON THE MANCHESTER TEST

The Test at Manchester leaves me with very mixed memories. Having struggled in the three years since my debut Test [in 1952–53], it was obviously a tremendous thrill to earn a place for the match, my first against England, after a solid run of scores in the county matches. My form and confidence were high but the latter was somewhat shattered when we saw the wicket as we took our places in the field, having lost the toss.

The previous Test at Leeds had proved a bonanza for the English spinners on a similar wicket and it was apparent that we would be in for a tough time, particularly having second use of the pitch and not having the type of bowlers who could exploit it. That it proved to be a 'dustbowl' was particularly disappointing as on the two other occasions we played at Old Trafford on that tour the wicket

NEGATIVE APPROACH:
Ian Craig

was both 'green' and lively. We struggled to make much impression on the English batsmen on the first day although there were signs of turn in the pitch which became more apparent as we moved into the second day.

My introduction came after the loss of two wickets in one Laker over including a magnificent delivery to bowl [Neil] Harvey. One certainly felt the pressure – nerves, a difficult pitch and a great bowler. A thick edge between the leg cordon got me off the mark, a respite came with the tea interval but immediately thereafter everything fell apart. [Jim] Burke succumbed to give [Tony] Lock his only wicket of the match and then [Jim] Laker cleaned up the rest of us as eight wickets fell for 22 runs.

Unquestionably the pitch contributed significantly to our demise, but our lack of experience under such conditions and a negative mental approach, born out of frustration at seeing our Ashes chances thwarted, were also factors. The game would probably have ended on the third day but for the intervention of the weather which limited play for two days. On the damp pitch and under grey skies much of the venom went out of the attack until lunch time on the final day. With defence of our wickets the only strategy left, Col McDonald and I managed to see through this period – never had one adopted such a negative approach to scoring runs with an average of only one run produced each over.

During lunch on the final day the sun finally appeared and the pitch took on a totally different character. Suddenly there was sharp turn and bounce – virtually a 'sticky' wicket – and batting became very challenging. Lock was perhaps turning too much to endanger the right-handed batsmen but Laker was a different proposition. Despite my determination to play forward to nullify the turn, Laker finally pushed me back with a virtual round arm delivery of lower trajectory, trapping me lbw [for 38 in 263 minutes – ed.] – a repeat of the first innings.

The loss of three more quick wickets pushed the game back in England's favour but McDonald and [Richie] Benaud fought valiantly through until the tea interval, with intermittent cloud cover nullifying some of Lock and Laker's effectiveness. However, the return of the sun during the tea interval signalled another difficult period and the loss of McDonald for a magnificent 89, to the second ball thereafter, sealed our fate.

Looking back on it all now (57 years on), it was a big disappointment losing to put the Ashes out of our reach. There was also a degree of frustration and anger that the series was not necessarily decided on the relative merits of the teams but on the quality of the pitches. There was also profound admiration for Laker's performance and the humility with which he accepted it, and finally a degree of satisfaction that my own debut had yielded an effort in which both I, and the media, saw promise. And the aftermath of the game? – an overnight train trip to the Oval to front up the following morning to guess who? – Lock and Laker as well as Eric Bedser who was hardly inferior to his more illustrious teammates! It was rubbing salt into the wounds!

Ten of Ian Craig's 11 Tests were overseas. He averaged 16 in first-class matches on his first English tour in 1953 and 36 in 1956. In his memories of the match and the tour he speaks of the 'deep antipathy' between captain Ian Johnson and vice-captain Keith Miller 'which did not contribute to team unity'. He penned his thoughts especially for this book, in 2013.

CRUCIAL: Having made a heroic 89, Colin McDonald finally succumbs to Jim Laker and his leg-trap, caught by Alan Oakman on a wicket the Australians likened to the beach at Bondi.

Laker had taken 19 wickets for the match and, whatever the Australian batsmen's deficiencies against good off-spin bowling and the appalling pitches prepared to haunt us, his performance was heroic and will remain forever as one of the greatest performances in the history of Ashes cricket.

Surrey spin 'twins' Jim Laker and Tony Lock were responsible for 38 of the 40 Australian wickets to fall in the two emphatic, much-debated English victories at Headingley and Old Trafford. England retained the Ashes 2-1.

C.C., the Colin McDonald Story, Colin McDonald
(Australian Scholarly Publications, Melbourne, 2009)

The First Day of Bodyline
Arthur Mailey

Having recaptured the Ashes emphatically in 1930
thanks to the record-breaking deeds of the boy wonder
Don Bradman, Australia entered the opening Test of
the 1932–33 summer full of hope and expectation.

First Day: The ground was almost filled at 11.45 a.m. The [Sydney] grandstand and the members' stand were packed, but there were small vacant spots on the Hill. A moderate southerly breeze was blowing. This was in favour of [Harold] Larwood, but from that particular end there is a rise to the wicket, which would have been a slight handicap to the fast bowler.

When one man was placed at silly square leg and four in the slips, it was thought that Larwood was going to bowl the off theory. Larwood, however, had other ideas. The first four balls were a good length, and were bowled on the leg. The fifth was straight, and the sixth, which was short-pitched, missed [Bill] Woodfull's head by inches. That was a signal that the battle had started. [Bill] Voce, at the other end, bowled unadulterated leg theory, without even one slip fielder.

Larwood's first two overs were very fast, but the bowler was not getting the assistance from the wicket he expected. In the third over two old rivals in [Bill] Ponsford and Larwood faced each other and the Nottinghamshire express bowler put every ounce of energy he possessed into his deliveries. The Victorian pair were not perturbed. Now and then, perhaps once each over, they ducked their heads and heard the ball whistling merrily past; but there was nothing sufficiently difficult in the bowling at that moment to cause any undue concern.

Larwood brought another man on the leg side, and made a supreme effort to dislodge the batsmen. He bowled a number of very fast, good-length balls. He dumped a short one straight at the leg stump. The same ball in Melbourne would have flown high over the batsman's head, but the 'dead' wicket killed the ball and it came along harmlessly at an ordinary height.

This was the last shot in Larwood's locker as far as that session was concerned. He finished the over, put on his sweater, and gave way to his understudy, ['Gubby'] Allen.

It was an interesting battle while it lasted. I could almost hear a sigh of relief come from the Victorian batsmen when Larwood was taken off.

Unleashing bodyline for the first time in a Test, Larwood took four of the first six Australian wickets to fall on the opening day overshadowed by one of the most gallant centuries of them all from Sydney's own Stan McCabe. Woodfull, 7, and Ponsford, 32, were separated in the first 40 minutes, by Voce.

And Then Came Larwood, Arthur Mailey
(The Bodley Head, Sydney, 1933)

It Wasn't Cricket
Alan Kippax

An eyewitness view of bodyline from one of the participants.

To say that Australian cricket received the shock of its life when it first saw the bodyline tactics in operation in a Test is to put the case mildly. The bitterest feelings of resentment were aroused first of all in the players, and not in [just] one or two. From No. 1 to No. 11 they were unanimous in feeling that they had had something 'put over them' which was not cricket.

Old cricketers and followers of the game did not at first know quite what to make of it. Many felt that it was better to say nothing and to see how the players were able to deal with the new methods. There was the cricketer's old and deep-rooted objection to anything in the nature of a protest.

It was felt that this was a new and ugly feature of cricket, but that it was better to try to defeat it on the field than to make it immediately the subject of a pen war.

It did not take long to convince most of the doubters that artistic batsmanship was more or less helpless in the face of this type of bowling and that physical endurance and acrobatics were to prove more important than skill. There were many hundreds of old players, however, who made no secret from the first of their objection to the new methods. Before the first Test match had been in progress two days, indignant letters were pouring in to the newspapers.

A clearly unnerved Alan Kippax, one of the ultimate stylists, played his last Australian-soil Test in Sydney in 1932–33, making 8 and 19.

Anti Body-line, Alan Kippax, with Eric Barbour (The Sydney & Melbourne Publishing Company, Sydney, 1933)

Chipper, McCabe & Other Legends
Ray Robinson

Australia's finest cricket writer of his era had a love
affair with England … and particularly Trent Bridge.

Of all the places on your match list the one that has the most, enduring memories for me is Trent Bridge, Nottingham. It was not only the scene of the first Test I saw outside Australia, but the human side of four happenings there made it memorable.

On the second day of the 1934 Test, I was sitting among rows of Notts folk, fascinated by the way they sound the 'g' in the middle of such words as Nottingham and wrong-un. Arthur Chipperfield played at several balls outside the off stump but missed them. On 99 at lunch, he played forward to the third ball to Ken Farnes and wicketkeeper Les Ames caught him. Missing 100 by one in his first Test innings prevented 'Chipper' from adding a third distinction to

100 in his first match against MCC in Australia and 100 in his first game against an English county.

The night before the Test ended I sent a telegram presumptuously trying to influence captain Bill Woodfull not to bat too long into the day.

I admired the team spirit of Stan McCabe and Len Darling. McCabe, 87, had a go at a ball and was caught. Sir Jack Hobbs praised Stan for sacrificing his chance of 100 in the interests of his side.

Hobbs noted that Darling did not trouble to play himself in but slung his bat at everything, not caring about the loss of his wicket. Being caught at 14 was especially unselfish of Darling. Last batsman chosen, he was the least sure of holding his place. (Alan Kippax replaced him for the fifth Test.)

By continuing the innings 90 minutes into the last day before closing, Woodfull gave his bowlers four and three quarters of an hour to get England out under 380 (80 runs an hour).

The Englishmen got within 10 minutes of playing out a draw. Out for 141, they lost by 238. It was one of the many times when time to take wickets was more important than setting a longer target.

In Bill O'Reilly and Clarrie Grimmett, Australia had two bowlers who proved they could do the job in a little more than four and a half hours, getting enough turn from the fourth day track. They shared all 10 wickets. The 'Tiger' was the match winner. He dismissed the opening pair (of Cyril Walters and Herbert Sutcliffe) and spun out five more. All except two edged his leg break to slip fielder Chipperfield or wicketkeeper [Bert] Oldfield. This gave him 11 wickets in his first Test in England. The Sydney branch of the Society is proud to have him as Patron.

Trent Bridge has atmosphere. In the white pavilion, as you come down the stairs from the dressing room your boots will be treading the steps McCabe trod on his way to play the greatest innings in Test history. Australia seemed doomed to follow-on here in 1938 until his 232 in 235 minutes plucked the Test from England's grasp. Stan skimmed his last 170 while his last four partners made 38. As a hook for 6 was being retrieved from behind square leg, fast bowler

Ken Farnes asked O'Reilly at the non-striker's end: 'What can I bowl now? What can I do next?'

O'Reilly: 'Well, you could run down and get his autograph.'

Upstairs on the balcony, captain Don Bradman called to the players in the room, 'Come and look at this! You will never see anything like this again.' This was one of the innings that inspired me to write a chapter, 'Never Say Die', in *Between Wickets*.

Down those same stairs in 1921 came Charlie Macartney to lash up the highest score by an Australian in England. Between 12.07 p.m. and 3.14 p.m. he plundered 345 runs from the Notts bowlers.

In 1996, shortly before his death, Bill O'Reilly wrote of the celebrated journalist and author 'Sugar Ray' Robinson: 'Of all the cricket writers I have read and tried to read, Ray Robinson was the unrivalled leader of the band.'

World Tour Souvenir Brochure (Australian Cricket Society, Sydney, June 1979)

Happy Reflections All
Arthur Gilligan

It remains one of England's most famous Golden Age Test wins of all, set up by a withering century from 'The Croucher'. A seven-year-old English captain-to-be witnessed the gripping finish – the start of a wonderful lifetime in the game.

I had my initiation into Test cricket 75 years ago, when my father took my two brothers and myself to see the fifth Test match at Kennington Oval, August 1902. It was a tremendous tussle with the issue in doubt right up until the last ball was bowled. In the end England triumphed by one wicket thanks to a 15-run stand after Wilfred Rhodes joined George Hirst. It had been an enthralling game: Australia made 324 in their first innings. Rain made England's task rather difficult and we were all out for 183. Some splendid

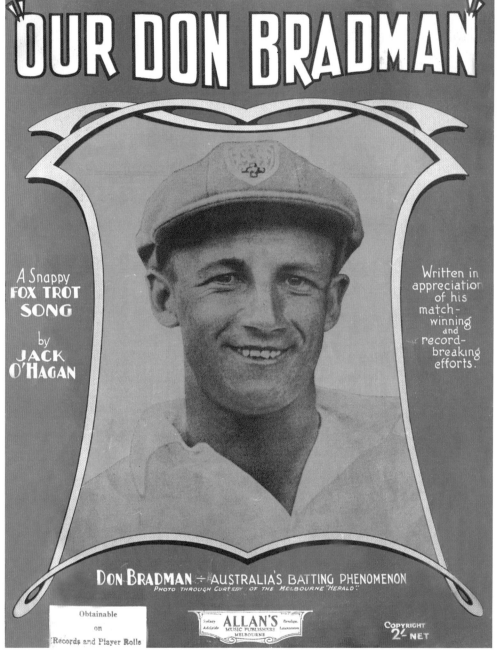

ASHES ICON: Life was never quite the same again for a young Don Bradman after his prodigious feats on his first English tour in 1930. The 21-year-old Don amassed a record 2960 runs at 98.66 and became known Australia-wide as 'Our Don'. His scores in the Tests were unparalleled: 8, 131, 254, 1, 334, 14 and 232.

'THIS THING CAN BE DONE' (above): Upset by the unsporting run out of teammate Sammy Jones by Dr W. G. Grace, the 'Demon' Fred Spofforth urged teammates to believe that Australia could still win, despite England requiring just 85 in its second innings. Famously he took his second 'seven-for' for the match as England collapsed for 77.

HANDS OF STEEL (above right and right): C. T. B. Turner's grip was so strong he could crush an orange between his thumb and forefinger. The first Australian to 100 Test wickets, he gathered his first 50 in just six Tests, a vicious breakback his trademark. He was one of three 19th century Australian Ashes cricketers to hail from bustling Bathurst and in 2013 was inducted into the Australian cricket Hall of Fame. Weeks earlier, a biography of his life, celebrating 150 years since his birth was also released, entitled *The Terror: Charlie Turner, Australia's greatest bowler.*

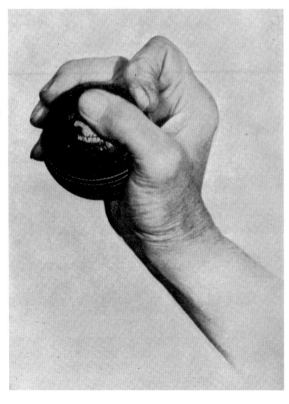

THE 1888 AUSTRALIANS: Having upset England at Lord's, Australia lost the next two Tests by an innings, the menacing combination of Charlie 'the Terror' Turner and Jack 'the Fiend' Ferris responsible for 32 of the 37 English wickets to fall in the three-Test series.

The team: Standing, left to right: 'Affie' Jarvis, Sammy Jones, Jack Lyons, Jack Worrall, C. W. Beale (manager), Jack Blackham, Harry Boyle, John Edwards (with bat). Sitting: George Bonnor, 'Terror' Turner, Percy McDonnell (captain), Harry Trott, Alick Bannerman.

THE 1897–98 ENGLISHMEN: Winning the opening Test in Sydney under acting captain Archie MacLaren, the visiting Englishmen lost the next four Tests in a row to go down 4-1 in a series notable for Joe Darling's power-packed hitting against the fastest bowler in the world, Tom Richardson.

The team: Standing, left to right: Frank Druce, Jack Mason, Tom Hayward, Jack Board, Jack Hearne. Sitting: Ted Wainwright, Prince Ranjitsinhji, Drewy Stoddart (captain), Tom Richardson, Bill Storer. Front: Johnny Briggs, George Hirst. Absent: Archie MacLaren.

(left) **WELCOMING:** Cricket-loving Lord Sheffield's feasts for the visiting Australian cricketers were lavish. Few matched his table for dimension or choice. From main courses of salmon, quail, lobster, ox tongue and roast lamb, followed by Venetian pudding and Maraschino jelly accompanied by the most expensive wines from around the world – all expertly served by a fleet of servants – the fare was invariably unforgettable.

(right) **HURRICANE HITTER:** Having missed selection for the 1896 Australian tour to England, Melburnian Albert Trott paid for his own fare to England and joined the groundstaff at Lord's, beginning an auspicious professional career, highlighted by his feat of hitting M. A. 'Monty' Noble over the Lord's Grandstand in 1899.

(left) **MUCH LOVED:** Harry Trott, Albert's younger brother, led the 1896 tourists to England, his 143 in the first Test at Lord's forcing the Test match into a third day after the Australians had been dismissed for just 53 in their first innings. He was a legendary figure in and around South Melbourne, where he worked as a postie.

(right) **GOOGLYMAN:** Albert Chevallier Tayler's famous watercolour portraits of the leading Anglo-Australian cricketers included this one of B. J. 'Bosie' Bosanquet, the famed each-way spinner who won the 1904 Test match in Sydney virtually singlehandedly with a riveting spell which saw him take a Down Under-best six for 51 from 15 wristy overs.

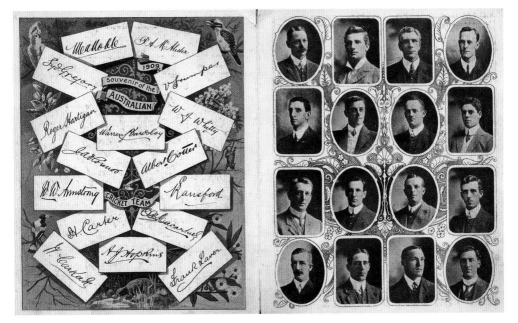

1909 ASHES MEN: On their way to a 2-1 series win, the Australians fielded just 14 men in the five Test series, compared with England's 25. The tour was dominated by the left-handers Warren Bardsley and Vernon Ransford who amassed 13 centuries between them, Bardsley, from Sydney, making twin tons in the decider at the Oval.

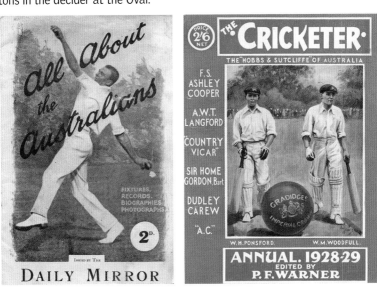

(left) **BIG JACK:** Jack Gregory was the fastest Australian bowler of the first 50 years of Ashes cricket who was noted for his giant kangaroo hop just before delivery. Only Bodyliner Harold Larwood was as menacing. Having taken 23 wickets in the 1920–21 home Tests, Gregory gathered 19 more in 1921 and formed one of the great combinations with Tasmanian-born Melburnian Ted McDonald.

(right) **HIGH PROFILE:** The feats of Victorian pair Bill Ponsford (left) and Bill Woodfull were recognised with front-cover recognition in the English *Cricketer* magazine in the late 1920s. Eight of their 23 century stands came in Melbourne, including their biggest three: 375, 236 and 227 at interstate level. They three times amassed 100-plus partnerships in Tests.

PROLIFIC: In 1928–29 the MCC's Walter Hammond ruled the crease like no-one else, even Don Bradman, with 1553 runs at an average of 90-plus. Two of his three double-centuries came in Sydney including this one, 225 against powerful New South Wales, an innings noted for his imperious driving and the ever-so-occasional miscalculation …

(above left) **BILL THE UNBOWLABLE:** Australia's Bodyline series captain Bill Woodfull as featured in the 16 February 1933 fourth Test special edition of the *Queenslander*. The Australians lost this game and the Ashes by four wickets after a brave innings from an ill Eddie Paynter, who was held back in the order to No. 8 and responded with a gritty near-century pivotal in England's win.

(above right) **BIRTHDAY BOY:** Captain Bill Woodfull, clutching a souvenir stump, dashes back to the pavilion at Kennington Oval after Australia's Ashes-regaining victory in the final Test of 1930. It was Woodfull's 33rd birthday. Fast bowler Tim Wall is on his left. Sadly, this was to be batting prodigy Archie Jackson's Ashes farewell. He was to die just two and a half years later.

(right) **THE FIRST 'ASHES' ABC:** The *ABC Cricket Book* has been an Australian institution for more than 80 years. This one, in 1934, was the first devoted to an Ashes tour and included short player profiles, records, scoresheets, listening times and cricketing terms for the uninitiated.

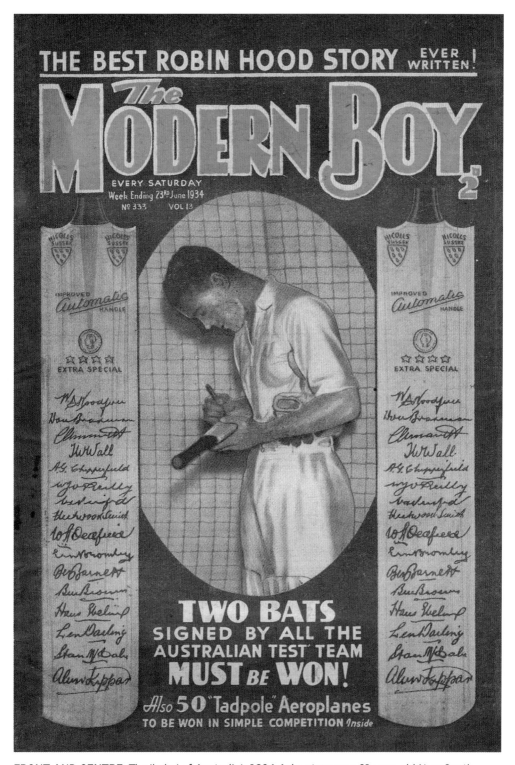

FRONT AND CENTRE: The 'baby' of Australia's 1934 Ashes tour was 21-year-old New South Welshman Bill Brown who is pictured on a specialist-cricket cover of *Modern Boy*, the popular boy's magazine of the late 1920s and 1930s. So successful was Brown that he opened in four of the five Tests, captain Bill Woodfull relegating himself to the middle-order.

THE KING AT A TEST MATCH, LORDS

(left) **THE KING AND I:** King George V is introduced to paceman Bill Bowes, who amassed 19 wickets in three Tests in 1934, including four at Lord's when the Australians suffered a rare defeat at the home of cricket.

(below) **GREATEST MOMENT:** Fitzroy's slow-medium bowler Morrie Sievers took full advantage of favourable conditions in 1936–37 to capture a Test-best five for 21 as England floundered in the Melbourne Test which was to attract a world record 350,000-plus fans over six epic days. *Ray Nichols*

(bottom) **HEROES OF THE NATION:** A between-the-wars confectionary tin depicts Australia's 1938 touring squad. After two draws and a washout the last two Tests were decided, one to Australia and one to England. *Charles Leski Auctions*

THE AGE, MONDAY, JANUARY 4, 1937. 11

ENGLAND FAILS ON "STICKY" WICKET.

SIEVERS OBTAINS FIVE FOR 21.

AUSTRALIA LEADS BY 124 ON FIRST INNINGS.

CAPTAINS' BATTLE OF TACTICS.

ANOTHER ENORMOUS ATTENDANCE.

BY MID-OFF.

As a result of a batting failure by England on a bad wicket on Saturday on the Melbourne ground, Australia led England by 124 runs on the first innings. Then Australia lost one wicket (O'Reilly's) for three runs in the second innings. In all the circumstances Australia is in a better position than it has occupied previously in this series of Tests. But those Australians who might be inclined to be mirthful should remember that cricket sometimes is a funny game (it was so on Saturday) with luck often counting for much more than pluck. He who laughs best laughs at the end of the game.

Although large sections of the huge crowd displayed understandable impatience in having to wait until 2.15 p.m. for the resumption of play—the delay having been caused by the unfit condition of the wicket—it was not long before the spectators were thoroughly enjoying a succession of thrills too infrequently associated with Test cricket. The atmosphere of sustained excitement

The score board at the end of England's first innings, indicating the English batsmen's

"ABOVE ALL"
AEROPLANE JELLIES

AUSTRALIAN TOURING TEAM - 1938

TOP ROW :- A.G.CHIPPERFIELD. L.O'B.FLEETWOOD-SMITH. D.G.BRADMAN. W.A.BROWN. S.G.BARNES.
CENTRE ROW :- E.C.S.WHITE. W.J.O'REILLY. C.L.BADCOCK. B.A.BARNETT.
BOTTOM ROW:- A.L.HASSETT. M.G.WAITE. C.W.WALKER. E.L.McCORMICK. J.H.FINGLETON. F.A.WARD. S.J.McCABE.

KEEPING THE CUSTOMERS SATISFIED: So high was interest in the cricket, that many of Australia's retail houses and leading manufacturers regularly produced fixture cards for Ashes summers.

(left) **TOSSING UP:** A Tony Rafty caricature from a 1953 *Sporting Life* magazine shows the two opposing captains Lindsay Hassett (Australia) and Len Hutton (England).

(right) **GENTLY FADES THE DON:** Don Bradman, circa 1948, as depicted by cartoonist-cricketer Arthur Mailey. Turning 40 late in the tour, the Don still averaged 72 for the Tests and 89 overall.

ARGUS BADGES: Four of the cricketing badges produced by the Melbourne *Argus* in 1950–51 included Ashes combatants, Australian Bill Johnston (left) and Englishmen Len Hutton and Alec Bedser.

CRICKET IMP: Diminutive Lindsay Hassett was noted for his sense of humour and love of touring life. He led the '53 Australians on their Coronation Year tour of the UK. It was his third and final tour. Later he became an ABC broadcaster.

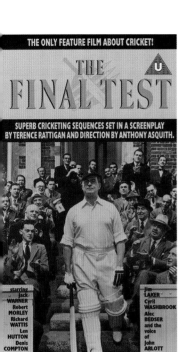

THE FINAL TEST

SUPERB CRICKETING SEQUENCES SET IN A SCREENPLAY BY TERENCE RATTIGAN AND DIRECTION BY ANTHONY ASQUITH.

starring
Jack WARNER
Robert MORLEY
Richard WATTIS
Len HUTTON
Denis COMPTON

Jim LAKER
Cyril WASHBROOK
Alec BEDSER
and the voice of John ARLOTT

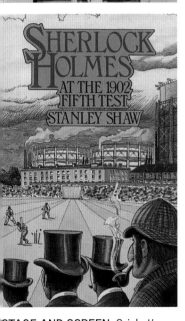

SHERLOCK HOLMES AT THE 1902 FIFTH TEST
STANLEY SHAW

STAGE AND SCREEN: Cricket's leading players and the Ashes have perennially been featured in general-interest films and books. *That's Cricket* was one of the early sporting films to celebrate the game and its leading Australian players.

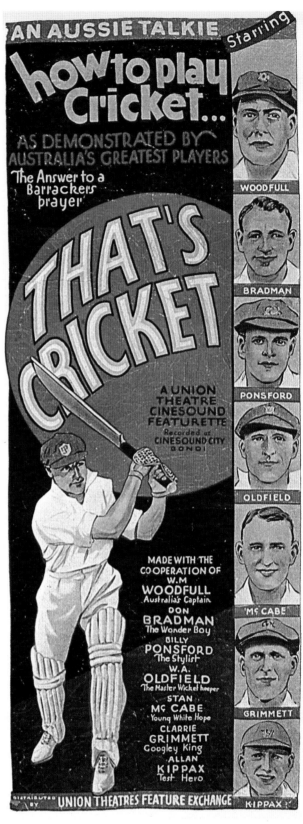

AN AUSSIE TALKIE Starring

how to play Cricket...
AS DEMONSTRATED BY AUSTRALIA'S GREATEST PLAYERS

The Answer to a Barrackers prayer

THAT'S CRICKET

A UNION THEATRE CINESOUND FEATURETTE
Recorded at CINESOUND CITY BONDI

MADE WITH THE CO-OPERATION OF
W.M WOODFULL
Australia's Captain
DON BRADMAN
The Wonder Boy
BILLY PONSFORD
The Stylist
W.A. OLDFIELD
The Master Wicket keeper
STAN MC CABE
Young White Hope
CLARRIE GRIMMETT
Googley King
ALLAN KIPPAX
Test Hero

DISTRIBUTED BY UNION THEATRES FEATURE EXCHANGE

WOODFULL
BRADMAN
PONSFORD
OLDFIELD
MCCABE
GRIMMETT
KIPPAX

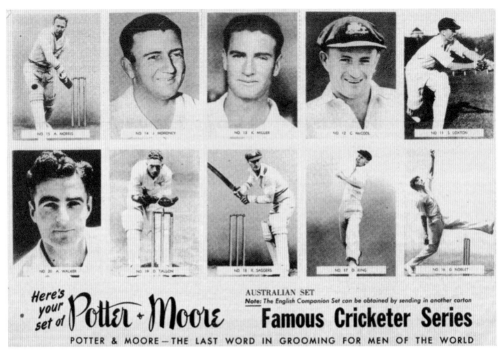

POTTER AND MOORE: Trade cards from the 1950–51 summer, featuring the most prominent Australian and English cricketers.

(left) **BUDDING CHAMPIONS:** A young Australian team from the Adelaide international of 1971–72 was building towards Ashes glory. In 1972 they squared the series 2-2 in England and two years later, back in Australia, re-won the Ashes 4-1.

Standing, left to right: Keith Stackpole, Ashley Mallett, Greg Chappell, John Benaud, Ashley Woodcock, Kerry O'Keeffe. Front: Ross Duncan, John Inverarity, Ian Chappell (captain), Rod Marsh, Doug Walters (12th man). Absent: Bob Massie.

(right) **FORTUNATE SON:** Under video replay analysis, Australian opener Keith Stackpole would have been run out before he'd reached 20 in the opening Test of 1970–71 in Brisbane. He went on to make 207, his highest Test score in a stellar summer. Later he worked for years with the ABC as a special comments expert.

Here's your set of Potter + Moore Famous Cricketer Series

ENGLISH SET
Note: The Australian Companion Set can be obtained by sending in another carton

POTTER & MOORE — THE LAST WORD IN GROOMING FOR MEN OF THE WORLD

(left) **BARGAIN BASED:** Ashes tickets to the member's enclosure at Lord's cost just two pounds to the opening day's play in 1977. Thirty-six years later for the second Test of 2013, they were more than 100 pounds each.

(right) **FORMIDABLE:** Greg (left) and Ian Chappell were pivotal in Australia's Ashes successes of the 1970s. Greg captained the Test team in three Ashes campaigns and Ian in two.

CALENDAR HEROES: A frontispiece to a Boy Scout's calendar for the 1982–83 Ashes summer by Australian painter and illustrator Cedric Baxter.

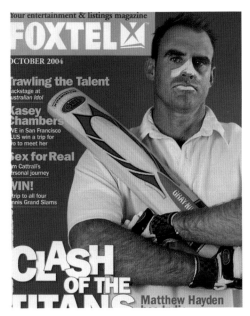

(left) **IMPROVING WITH AGE:** After a modest beginning to his Test career, Matthew Hayden formed one of the great opening stands with fellow left-hander Justin Langer, four of their 14 century starts coming in Ashes contests, including a high of 195 in the Boxing Day Test in Melbourne in 2002–03.

(right) **EXTROVERT:** Some considered his antics boorish, but Shane Warne made the most of Australia's Ashes-winning Test at Trent Bridge in 1997. So many of Warne's mega performances occurred on English wickets against batsmen who often refused to leave their crease and fell like flies against the beefy conjurer.

ONE LAST HURRAH: Steve Waugh leads the Australians on to the Sydney Cricket Ground for his last Ashes Test in 2003, the game in which he famously reached his final century against England on the last ball of the second day's play. *Patrick Eagar*

MAESTRO: Ricky Ponting averaged 44 in Tests against England and 51 overall, eight of his 41 Test centuries coming in Ashes battle including his most important, 156 in the drawn third Test at Old Trafford in 2005. *Patrick Eagar*

SCAPEGOAT: Harold Larwood refused to apologise for his hand in the acrimonious Bodyline summer, saying he'd only been following orders. He was never selected for England again and in 1950 he sold his confectionary shop in Blackpool and with his wife and five children moved to Australia where he found little of the resentment which had forced his premature exit from professional ranks in England.

PRIZE SCALP: Chasing 315 in the fourth innings of the mid-series Test in Adelaide, the 1901–02 Australians lost Reggie Duff at 5 and Victor Trumper at 50, bowled by John Gunn (above), before a recovery led by locals Joe Darling and Clem Hill resulted in Australia's four wicket win. Gunn, from Nottinghamshire, took eight wickets for the game. Fifteen thousand fans attended the second day's play and almost 50,000 over the six days of the game. *The Australasian*

THE 1903–04 AUSTRALIANS: Adelaide Test, mid-summer: Standing, left to right: Algie Gehrs (12th man), Warwick Armstrong, Bill Howell, Hugh Trumble, Bert Hopkins, Charlie McLeod, Victor Trumper. Sitting: Jim Kelly, Clem Hill, 'Monty' Noble (captain), Reggie Duff, Syd Gregory.

GOLDEN AGE HEROES: Leading Australian and English cricketers from the 1911 Wills release, from left: Warren Bardsley, Victor Trumper, Bill Whitty (all Australia) and C. B. Fry and Wilfred Rhodes (England)

HOMAGE TO CLARRIE: President of the South Australian Cricket Association Mr H. Fisher makes a presentation to Clarrie Grimmett in honour of his remarkable Test debut in which he took 11 wickets in the fifth and final Test in Sydney in 1924-25. His SA captain Vic Richardson watches on approvingly. *Charles Leski Auctions*

FORMIDABLE: Jack Hobbs and Wilfred Rhodes open England's batting against the 1920–21 Australians in Adelaide. Hobbs' 123 in the second innings saw England reach 370 but Australia still won comfortably in the timeless Test which stretched into a sixth day. *The Australasian*

(left) **JOHNNY WON'T HIT TODAY:** J. W. H. T. Douglas was a born leader who had an 8-8 captaincy record for England, including a 4-1 series win in the 1911–12 Ashes summer dominated by pacemen Syd Barnes and Frank Foster.

(above right) **A YOUNG WALLY:** Jack Hobbs aside, Walter Hammond was England's finest between-the-wars batsman who was to tour Down Under four times for Test series averages of 113 (in 1928–29), 55 (1932–33), 58 (1936–37) and 21 (1946–47).

(below right) **TOUGH AS TEAK:** Maurice Leyland had to wait eight years for an opportunity to represent England. Seven of his nine Test 100s were to come in Ashes battles, his average of 56 against Australia a ready reckoner of his love of the challenge of opposing the Cornstalks, the nickname Brits bestowed on early Australian teams.

A SEVEN-DAY TEST: Having convincingly lost the first two Tests of 1928–29, Australia included two more debutants, all-rounders Ted a'Beckett and Ron Oxenham into its XI for Melbourne. In a fierce contest that lasted for seven days – Tests in Australia being timeless – England won narrowly after chasing 332 in the fourth innings. Herbert Sutcliffe's 145 was his fourth Ashes century in five consecutive Test innings in Melbourne.

Australia's team: Standing, left to right: Alan Kippax, 'Stork' Hendry, Don Blackie, Ted a'Beckett. Tommy Andrews (12th man). Front: Ron Oxenham, Clarrie Grimmett, Bert Oldfield, Jack Ryder (captain), Bill Woodfull, Don Bradman, Victor Richardson.

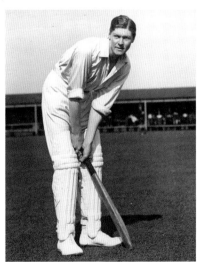

NINE IN A ROW: Percy Chapman won his first nine Tests in a row as England's captain having been handed the captaincy for the final Ashes Test of 1926. While he was to average under 30 in Tests, he could be dominant, as shown by his 121 in the second innings at Lord's in 1930.

BODYLINE CAPTAINS: Douglas Jardine and Bill Woodfull toss for the first time in Melbourne during the MCC–Victoria international in November 1932. Woodfull won five of their six tosses for the summer, but the English XI won five of the six matches.

ENJOY YOURSELF AT AUSTRALIA'S PREMIER SEASIDE RESORT
HOTEL ASTRA
BONDI, SYDNEY
Tel. FW8112.

PRICE 4d

Smith's Weekly

FOUNDED BY JOYNTON SMITH — The Public Guardian

CHAMPION'S
PURE MALT
VINEGAR
BREWED IN AUSTRALIA
FROM OUR
OLD ENGLISH FORMULA

Vol. XIV, No. 29 (Copyright) • • • Saturday, January 14, 1933

How Woodfull Made His Way Into Third Test Team

DROPPED FROM SECOND, HE WAS REINSTATED AT LAST MINUTE

Irritating Tactics Of Board Of Control And Selection Committee Wrecked Players' Nerves

Win Was a Prodigious Feat, So What About a Bob-in For Jardine?

WOODFULL'S OFFER: *Smith's Weekly* reported that Bill Woodfull had offered to step down in the wake of Australia's humbling first Bodyline series defeat in Sydney, a decision initially accepted by the selectors before Woodfull told them that he would not be making any comebacks. He continued as captain.

IMPREGNABLE: With his hands wide apart on the handle, Bill Woodfull was hardly a stylist but he was a fine and spirited competitor who averaged 75 for Victoria, 46 for Australia and toured England three times. His finest Ashes innings came at Lord's in 1930 when he scored 155 on the day Don Bradman made a peerless 254.

CLOSE CALL: Umpire Bill Parry is not needed to adjudicate as a throw from side-on to run-out Herbert Sutcliffe flies wide of wicketkeeper Bert Oldfield at Kennington Oval in 1930. Sutcliffe made 161 and 54 in a mighty double but Australia won by an innings to regain the Ashes on captain Bill Woodfull's 33rd birthday.

TELEGRAMS AND CABLES:
"CRICKET" ADELAIDE

TELEPHONE:
CENT. 1111 (2 LINES)

SECRETARY:
W. H. JEANES

MANUFACTURES BUILDING
14 PIRIE STREET
ADELAIDE
SOUTH AUSTRALIA   17th February. 1933.

Mr. L. O'Brien,
C/- Victorian Cricket Association,
Cr. Collins Place & Flinders St.,
MELBOURNE.

Dear Sir,

The Australian Selectors have chosen 12 players
from whom the team to play England in the Fifth Test
Match, commencing in Sydney on the 23rd inst. will
be selected.   These players are -

W.M. Woodfull	H. Ironmonger
V.Y. Richardson	W.J. O'Reilly
L. Darling	T.W. Wall
W.A. Oldfield	L. Nagel
D.G. Bradman	E.H. Bromley
S.J. McCabe	L. O'Brien

The allowances to players will be £30. for the
Match plus 30/- per day and travelling expenses when
out of their home State.   Players are expected to
arrive in Sydney on February 21st.   For the purpose
of determining the daily allowance the day of departure
from and return to the player's home State will count
as one day.   Selected players should get into touch
with their State Association Secretary regarding
travelling arrangements.   Travelling expenses to be
allowed comprise First Class Railway Tickets, Sleeping
Berths, and Parlor Car Seats.   Players visiting Sydney
are to arrange their own hotel accommodation and pay
for same.   They are requested to report to the
Secretary of the New South Wales Cricket Association
prior to or immediately after their arrival, their
addresses and also to advise any subsequent change
thereof.

If there is any doubt about your being able to
play in the match please let me know as quickly as
possible.

The team to take the field will probably
be chosen shortly before the hour appointed for
the game to commence.

Yours faithfully,

Secretary.

MODEST MONIES: An invitation for Leo O'Brien to play in the fifth Bodyline Test in Sydney. Players often had to take leave without pay from their normal jobs and rarely did better than 'break even'. O'Brien, a Melbourne-based taxation clerk, would have played for nothing. He made a Test-best 61 and 5 in this match which England won by eight wickets.

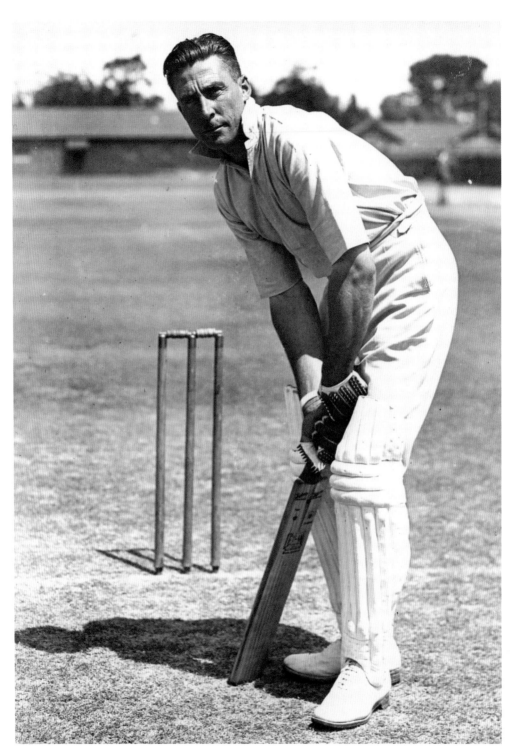

WARRIOR: One of Australia's outstanding and most charismatic sportsmen of the 1920s and 1930s, Vic Richardson made a century in his second Ashes Test in Melbourne in 1925, toured England in 1930 and was Bill Woodfull's deputy-captain in 1932–33 where his 83 opening up with Woodfull in the Brisbane Test was pivotal in Australia's only 100-plus score for the first wicket all summer.

THE McCABE EPIC: Day 2 of the first Bodyline Test and 22-year-old rising champion Stan McCabe (pictured right, on 127) resumes with Clarrie Grimmett (17). Scoring almost at will, McCabe was to make 60 out of 70 in a frenetic first hour's play in his greatest Test innings in Australia.

UNMISTAKEABLE: With the SS *Orontes* just days from the White Cliffs, Don Bradman looks typically assured and confident. He was to begin the '38 tour as he had begun the 1930 and 1934 trips, with a double century at Worcester.

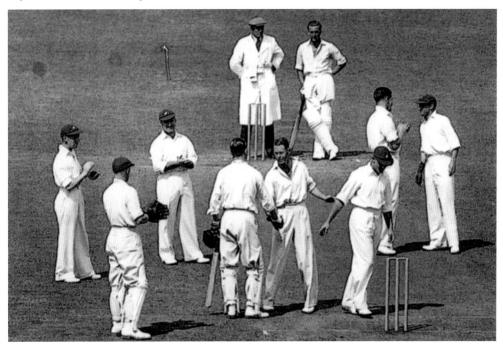

CONGRATULATIONS: Bill Brown shakes hands with Len Hutton after the Yorkshireman has broken Don Bradman's 334 as Test cricket's highest individual score. All the Australians, including the Don, applauded and congratulated Hutton on his remarkable feat of skill and stamina, the high point of the final Ashes Test before World War Two.

THE OLD PROS: Len Hutton and Cyril Washbrook built the finest record since 'Obbs and Sutcliffe, three of their eight century stands in Tests coming in consecutive innings in Australia in 1946–47. At Leeds in 1948 they started with 169 and 129 yet still played on the losing side.

IVERSONED: The 1950–51 MCC team may have lost 4-1 but they encountered the worst of a Brisbane sticky in the opening Test and went down by just 28 runs in the following Test in Melbourne, after Australian newcomer Jack Iverson took six wickets in front of his own home crowd.

The team: Back row, left to right: Bill Ferguson (scorer), Bob Berry, Arthur McIntyre, Trevor Bailey, Gilbert Parkhouse, Eric Hollies. Middle: John Dewes, David Sheppard, John Warr, Alec Bedser, Brian Close, Reg Simpson, Doug Wright. Front: Brigadier Michael Green (joint-manager), Cyril Washbrook, Denis Compton, Freddie Brown (captain), Len Hutton, Godfrey Evans, John Nash (joint-manager).

MATCHSAVERS: Willie Watson (on strike to Richie Benaud) and Trevor Bailey saved England at Lord's with an epic fifth day partnership which begun at 12.42 p.m. and ended at 5.50 p.m on 30 June 1953.

COMPO: Denis Compton toured Australia three times after the war, his twin centuries in Adelaide in the fourth Test of 1946–47 his personal highlight.

UNPLAYABLE: Jim Laker's famous 19 wicket haul at Old Trafford in 1956 included Ron Archer (above) caught by Alan Oakman in the leg trap. England won by an innings.

(left) **RIVAL CAPTAINS:** Len Hutton calls incorrectly in Adelaide, 1954–55 and Ian Johnson's Australians bat first. But none of the top six can make even a half-century in either innings and Australia is well beaten.

(right) **FOCUSED:** England's captain Peter May at the nets at the WACA Ground in Perth in 1958–59. He played one glorious innings, 113, in Melbourne and followed with 92 in Sydney in a draw. Australia won the first two and the last two Tests.

MATCHWINNERS: Alan Davidson (right) with first-time tourist Graham McKenzie in England in 1961. Their 98 run stand for the final wicket at Old Trafford provided the impetus for one of the great comeback victories of all.

300-WICKETS MAN: Fred Trueman is congratulated by England's captain Ted Dexter after becoming the first to 300 wickets during the fifth Test at the Oval in 1964.

234 RUN STAND: England openers Geoff Boycott and Bob Barber set up an innings victory on the opening day in Sydney in 1965–66 with a stand of 234. John Edrich joined the run feast, at one stage the Englishmen being 1-303 on their way to an imposing 488. In reply Australia was bowled out for just 221 and 174.

GOOD SPORTS: England was led by Mike Smith and Australia by Brian Booth in the absence of the injured Bobby Simpson in the Sydney Test of 1965–66. Booth lost the toss, made just 8 and 27 and was dropped, never to play at international level again.

1968 Australian Touring Test Team

Bill Lawry, Victoria Captain.

'all the best from the best of all beers!'

CARLTON DRAUGHT

Enjoyed by Victorians for over 100 years

ANOTHER CARLTON PRODUCT

LAWRY'S HEROES: A brewery poster produced for Bill Lawry's 1968 touring Australians to England. *Jim Rutherford*

MATCHWINNER: Dennis Lillee is chaired from the MCG after his 12 wicket haul in the 1977 Centenary Test. *Cricketer* magazine

The Daily Telegraph

JULY25, 2005 sport.telegraph.co.uk

Brutal Australia on the march

HEADLINERS: The *Daily Telegraph* front page after Australia's Glenn McGrath–inspired triumph in the opening Test at Lord's in 2005.

English bowling saw Australia out for 121. England had to get 263 to win, but we made an appalling start. Archie MacLaren, Lionel Palairet, Johnny Tyldesley, Tom Hayward and Len Braund all out with the scoreboard 48 for five. The Hon. F. S. Jackson had propped up the debacle until Gilbert Jessop came in to join him.

In 1936, I was playing golf with Stanley Jackson at the Berkshire Golf Club and I had the most interesting talk with him; how he and Jessop had weathered the storm (that afternoon, back in 1902). This is what he told me: 'At tea time I was 29 not out and "Jessopus" 19 not out. Then Gilbert got going in his own inimitable style and he reached his 50 when I was 40. The tragedy came when I was caught and bowled by Hughie Trumble for 49. "The Croucher" found a useful partner in [Dick] Lilley, but when Gilbert was out [for 104, the fastest century in Ashes Tests to that time − ed.], Hirst batted superbly until the ninth wicket fell with England needing just 15 runs for victory. Hirst and Rhodes, as legend has it, did it [almost] in singles, Hirst being 55 not out with victory to England. It was a marvellous match in every way.'

It was 22 years later that I had the honour of being elected captain of the MCC touring team in Australia for the 1924−25 tour. We had a great team, but Australia were even stronger and we went down 4-1. I lost four of the five tosses and it meant two to three days in the field. All matches then were played to a finish and three of them lasted seven days and the final two five days.

When I managed to call correctly at Melbourne in January 1925, we won by an innings and 27 runs − our first win for 13 years. Herbie Collins was Australia's skipper and he was a generous opponent. In 1968, at Sydney, I remember sitting with Sir Robert Menzies and Syd Smith (long-time president of the New South Wales Cricket Association) in the Committee room and the discussion took place as to whom were the three best Australian captains ever and the unanimous verdict by all three of us was 'Monty' Noble, Collins and Richie Benaud.

In 1924−25, England was practically always given a fine start by Jack Hobbs and Herbert Sutcliffe, with Frank Woolley and 'Patsy' Hendren as our star batsmen. We relied very much on Maurice

Tate, who then broke Arthur Mailey's record of 36 wickets by taking 38 on the tour. At Melbourne, he actually clean bowled Mailey for his 37th victim and Mailey — a great sportsman — walked up the pitch and shook Maurice warmly by the hand. I must not forget Herbert Strudwick who did a great job behind the stumps. We had a wonderful tour and I shall always remember and appreciate the great kindness shown to me and my team by the Australian people.

I didn't go again to Australia until 1936, when I joined the Australian Broadcasting Commission's team led by Vic Richardson, Alan McGilvray and Hal Hooker. I had a worrying time at Brisbane when I was to contribute 10 minutes to a summary after the first day's play. At a moment's notice, Eric Sholl who was the head honcho of the ABC team came up to me and said, 'You will have to take C. B. Fry's place as he is unable to broadcast the highlights — 17 minutes in all.' I had prepared for 10 minutes — and at the end of that time I had completed all I had in my notes. So I started again, giving a more detailed account of what I had already said and I lasted out, with perspiration pouring off my head. I don't think I shall ever forget that talk.

At the start the announcer said, 'Unfortunately Capt. C. B. Fry is unable to broadcast and in his place Arthur Gilligan is giving you the highlights of the first day's play. Arthur Gilligan captained both England and Australia.'

So valuable seconds were taken up when I said, 'Thank you Mr Announcer, I have had the pleasure of captaining England, but *never* have I had the honour of captaining Australia.'

In the years to come, I did some four or five tours with the ABC and also did several for the BBC in England — most memorably in 1930 when Sir Donald Bradman made his 334. He was 309 not out on the first day and on entering the Australian dressing room he is supposed to have said, 'That's a nice bit of practice for Monday.' When I met Don two years ago (1975) in England he told me how that story was untrue but all the same, at the time, many believed it.

I also saw his 304; both those triple centuries came at Headingley and later on I watched eight of his double centuries — some in Australia and some in England — and quite a few of his single hundreds. I also saw his final 'duck' at the Oval, when Eric Hollies bowled him with a googly.

I thoroughly enjoyed my broadcasting days in Australia with Vic Richardson and Alan McGilvray in 1946, 1950, 1954 and 1958 with Bernie Kerr in charge and my dear good friend the late Johnnie Moyes, a fine summariser and so very fair to both sides.

I well remember the Test at Sydney during Freddie Brown's 1950–51 tour when both Doug Wright and Trevor Bailey were injured, which meant that the England attack was badly crippled. Freddie did a Herculean task in bowling – at the age of 40 – [sending down] 44 eight-ball overs to take four for 153. The following day a hawker selling lettuces outside Australia Hotel in Castlereagh Street was calling, 'Wonderful lettuces – hearts as big as Freddie Brown's!'

I was at Adelaide in 1954–55, when Len Hutton regained the Ashes despite some fine bowling by that great cricketer Keith Miller who also caught two fine catches.

I have fond memories, too, of Peter May and Colin Cowdrey scoring centuries at Melbourne in different tours and I shall never forget Stan McCabe's brilliant double century at Trent Bridge (in 1938) when Australia were in dire trouble.

One of my most pleasant memories took place in 1936, when I sat at Trent Bridge for the whole three days with Sir Robert Menzies whom I shall always regard as the greatest cricket lover in the world. I can remember him describing cricket as a 'reflective' game because you could sit and watch the play and discuss many wonderful feats of the past in Test cricket between England and Australia.

Bob Menzies loved telling me the story in later years of the match between his Prime Minister's XI v. MCC at Canberra when he had Lindsay Hassett and Tiger O'Reilly in his team. He said to Lindsay, 'I well remember your century against Tiger – Victoria v. New South Wales.' To Tiger's extreme disgust, Lindsay said: 'Thank you Prime Minister. To which of the three occasions are you referring?'

Finally, I saw every ball bowled at the Oval when Len Hutton broke Don Bradman's record score of 334. With Don standing four yards from the bat at silly mid-off, Len cut a ball for 4 off 'Chuck' Fleetwood-Smith and that was a new record for the highest score for England and Australian Tests. Don was the first to congratulate Len.

So over 75 years I have many happy memories to think over and I only wish I could have written more about these happy occasions.

I must not forget the kindness and help given to me on my 1924 Australian tour by that great captain, 'Monty' Noble, who gave me many tips, which proved to be most valuable to me and my team.

Despite popular opinion, Wilfred Rhodes never did say to George Hirst, 'Let's get them in singles' … Rhodes hit one boundary and Hirst a 'two' as the pair steered England to one of its great wins of the Golden Age.

Cricket '77 (Test & County Cricket Board, London, 1977)

Billy Bates' Match
A Country Vicar (R. L. Hodgson)

His fielding was so chancy that he was never chosen for one home
Test, yet he toured Australia five times and in the 1883
New Year became the first Englishman to secure the hat-trick.

This might well be called Billy Bates' match, since he made the second-highest score (of 55) and captured 14 wickets for 102 runs. He also performed the hat-trick in the first innings — his victims being Percy McDonnell, George Giffen and George Bonnor.

Bonnor, the great hitter, was defeated by means of a little plot. All the English team were desperately keen that Bates should bag his third wicket and someone suggested that the 'Giant', anxious to avert the hat-trick, would be certain to play forward slowly to the first ball he received, whatever its length might be.

Walter Read volunteered to stand at short mid-on, and creep

gradually nearer, if Bates could be certain of bowling a short-pitched ball on the leg-stump. The bowler promised to do this, did it, and the trick succeeded. Bonnor played the ball into Read's hands and walked off in wonderment that any human being should dare to stand so close up to him!

A tallish man, 5 feet 10 inches (178 cm) in height, he bowled right-hand slows very well indeed, and was a fine batsman, hitting with great freedom. He was also in his zenith, having reached the age of 27 by the time of the tour in Australia.

This 1882–83 Melbourne Test produced Test cricket's first 'innings' result, Bates, used at third change in the first innings, taking seven for 28 and in the second seven for 74 in the game of his career. Fourteen of his 15 Tests were played in Melbourne or Sydney. He also played in the first Test in Adelaide in 1884–85. Bates was selected for five tours Down Under.

The Cricketer (W. H. Hillman & Co., London, 27 July 1940)

How the Ashes Began
Reg Hayter

The Ashes have officially been in
existence since Christmas, 1881.

Cricket from the daisied turf of the village pitch to the almost sacred green sward of Lord's, is so rich in character and charm that it has no need of symbolic awards to mark its triumphs. While other sports possess their cups and medals, cricket flourishes upon the delights of hard-fought struggles in seasons of sunshine and shower. Such is the measure of its stature. I am positive that few of those who have the spirit of cricket close to their heart would wish to see any change.

Perhaps the nearest approach cricket makes to acknowledging success is expressed in the romantic story of the Ashes which, though never actually awarded, exist as a permanent challenge to the cricketers of England and Australia.

To appreciate the full significance of this unique emblem it is necessary to retrace one's steps through the colourful pages of cricket history, to the year 1861 when an England team first visited the shores of Australia.

H. H. Stephenson, the Surrey cricketer and an accomplished huntsman, led this side which was composed entirely of professionals. Three years later another all-professional team ventured 'down under', this time captained by George Parr, a great personality. To this day a tree behind the pavilion on the Trent Bridge ground, Nottingham is referred to as 'George Parr's tree' because it is said that he once hit a ball over it. This must have been a tremendous hit and whenever I visit Nottingham I picture in my mind's eye the spectacle of the mighty George Parr opening his burly shoulders and scattering the sparrows with such a terrific blow.

The immortal W. G. Grace — the Grand Old Man of Cricket — also toured Australia before the first Great Match between the two countries took place in March 1877. Australia won this game at Melbourne where James Lillywhite's XI was beaten by 45 runs. But a fortnight later England avenged the defeat with a victory by four wickets.

Australia came to England for the first time in 1880 and lost the only Test match at Kennington Oval by five wickets. Lord Harris led England in a match notable for centuries by 'W. G.' and W. L. Murdoch, Australia's captain. Yet the result might have been different had F. R. Spofforth, the Australian's demon fast bowler, been fit to play.

Two years later, on 29 August 1882, Australia struck what seemed to be a mortal blow at English cricket by winning at the Oval by seven runs in one of the most dramatic games recorded by the chroniclers of cricket. Indeed, according to a contemporary writer, such was the tension on the last afternoon that one spectator bit clean through the handle of his umbrella. Another died of excitement. One description recounted how men noted for their coolness at critical moments 'shivered and trembled like leaves'.

I shivered and trembled like a leaf in the early weeks of the 1951 season but through an entirely different reason — the icy cold (British) weather!

Billy Murdoch, considered to be one of the finest captains Australia has produced and a batsman of outstanding qualities, led the 1882 team. With him were such personalities as George Giffen, a magnificent all-rounder, who later was called the 'Grace' of Australia, H. H. Massie and G. J. Bonnor, both of whom became great favourites with the crowd because of their mighty hitting. Another of the side was J. M. Blackham, a prince among wicketkeepers.

From the start of play the pitch played queer tricks. Australia batted first but, against the splendid bowling of R. G. Barlow, the Lancashire professional, who took five for 19 in 31 four-ball overs they were out for 63. Next came the turn of the English batsmen to struggle on the lively turf. This time Spofforth caused the damage. 'The Demon' maintained a most hostile attack and when the last England wicket fell at 101, he had the remarkable analysis of seven for 46 in 36 overs.

A masterly 55 by Massie raised Australia's hope in the second innings, but the remainder of the team collapsed. England was left to score only 85 runs. Spofforth sent back 'Monkey' Hornby and Dick Barlow with 15 runs on the board but vigorous hitting by Grace and George Ulyett took the score to 51 before the third wicket fell. Thirty-four runs were required with seven wickets left. Victory looked fairly certain for England, but it was not to be. Knowing the terrific fighting qualities of the Aussies, not many people would feel happy now until the last run had been scored.

As it was, most folk reckoned without Spofforth. The great Australian fast bowler doubled his efforts. Amid scenes of mounting excitement, he dismissed one batsman after another. When the last man, Teddy Peate, nervously traced his steps to the crease, his face ashen white, England needed 10 to win. He showed typical Yorkshire dourness by hitting 2 runs to square leg. For a few brief moments England looked as though they might succeed but soon Peate's stumps were shattered. Australia had won — by seven runs.

How much they owed to Spofforth can be gained from a glance at his match analysis of 14 wickets for 90.

This sensational result captured the imagination of the press and public alike. The *Sporting Times,* popularly known as the 'Pink 'Un', published the following mock *In Memoriam* notice:

> In affectionate remembrance of English Cricket which died at the Oval on 29th August, 1882. Deeply lamented by a large circle of sorrowing friends and acquaintances. R.I.P.
>
> N.B. The body will be cremated and the ashes taken to Australia.

Immediately afterwards the Hon. Ivo Bligh, who became the Irish earl, Lord Darnley – 'St Ivo' as *Punch* called him – set out on a pilgrimage to recover England's lost prestige.

The side played three matches against Murdoch's team and won two. After a fun game at Christmas-time outside Melbourne (at Rupertswood, Sunbury), Lady Clarke, wife of Dr W. J. Clarke, the president of the Melbourne Cricket Club who had entertained the English party, burnt a bail used in the game as a mock tribute to the English visitors and stored them in a small urn, handing them to the winning captain Bligh [and they were to remain on his mantelpiece at his country property, Cobham Hall in Kent for years until his death – ed.].

When Lord Darnley died, the urn containing the ashes was given to the MCC. It now rests under a glass case in the Long Room of Lord's – together with an original scorecard of the 1882 match and a photograph of Bligh's successful team.

So really 'the Ashes' are not as mythical as some of you may have heard.

Denis Compton's Annual 1952 (Stanley Paul & Co., London, 1952). Edited excerpts from 'How the Ashes Began' by Reg Hayter.

HIS LORDSHIP: The Hon. Ivo Bligh was England's captain in all four of his Tests, winning two and losing two of the games against the 1882–83 Australians. While his average was just 10, he remains intrinsic to the Ashes story, having been the recipient of the tiny Ashes urn at Rupertswood Mansion at Christmas-time, 1882.

6

Laugh-time

A Storm in a Teacup

When England's so-called 'secret' bowling plan to unsettle the Australian batsmen was leaked to an Australian newspaper at Christmas-time, 2006, Matthew Hoggard, the most whimsical of all the English tourists was chosen to front the 'please explain' press conference. 'And when we find the culprit,' said Hoggy, hiding for a moment his trademark grin, 'we're going to string him up by the Ding-Dang-Doos and chop them off. Gentlemen, you can rest assured, we've got our finest detectives on the case — Inspector Morse, Sherlock Holmes … and … Miss Marple,' before he and the assembled press gallery lapsed into uncontrollable laughter.

Stellar Finish

'You know how to write your scripts well,' England's wicketkeeper Alec Stewart told Steve Waugh as the Australian closed in on his epic farewell Ashes century in Sydney in 2002–03. 'Mate, you're right, but I've had a pretty tough last 12 months,' came the reply.

The pair laughed and Waugh proceeded to punch the final ball from Richard Dawson through the covers for a fairytale final

THE REV.: David Sheppard (left) opens England's batting with Geoff Pullar in Sydney in 1962–63. A fine batsman, his catching woes on the tour drew the wrath of teammate Freddie Trueman …

boundary to give him one of the sweetest of all his three figure scores. Stewart, one of the great sportsmen, said few centuries had ever been more richly deserved.

Happy Chappies

To say that Stuart MacGill was chuffed was a classic under-statement after he took a career-best 12 wickets in an Ashes Test at the Sydney Cricket Ground (in 1998–99). MacGill announced he'd be excited to take 12 wickets in a grade match, 'so heaven knows what I will get up to tonight', he said after he'd masterminded a 98 run Australian win in his adopted hometown.

Captain Mark Taylor, in his 50th and final Test as Australia's captain, was equally happy, telling the world how he'd advised Lord McLaurin, the chairman of the English and Wales Cricket Board that the new glass Ashes replica should be smashed and all the pieces put into an urn to be the new Ashes.

You've Been Warned

Robert Croft couldn't help but watch the instant replay. After all it's not every day you hit Shane Warne for 6. 'Hey Crofty,' said Warne, 'don't worry mate. You'll be able to see the replay again in a couple of minutes.' He did: c. McGrath, b. Warne 6 … Trent Bridge, 1997.

Alderman's Bunny

So regularly did Graham Gooch fall to Terry Alderman during the 1989 Ashes tour that he recorded a home telephone message: 'Sorry, I'm out at the moment, lbw Alderman.'

Pig Stops Play

It was yet another 'first' for the Gabba, the afternoon (in 1982—83) some Brisbane veterinary students smuggled a tranquilised piglet into the ground in a portable esky and proceeded to let it loose on the oval. Much to everyone's amusement — especially the English fieldsmen — scrawled on one flank was EDDIE and on the other BEEFY, in honour of two of the more robust tourists Eddie Hemmings and Ian Botham. Completing the picture was a Union Jack flying happily from the piglet's tail.

Pinting Them Up

Northamptonshire's Peter Willey received seven barrels of beer (2016 pints or 1145 litres) from a local brewery in recognition of helping England to a record 5-1 Ashes victory in Australia in 1978—79.

Still Good, at 71!

Mike Brearley's 1978—79 Englishmen had just been dismissed in two sessions by Western Australia on a WACA greentop. 'Don't worry lads,' said Brearley, breezing into the rooms. 'On that wicket even Don Bradman wouldn't have got runs!'

At which fast bowler Bob Willis piped up: 'I should bloody well think he wouldn't. He was born in 1908. He'd have to be into his 70s by now.'

Oops!

'All the best Steelo,' chorused David Steele's teammates as he picked up his gear and headed for the famous stairs at Lord's to begin his Test career at the ripe old age of 33. Focusing only on his immediate task of dulling the menace of Dennis Lillee and Co., Steele tripped down the first set of stairs and then a second and found himself in the men's toilets! True. 1975.

Streaking at Lord's

John Arlott was the 'Bradman' of commentators, his humour ever present, whether he was counting the trains leaving the Warwick Rd station to one wacky occasion at Lord's (in 1975) when cricket had its first streaker.

The merchant seaman, 'strappingly built', as Arlott described him, appeared from the grandstand side of the ground and sprinted for the middle to amazed oohs and arrs from the crowd.

'My goodness me,' said Arlott, interrupting his description of a consummate Greg Chappell on drive, 'we've got an intruder from underneath Father Time in the person of a strapping young man rippling with muscles. The most remarkable thing about him is that he does not have any clothes on. There he goes, striding out towards the middle to what I can only describe as the puzzled delight of a big crowd.

'He's making for the wicket at the nursery end and umpire Tom Spencer doesn't quite know what to do. Ooh, would you believe it, he jumps the stumps! But all's well, umpire Spencer hasn't signalled "one short".

'And now the amply proportioned young man goes galloping away towards the Mound Stand with his arms outstretched, showing 25,000 people something they've never seen before. And now a young copper comes across and spoils it all. He's taken off his helmet, placed it over the offending weapon and now he leads the young man off the field to a night in the cells and a visit to the Marylebone Magistrates Court in the morning.'

Classic Arlott.

The young man? He was fined his winnings.

Giving 'Im Another

Dennis Lillee was in his comeback Tests and bowling bouncers at a rate of two or three an over. On fast, bouncy greentops, England had been steamrolled in the opening two (1974–75) internationals thanks to Lillee and his even-faster sidekick Jeff Thomson.

One of the few Englishmen enjoying the competition was Tony Greig who made a brave century on the opening day in Brisbane and on first sight of Lillee coming into bat in Sydney, unleashing a first-ball bouncer which caught him on the point of the elbow. Much to the consternation of those around him, Keith Fletcher from close-in yelled, 'Well done Greigy, give 'im another!'

Lillee was unimpressed and as soon as Fletcher came in the next day, unleashed a torrent of bouncers, most of which Fletcher ducked before one zeroed straight at his skull, striking him flush on his cap.

'Blimey,' said Geoff Arnold in the rooms, 'he's just knocked St George off his 'orse!'

'How Do You Do? ... I'm Colin Cowdrey'

It was impossible not to love Colin Cowdrey. He had the gift to make you feel important with his warm handshake and ever present smile.

In 1974–75 he answered an SOS from Mike Denness and the English hierarchy to reinforce the MCC touring party after Dennis Amiss and John Edrich were badly injured in the opening Test in Brisbane. It was his record-equalling sixth tour and he arrived not only with his favourite two bats but with enough foam rubber to line just about every part of his upper torso. Asked by the local press at Perth Airport how he intended to cope with the dual menace of Lillee and Thomson, Cowdrey, 41, said, 'Why should I worry? After all I faced Gregory and McDonald!'

Looking like the Michelin man as we walked out at No. 3 on the first morning, he immediately introduced himself to Jeff Thomson: 'How do you do?' he said. 'I'm Colin Cowdrey.'

Thommo's reply was slightly less polite.

Later in England's second innings he doffed his cap to one barracker, who insisted on calling him 'Cowboy' to which came the immediate reply: 'Cowboy, I used to come here and watch your father and he wasn't much good either!'

A Hunch which Paid Off

Basil D'Oliveira's military mediums were never confronting. But he could swing it, especially under cloud cover. Captain Ray Illingworth had little need for him with John Snow in such intimidating form in the opening Tests of 1970–71, but having ignored his hints to bowl late one night in mid-series in Sydney, he threw the ball to D'Oliveira to start the following morning. 'Are you kidding man,' said Dolly, the supreme team man. 'Surely Snowy's got to start from this end. The blokes in the press box will crucify you ...'

'Just get on with it,' said Illie.

D'Oliveira dismissed Ian Redpath with his second ball and John Gleeson shortly afterwards. 'Right,' said Illingworth. 'Back to third man for you,' and Snow cleaned up the tail.

DOLLY: Basil D'Oliveira, one of England's most valuable and astute all-rounders of the late '60s and early '70s.

'Now *that's* a Bloody Bouncer!'

Umpire Lou Rowan was unimpressed as another short-pitched delivery from England's expressman John Snow whistled past Doug Walters' ear at the WACA Ground (1970–71). 'But they're not bouncers,' said Snow. 'It's just that your batsmen can't play them.' Rowan still issued a warning and informed MCC captain Ray Illingworth that Snow risked being banned from the crease. The next over Snow really let one go – and turned to Rowan and said, 'Now *that's* a bloody bouncer!'

Mum's the Word

The 200th Test between England and Australia was a merry old occasion, especially for the boys from Down Under who felt the historic match could surely end only in a draw with England still seven down after the first three rain-interrupted days. Eyewitness Ian Wooldridge was present as the colonial lads opted to attend a mid-match wedding party in honour of the cricket writer from the *Australian* Bob Gray and his West Indian wife Grace ...

'One of the more historic and significant sportswriting binges deserves slightly more attention than its consequences were later to receive,' Wooldridge later wrote.

'It started around five o'clock on the afternoon of Sunday, 23 June 1968, in a flat just north of Fleet Street and was roaring along quite sociably at 2.30 the following morning when I made the unpopular unilateral decision to take a taxi home. In retrospect this was an amazingly responsible act since at 11.30 the same morning England and Australia were to resume hostilities on the fourth day of the Lord's Test.

'It was the sort of day you needed such wits as you had about you. It was the 200th Test between the oldest enemies in cricket and Australia was promptly bowled out for 78, its lowest score in England since 1912. Even the *Times* promoted the sensation to its front page, with photographs of the fall of all 10 wickets. What neither the *Times* nor any other newspaper spelled out was that a contributory factor to the batting debacle may just have been the presence of almost every member of the Australian team at the Sunday night to Monday morning party, celebrating the wedding of one of Australia's most notoriously hard-living cricket writers [Gray]. Many were still there at the time of my departure and revealing marked reluctance to go anywhere before the last bottle of champagne had had its neck wrung. One of them confided subsequently that he found it disturbingly difficult even to see where the stumps were when he walked out to bat.

'In the circumstances, 78 was possibly an heroic total, but equally heroic, I like to think, were the efforts of the sportswriters of both countries in attributing Australia's totally unexpected collapse to a freak combination of low cloud-base and sudden rush of warm southerly air which produced the rare atmospheric conditions in which a cricket ball swings like a boomerang. This seemed to satisfy an English public who were ecstatic anyway and go in some way to appeasing those Australians who rated it their blackest national day since Gallipoli. It is not often that the sporting press so protects international sporting idols but on this occasion there was the self-interest that comes from complicity. Beyond that, Australian cricketers down the years have proved themselves friendlier and less sensitive to honest criticism than most sportspersons.

'That Monday evening at Lord's a hastily prepared scroll was presented by English sportswriters to the Australian bridegroom who had given the party, acknowledging his services to English cricket.'

Forced to follow-on, the Australians escaped with a draw on the Tuesday, Paul Sheahan being most unSheahan-like, batting almost an hour and facing 44 balls without scoring on the final afternoon. He always rated it the best 0 of his life.

Do-gooder Rowdy

It was 22-year-old tour rookie Ashley Mallett's first day in England and he joined some of his teammates in a cafe for lunch. Midway through their meal, some others on an adjourning table all left as one and paid their bill at the desk near the door. Noticing a number of coins had been left on their table, Mallett gathered them up and scampered after the group to return their monies only to find they had disappeared into the busy street. On return he was greeted by glares from the restaurant staff. Welcome to tipping, Rowdy.

First-time tourist to England Ashley Mallett was so quiet that teammates kept on telling him to shut up. 'You're too rowdy,' they said. Ashley has answered to 'Rowdy' ever since.

Mistaken Identity

Mallett was short-sighted and if he ever happened to lose his direction, captains would ask if he had his contacts in. A cocktail party celebrating the 200th Test between England and Australia had been arranged at the Queen Mother's official residence in London, dignitaries from the Royals to distinguished politicians including Sir Robert Menzies all present.

Mallett was chatting with his teammates when he saw an elegantly dressed woman approaching from about 10 yards (9 m) away. He couldn't make out who the woman was but called out, 'I say my dear. Will you not join us here?' It was Queen Elizabeth!

Let's Keep It Secret

Basil D'Oliveira had some extra pep in his step as he met batting partner Geoff Boycott in mid-pitch. 'I think I've worked him out,' he said motioning towards Australia's each-way spinner John Gleeson. 'Yaas,' said Boycott. 'Arr did several Tests ago, but don't tell the other boogers!'

An Enforced Holiday

Jack Potter toured England in 1964 as a back-up batsman without playing any of the nine Tests, either in England or on the way home, on the sub-continent.

'"Simmo" [captain Bobby Simpson] said that everyone who hadn't played [a Test] in England would get their opportunity in the Tests on the way home, but I suffered a hairline fracture of my skull in a semi-serious game on the Continent which cost me a chance,' Potter said. 'My face dropped on one side, causing me to dribble and slur. During the treatment the doctor told me I wasn't going back home until I could say MASSACHUSETTS INSTITUTION without slurring. I didn't get back to Melbourne until November. There were a lot of good batsmen around at the time. While I continued to play well, I never got another chance.'

Gee, I *Am* Tired Tonight

Australia's captain Richie Benaud came in late, cursing Sydney's traffic, changing as quickly as he could and bolting out to join Ted Dexter for the toss of the coin.

Back in the rooms, Bill Lawry saw that Benaud had come in with a nice new pair of black slip-on dress shoes and alerting perennial prankster Frank Misson to some potential fun to be had, borrowed a couple of three inch nails and a hammer from tradesmen doing repairs in the member's bar. At the tea break, when Benaud was absent, they nailed his pride-and-joy new shoes to the floor.

Looking to cover his tracks, Lawry told nine teammates of 'Frank Misson's prank on Rich' ... the only two oblivious to it all were Misson and of course, Benaud!

Showering that night and finally putting on his trousers and socks and calling his players to follow him for a function, Benaud found that he couldn't lift one foot ... or the other. 'Gee, I *am* tired tonight,' he said, before spying the nail heads. 'BLOODY MISSON,' he roared.

The whole room broke up in hysterics.

Fiery Freddie

The first to 300 Test wickets, Freddie Trueman insisted he would surely have taken 500-plus if all the %#$&ing chances from his bowling had been held.

During the 1962–63 summer Down Under, the Rev. David Sheppard and the normally ever-so-sure Colin 'Kipper' Cowdrey both grassed slips catches which should have been taken, Sheppard a multiple offender.

'Kid yourself it's a Sunday, Rev.,' said an unimpressed Trueman, 'and put your hands together!'

Cowdrey's miss resulted in the ball flying all the way to the fence for a boundary. 'Sorry Fred, I should have crossed my legs,' said an apologetic Cowdrey.

'Noo Kip,' said Trueman, 'but thee bluddy mother should 'ave.'

It was during that tour, in Melbourne, that Sheppard, banished to fine leg took a fine running catch and in his joy hoisted it high to show the MCC members. To roars of acclamation, he was on to his third or fourth jig of delight when he was tapped on the shoulder. It was Freddie. 'Great catch Rev., but can thee throw the bluddy thing in? It's a no-ball and they've already run five!'

Name Dropping

Australia's bubbly wicketkeeper of the late '50s and early '60s, Wally Grout was virtually unflappable, unless you happened to address him as 'Grouty' or worse still 'Grout'.

He loved everything about England and Englishmen, except for the old school tie.

G. O. B. 'Gubby' Allen, later Sir Gubby, was never going to endear himself to Wally. Allen was from a wealthy family of bluebloods and had been educated at Eton and Cambridge. Once Gubby greeted Wal with a 'Hello Grouty' to which Wal responded with a 'Hello Allen'. Gubby hated being called by his surname just as much as Wal did.

Even Robert Menzies, Australia's longtime Prime Minister once made the faux pas, greeting him once with a 'How's my friend Grouty, today?'

'Sir,' said Grout, thinking on his feet. 'You have just lost two votes. Mine and my wife's.'

Body Beautiful

So well-built was teenage Ashes debutant Graham McKenzie that he was soon dubbed 'Garth' after the comic book superhero of the late '50s. When Australian teammate Norm O'Neill first saw him in shorts, he said: 'Jeez, if I had a physique like that, I'd sleep with the lights on!'

Land Legs

The 1958–59 MCC team was only just off the SS *Iberia* and bunkered up at their Perth hotel when first-time opener Arthur Milton wandered across the hotel lobby sideways. To everyone's amusement, try as he might, he could barely walk forward – the result of six weeks on board ship. 'The boys thought I was paralysed or had had one or two more to drink than I ought – except many of them were in the same condition,' Milton said. 'It took us days to get our land legs.'

The Little Imp

So successful was Ashes hero Arthur Morris in his Sydney grade comeback with Paddington that he was invited by Prime Minister Robert Menzies to play one last international, alongside his old mate Lindsay Hassett for the PM's XI against the touring MCC (in 1958–59).

Armed with a new pride-and-joy bat he'd just purchased, Arthur opened with a rollicking 79. Hassett, who had retired years earlier, was also in the top order and asked if anyone could loan him a bat. Feeling particularly benevolent after his sparkling display, Arthur agreed to lend him his, thinking little Lindsay was unlikely to do much damage. 'Of course old fellow, have mine,' he said.

Morris was chatting with the PM and Australia's captain Richie

Benaud when Hassett was dismissed, having made 18. Menzies followed his every step as he returned to the pavilion. 'Oh, look at that. What a wonderful gesture from Lindsay,' said the PM suddenly.

'What's that, sir?' said Morris turning around.

'Didn't you see? Lindsay just presented his bat to a little boy in the crowd!'

'His bat!' said Arthur, seeing red. 'With all respect sir, it was *my* bloody bat.'

During the change of innings the little boy knocked on the dressing-room door and asked if the team could please sign his new prized possession. Hassett walked him across to Morris and said: 'And Mr Morris would *particularly* like to sign it for you son!'

An Underwhelming Reception

Finally the champagne arrived in the Australian rooms. It had been a magnificent come-from-behind victory triggered by Richie Benaud going around the wicket. Manager Ray Steele handed out 17 bottles, one for each of the tourists and suggested that the players acknowledge the large crowd downstairs by popping their corks simultaneously. At Old Trafford five years earlier, 10,000 deliriously happy Englishmen had gathered on the ground below, swept up in the euphoria of England's Jim Laker—inspired victory. The Australians trooped onto the balcony as one, popped their corks and looked down ... to see just one person below in a grey jacket, head down, picking up litter!

Nugget to the Rescue

Maybe it was the Boy Scout in Keith Miller. He was always prepared ...

Australia's stocky wicketkeeper Gil Langley scrambled to take a Miller off-break on a drying wicket at the Oval (in 1956) and heard a big RIPPP as his trousers tore from the seat.

Not wanting to hold up the game by going off the ground, Langley was relieved when Miller strolled up and said: 'This may help Gil,' and producing a large safety pin proceeded to expertly thread it, adding a touch of decency again to Langley's posterior. Nugget's mates always wondered how he came to possess it.

Miller was dubbed 'Nugget' by esteemed English cricket writer Ian Wooldridge who regarded him as cricket's golden boy, the best and most charismatic player – when he wanted to be – since the Don.

Touché

Arthur Morris may have been Australia's first great post-war left-hander but he had a propensity for falling to the 'Lion of Surrey', England's long-time new-ball leader Alec Bedser.

Bedser captured his wicket on 22 occasions, including seven times throughout the 1950–51 tour, once even on Morris's 29th birthday. That night, in Launceston, Bedser presented his old rival with a nicely wrapped present. 'Here Arthur,' he said, 'I hope you like this. It may help.'

Thanking him profusely, Morris unwrapped the gift to find a copy of *Better Cricket* by Lindsay Hassett and Ian Johnson. Opening the book he saw on the contents page that the reference to batting had been underlined!

Two weeks later, in the Adelaide Test, Morris made a memorable career-best double century and that night, found Bedser and handed the booklet

THE LION OF SURREY: Alec Bedser, who opposed the Australians as England's frontline seamer in the first four post-war Ashes contests.

back, this time with the bowling instructions highlighted. 'Here Alec,' he said, 'this may help you.'

Royalty Awaits

It was Saturday night in Southampton and with no Sunday play, the 1953 Aussies were preparing to go out for the evening. Captain Ian Johnson was busily dressing himself in a dinner suit. 'What are you doing tonight, Johnno? Where are you off to?' said one of the players.

'As a matter of fact I'm going up to London to dine with the Prime Minister in the House of Lords.'

'Jeez,' came the reply. 'Are you? Not bad ...'

At the other end of the room Keith Miller smiled and also continued to get ready. Like Johnson he also had a penguin suit on. 'You off somewhere special too Nug?'

'As it so happens yes,' said Nugget. 'I'm also going up to London. I'm dining at the [Buckingham] Palace ... Princess Margaret awaits.'

Word got back to his wife Peg in Sydney about Keith's dalliance.

'Oh, that's Keith for you,' she said. 'He always has had a way with the girls.'

The Red Inks King

To his teammates' amazement and amusement and much to his own delight, batting bunny Bill Johnston averaged 100-plus from No. 11 on the 1953 tour of England thanks to a spate of 'red inks'.

Undismissed in the Tests, 'Big Bill' was out only once all tour, his aggregate of 102 seeing him lead the Australian batting averages ahead of the likes of captain Lindsay Hassett, Neil Harvey, Arthur Morris and Keith Miller.

Years later Hassett came to visit the Johnston family in Sandringham and involved himself in some backyard cricket with Bill's son, David.

Within minutes he'd stepped in. 'Give me a look at that bat,' he said to young David. 'You're batting like your old man. Don't ever do that again!'

'Hang on a minute,' said Big Bill. 'I did bat at No. 4 at school!'

The Bottom Line

'I understand, Mr Craig,' said Queen Elizabeth to Australia's 18-year-old Coronation Year tourist Ian Craig, 'that this is your first visit to England.'

'Yes your Majesty,' said Craig, 'and unless my batting improves, it will also be my last!'

Later that night, in his tour diary, Craig wrote of his excitement at meeting the young Queen in mid-match at Lord's: 'I nearly died of fright when she talked to me!'

100 and Out

Representing the Australian XI against Freddie Brown's 1950–51 MCC tourists, Arthur Morris reached his century and turning to his big mate Alec Bedser said: 'Bob Berry hasn't got a wicket and John Warr hasn't taken a catch all tour … I'll see what can be done.' Soon the scoreline entry read: A. R. Morris, c. Warr, b. Berry 100.

Elephant Memory

Morris was surprised when Don Bradman asked him to field five yards finer at square leg as Ray Lindwall was preparing to bowl to Denis Compton at the Oval in 1948. It was short and Compton hooked the ball … straight to Morris!

'What prompted you to move me Don?' asked Morris.

'Compton hooked Ernie McCormick to that very same possie here in 1938!' he said.

The Full Monty

A cyclonic storm hit the Gabba and the English players watched in amazement, many covering their ears as hailstones pelted on the old corrugated iron roof of the pavilion. Fun-loving Australian Sid Barnes was among them, saying this was typical of cricket in the tropics. The hailstones, he said, were often as big as your hand. At the height of the storm he ducked out of the viewing area and extracting one of the large square blocks of ice used to cool the drinks in a bathtub, he hurled it onto the roof and watched in delight as it slid down the roof and descended with a crash in full view of the shocked Englishmen. Rejoining them just as it was smashing onto the concrete below, Barnes grinned and said: 'Now lads, that's what I call a hailstone.'

Barnes, of course, was famous for picking a stray dog up one day and handing it to the umpires with a 'Here you are. All you need now is a white stick!' [insinuating that the umpires were blind and the dog could be their guide dog].

A Little Knowledge ...

The Australians were at an official dinner and Clarrie Grimmett got talking with a pretty woman. Asked about her cricket knowledge, the woman said, 'Oh yes, I know all about a maiden over!'

'And what exactly,' Clarrie asked, 'is a maiden over?'

'It's his first!'

The Last Word

Maurice Tate was a delightful character known for his geniality. During a baking hot day in Australia, he was seen to say something to the Australian batsman Bert Oldfield after a series of appeals had been rejected. Several Australian pressmen accused him of abuse. Summoned by the manager to explain, Tate struggled to recall what he had said, then remembered: 'Bloody hot, ain't it Bert? I could do with a cuppa …'

Rules for One …

Having made his second century in consecutive post-war Tests, the iconic Jack Hobbs was asked to meet the South Australian state governor Sir Archibald Weigall, who presented him with a diamond scarfpin to commemorate the occasion. Soon England's most successful bowler Cecil Parkin, who had taken seven wickets for the match, was also invited to meet Sir Archie.

'Out I marched,' he said, 'the band again struck up "See the Conquering Hero Comes" and 30,000 people assembled in front of the Royal box, saw me shake hands with the Governor-General, state governors, their wives and ladies-in-waiting. I stood to attention, waited for *my* diamond scarfpin, but the only thing I got was a: "Well played Parkin."

'To crown it all, when I got back to the dressing room, Johnny Douglas said, "Let's have a look at it Ciss!"

'"I've got nowt."

'"Don't be silly. You must have got something."

'"No, nothing."

CISS: Cecil Parkin added colour and humour to every dressing room he entered.

'Jack Hobbs walked by and said: "Well Ciss, you would be a bowler!"'

A Memorable Steal

During the 1920—21 tour young Jack Hearne was struggling to middle the ball against the likes of Jack Gregory, Ted McDonald, Arthur Mailey and Co. Suddenly he stole a quick single into the off side. Watching from his normal position on the Hill, the famous barracker Yabba yelled: 'Whoa! He's bolted!'

Sydney 'rabbitoh' Stephen Harold Gascoigne was dubbed 'Yabba' because he was a 'bit of a talker'. His gravelly voice could be heard from every point of the Sydney Cricket Ground in the '20s and '30s.

A Bird in the Hand

Yabba's all-time favourite was 'Patsy' Hendren, who loved the good-humour and the banter of the fans. He camped himself under a catch one day to the call from one fan from the Hill: 'Patsy, Patsy, if you drop it, I'll let you kiss my sister!'

Asked later what he had done, Patsy said, 'As I hadn't seen his sister, I caught it!'

Do It for England

Arthur Gilligan loved cricket and could not understand anybody playing the game who did not regard it as fondly. There was one occasion when Arthur was in charge of a side, and he asked a member of his XI to come very close in — to silly point. The player looked at the batsman, who looked capable of doing some very hefty driving.

FUN-LOVING: One of the perennial favourites of the Sydney Hill, Elias Henry 'Patsy' Hendren.

'But, Mr Gilligan,' said the man who had been asked to go close up, 'I can't field at silly point to that fellow. I should get killed.'

'Perhaps so,' said England's captain, 'but what a death — and all for England!'

The player went to the required position.

Brevity at All Times

It could have been the shortest speech on record — and yet he received a standing ovation. The MCC's stand-in captain Johnny Douglas was responding to a toast to the English cricket team at the Melbourne Town Hall. It had been a lengthy night and Johnny, always light on his feet — he'd won an Olympic Gold Medal as a boxer — rose and nodding his thanks simply said: 'I hate speeches' before promptly sitting down again.

Your Call, Joe

So frustrated was Joe Darling at losing all five Test tosses to the Hon. F. S. 'Jacker' Jackson in 1905 that at the tour end fixture at Scarborough, he challenged Jackson to wrestle him for the choice of innings. For the entire tour, Jackson's record against Darling was a definitive 8-0!

'I Should Have Hit the Perisher!'

The only batsman to be caught while turning for a third run — at the Oval in 1880 — big-hitting George Bonnor was consoled by teammates on his ill-luck to have picked out Fred Grace way away in the outfield a good 80 metres away. 'Hard luck, Bon,' said one.

'Hard luck nothing,' said Bonnor. 'I should have hit the perisher!'

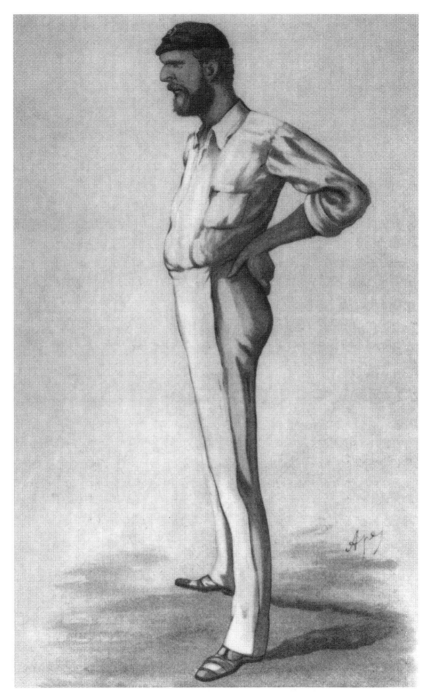

BIG-HITTER: George Bonnor as depicted by Spy (Sir Leslie Ward), the famous English caricaturist.

7
Lists & Letters

One Silent Movie with Ashes References

One of Australia's earliest films, a silent cartoon made by G. B. Savi, thought to be made in 1921, deals with a Test cricket match between England and Australia and caricatures two Ashes legends Arthur Mailey and 'Patsy' Hendren. Cricket historian Stephen Gibbs says the film begins with subtitles: 'Cartoons by Hiscocks (Australia), edited and titled by G. B. Savi, animated by Publicity Pictures, H. Luscombe Toms and Co. Ltd.'

Two Batsmen Rated as the 'Next Bradman'

Ian Craig, Norman O'Neill

Two TV Miniseries with Ashes References

Howzat (2012)

The fascinating four-hour miniseries contains highlight footage of the 1977 Centenary Test just before the story of the World Series Cricket breakaway and signings was exclusively made public by Australian cricket writers Peter McFarline and Alan Shiell. Amidst

TECHNICIAN: Norman O'Neill was a darling of Australian cricket from the time he made 71 not out on his unforgettable Ashes debut in Brisbane in 1958–59 — the first Ashes Test Down Under to be televised.

the fallout and player bans, including Tony Greig being stripped of the English captaincy, Kerry Packer (Lachy Hulme) is shown walking onto Lord's and enthusing about cricket and its wonderful history. Ex-Test fast bowler Brendon Julian does some in-studio TV commentary work. The rest of the extended cast are all non-cricketers.

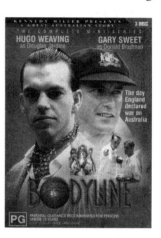

Bodyline (1982)

Detailed television miniseries covering the 1932–33 Bodyline tour by Douglas Jardine's Englishmen. It's popular and entertaining with typical 'Hollywood licence' with the facts. Gary Sweet plays Don Bradman while Peter Philpott is among the few regular cricketers to appear – as crack leg spinner Clarrie Grimmett.

Three Feature Films with Ashes References

The Ladykillers (1955)

Alexander Mackendrick's superb Ealing Studios black comedy stars Alec Guinness, Peter Sellers and Cecil Parker and includes the scene where Mrs Wilberforce realises her tenants have committed an armed robbery. Another elderly lady is reading a newspaper report of the robbery when an agitated Professor Marcus (Alec Guinness) snatches the newspaper from her to check the cricket score and calls out: 'Australia all out for 60,000' – the amount of money stolen.

The Final Test (1953)

This is the only actual feature film dedicated to cricket, starring Jack Warner, Robert Morley and Richard Wattis; an English version of what happened to Sir Donald Bradman in his final Test. The 88-minute film includes footage of the 1953 Ashes decider at Kennington Oval. Len Hutton, Alec Bedser and Denis Compton are among the contemporary English cricketers to have cameo roles.

The familiar voice of John Arlott adds further authenticity.

The Lady Vanishes (1938)
This classic Alfred Hitchcock spy mystery stars Michael Redgrave and Margaret Lockwood and includes the predicament of two very-English gentlemen (Charters and Caldicott) a long way from home on a cross-Europe train trying to make it back in time for an Ashes Test in Manchester. When they finally return, the Test is washed out – coincidently, just as it occurred at Manchester in 1938!

Four Ashes Signs Seen in Australia

'Bring Back Deano.'
(A sign paraded most years at the Christmas Test in Dean Jones' old hometown of Melbourne)

'If the Poms win the toss and bat, keep the taxi running.'
(1994–95)

'The Phil Tufnell Fielding Academy.'
(1990–91, the much-loved 'Tuffers' was a magnificent bowler on his day but one of cricket's clumsiest fieldsmen)

'Gold Medallion Award for Greatest Whinger Would Have To Be Won by J. M. Brearley, Classical Music Lover.'
(Melbourne, 1979–80)

Five Ashes Fiction Books

Stanley Shaw: *Sherlock Holmes at the 1902 Fifth Test* (1985)
Allen Synge: *Bowler, Batsman, Spy* (1985)
Paul Wheeler: *Bodyline: The Novel* (1983)
William Godfrey: *Malleson at Melbourne* (1956)
Jack Hobbs: *The Test Match Surprise* (1926)

Six Ashes Catchphrases

2010–11: History Will Be Made
2006–07: It's Definitely On
2002–03: The Prize
1998–99: The Quest for the Ashes
1986–87: The Clashes for the Ashes
1982–83: The Hottest Cricket in 100 Summers

Nine Must-Read Ashes Tour Books

One Summer, Every Summer: An Ashes Journal
   (1994–95), Gideon Haigh
Phoenix from the Ashes (1981), Mike Brearley
The Fight for the Ashes (1961), Ron Roberts
Australia '55 (1955), Alan Ross
Brightly Fades the Don (1948),
   Jack Fingleton
Ashes – And Dust (1934), Douglas Jardine
Bodyline Autopsy (1932–33), David Frith
The Turn of the Wheel (1928–29),
   Percy Fender
With Stoddart's Team in Australia (1897–98),
   Prince K. S. Ranjitsinhji

ANOTHER MUST READ: Douglas Jardine's *Ashes and Dust.*

Nine Favourite Movies

David Boon: *Uncommon Valour*
Allan Border: *The Sting*
Ian Healy: *The Man from Snowy River*
David Hookes: *An Officer and a Gentleman*
Jack Russell: *The Battle of Britain*
Phil Tufnell: *Apocalypse Now*
Mark Waugh: *Caddyshack*
Graeme Wood: *Midnight Express*
Graham Yallop: *Raiders of the Lost Arc*

Ten Ashes Letters

Australia-made
From Peter West (Bosham) to the *Times*, September 2005:

> SIR — I am the proud owner of a new MCC cricket cap, purchased
> in the members' shop in the Pavilion at Lord's, clearly marked
> 'Made in Australia'.

Honeymoon thrill
From Joyce Mantell (Tamworth) to the *Times*, September 2005:

> SIR — When I got married in 1955 my husband told me he was
> going to give me the greatest thrill a girl could have on her
> honeymoon: he took me to Lord's.

Royal Ashes
From Mrs Stella Braithwaite (Balmul) to the *Times*, August 1977:

> SIR — It is interesting to note that the last three times the Ashes
> have been regained by England have been Royal occasions: the
> first, in 1926, was the year of the Queen's birth; the second,

in 1953, was the Coronation; and the third, in 1977, is Jubilee Year.

From Marjorie Millman (London) to the *Times,* also August 1977:

SIR — England also regained the Ashes here in 1893 and this was again a Royal occasion, the year of the marriage of the Duke of York to Princess Victoria Mary of Teck, later to become King George V and Queen Mary.

Sorry Mike, but you're out

From Alec Bedser, England's selection chairman, to Mike Denness, July 1975:

DEAR MIKE — I'm sorry it had to be me whose duty it was to pass on the sad news to you. However, that is life. I would like to say how much I have enjoyed our association over the last two years or so. At all times you have been most cooperative and helpful and I would like to thank you for all your efforts which I appreciated very much. We shall be seeing something of each other from time to time. With all good luck to you, kindest regards to Molly, no doubt in some ways she will be glad not to have reporters phoning all day.

Kindest regards
Yours Alec

I Declare, Mike Denness (Arthur Barker Ltd., London, 1977)

THANKS BUT NO THANKS: Mike Denness lost his captaincy midway through the '75 Ashes summer.

Chuck danced to a different drum

From Bill O'Reilly to Father Paddy Stephenson, editor of the *Xaverian,* Xavier College, April 1971:

DEAR PADDY — I am glad to try to help in your assignment in regard to the obituary about my old mate 'Chuck' for inclusion in the *Xaverian.*

Chuck Smith could spin the ball more than any bowler I have seen. His ability to do this to the 'nth' degree detracted of course from his ability to control some of the other essentials which go to make up top-class bowling, but that has always been an accepted penalty and is always cheerfully accepted and borne by the man who goes out full belt for exploiting all the great advantages that spin can give.

When Chuck bowled at the nets at Launceston in 1934 when the Australian team for that year was on its first official match of the tour of England — in those days the team assembled in Melbourne and made off to Tasmania for a match in Launceston and one in Hobart — he spun the ball so wide on a holding practice pitch that several batsmen asked for him to stop bowling so that they really could get a feel of the bat on ball.

At Scarborough on the far North Sea Coast of England in 1934 in the concluding match of tour, he succeeded in making Maurice Leyland look like a beginner. Leyland had taken three Test centuries that season against Grimmett and myself, and Chuck, enjoying one of those days when all things clicked with him, had the left-hander clawing the air.

I suppose the best ball he bowled on an important occasion was the one with which he rolled Walter Hammond's wicket in the Adelaide Test in the 1936–37 series. This ball had a tremendous influence on Australia's winning of that series. We had lost the first two Tests in Brisbane and Sydney, had won the third and this Adelaide one was vital.

[On the final day] Chuck knocked Hammond over with a ball which beat England's star batsman through his strength

— he left him stranded in an attempted powerful cover drive; a performance to be seen before being believed.

Chuck had a 'devil-may-care' outlook in excelsis. Attention to detail to him was a gross waste of good time. That is why his batting made no attempt to conform. A duck meant no more to him than a walk out to the centre. He was a No. 11 in any team. Batting with him at Northampton in 1934 on a tour when it was no easy matter for one of the tailenders to have a 'go' with the bat — opportunities were made scarce by the fact that we had a string of runmakers like Woodfull, Ponsford, Bradman, McCabe, Kippax, Brown, Chipperfield, Darling to satisfy first — Chuck came in last as usual and joined me who had been making bold plans to have a bit of fun with the bat. I hit one to square leg and as I passed him, I said, 'Take a look Chuck … maybe 2'. The local boy on the square-leg boundary galloped quickly to the ball, collected it well and hurled it back right over the top of the stumps. In the meantime Chuck had grounded his bat, turned and begun his return to base without even acknowledging the fieldsman constituted a threat to his safety. After the bails had been taken off quietly and he had joined me on the return walk to the pavilion, I asked him, 'Why didn't you look to see what square leg was doing Chuck?' His characteristic answer was, 'Ah Tige … what the hell does it matter. There's no need for you and me to bother about runs.'

At golf he generally amazed the gazing rustics ranged around by affecting a 'walk-in' start [à la Happy Gilmore — *ed.*] in hitting off from the first tee. He would tee his ball up, step back and survey the surroundings majestically, then walk in and belt the ball in his stride. Sometimes it came off but it never failed to be an eye-catching act.

He always looked the part — tall, strong and handsome enough for the English press always to refer to him as the 'Guardsman'.

'Nonchalant' was an adjective they used often, and it was an appropriate one. He had a profuse thatch of jet black hair which trespassed well below the customary forehead hairline. His eyebrows were beetling, and his smartly trimmed moustache always added to the glamour of our Australian sides in the '30s. I smile now to think what a sight he would have been had he cultivated the hairstyles of the '70s. He might have been a classical example of the 'Hairy man from Koorawatha'.

Finally, one must mention that Chuck had a definite 'air' about him. His very presence seemed to denote authority, breeding and cultivated capacities to handle any difficult situation which might arise. All this made him an unforgettable character who enriched the wonderful days I spent in the sun back in the faraway '30s when Chuck was a very good mate of mine and a very highly talented bowler.

With every personal good wish
Yours sincerely
Bill O'Reilly

Timing is everything

From Percy Fender (London) to the *Times*, August 1967:

SIR — I write in defence of cricketers who cannot answer back to those critics who take freedom to castigate the players in circumstances of which they (the critics) have no knowledge.

On 14 August, I was disgusted to read such twaddle as appeared in your paper (and in the *Guardian*) about the performances, on Saturday, of [Ken] Barrington and [Brian] Close.

Writers who have never played in a Test and who have no idea of the difficulties and responsibilities of the players in such a game should not be allowed to pontificate (and so mislead the reader) on a matter of which they know so little.

The first duty of a player in a Test is towards his side and its best interests. He is not there to pander either to the public or to the critics by fireworks at the expense of that duty.

Having bowled out their opponents for 140, and then having to bat on a wicket which has had '240 tons' of water on it, it was the duty of the batsmen to ensure, if they could, a total of about

300 to win the match, and that the methods employed to this end were what the captain approved was obvious.

By what right do writers call such an effort 'tedious to death'?

In the 'Verity Test' at Lord's [in 1934], Don Bradman showed what can happen to those who take the line advocated by critics when on a 'slow turner' [Australia losing outright by an innings, Verity taking 15 wickets for the game − ed.].

Only those who have played on such a wicket can know what pitfalls await a batsman who takes a chance for the sake of a little applause from such critics − you can easily be 'out' off a full toss (see Barrington's first over at Lord's) or off a long hop which 'stops'.

All batsmen like to score runs if they can reasonably do so − they do not refrain for the sake of annoying critics. It is just not playing the game to slang a man who cannot answer back if he has put up the shutters in the interests of his side (and with the approval of his captain on the spot).

I am no advocate of slow batting, but there are times when the demands of the situation and the interests of the side make it necessary − and critics should understand this.

Sorry Brian, you're out

From Sir Donald Bradman to Brian Booth, January 1966:

DEAR BRIAN − Never before have I written to a player to express my regret at his omission from an Australian eleven. In your case I am making an exception because I want you to know how much my colleagues and I disliked having to make this move.

Captain one match and out of the side the next looks like ingratitude but you understand the circumstances and will be the first to admit that your form has not been good. I sincerely hope that your form will return quickly and in good measure and in any event assure you of the high personal regard in which you are held by us all and our appreciation of the way you have always tried to do everything in your power to uphold the good name and prestige of Australia.

Yours sincerely
Don Bradman

Booth was not to be recalled and was soon to retire from first-class cricket with the advent of Sunday play. He continued in grade ranks at St George where he is an icon of the club.

Booth to Bat: An Autobiography, Brian Booth & Paul White (Anzea Publishers, Homebush West, 1983)

The best Australian team?
From E. J. Metcalfe to the editor of the *Cricketer,* 1948:

SIR — I saw three of the five Test Matches this year, and have been fortunate in seeing, either here or in Australia, practically all the Australian sides since the famous match at the Oval in 1880. It was therefore with some surprise that I read Bradman to say (if he was properly reported) that this year's team was possibly the best that had visited this country. Everyone must admit they were a very fine side, but was not their greatness increased by the weakness of the opposition? They had batting down to No. 10, the first six all being exceptionally good. But can one say they were better than Trumper, Darling, Hill, Noble, Giffen and S. E. Gregory [at] No. 6? Then as regards bowling, Lindwall is a very good bowler but is he better than Cotter and Ernie Jones, and had he had to bowl, as they did, against Hayward, MacLaren, Fry, Ranji and Jackson, would he have been quite so successful? With reference to the other bowlers, are they as good as Trumble, Noble and Giffen?

I have always found it is quite impossible to get the present generation to believe that the players of the past were any better or as good as those of the present day, but having seen the sides that defeated Stoddart's and MacLaren's teams in the '90s I am afraid I cannot admit that, good as they were, the recent side were their equal.

Not so graceful in defeat

A letter home from Arthur Shrewsbury to his sister, Amelia, February 1887:

> We have just finished a match against the Combined Team of Australia [in Sydney] and I don't think that during the time I have played cricket, I ever played in a match that was literally pulled out of the fire, as this one was. It was so entirely unexpected that the people out here could scarcely realise that we had won.
>
> It was a glorious victory and I am sure the cricket public at home will be more than pleased with the result, considering the uphill game we had to fight. All our players during the Combined last innings worked and fielded like a high machine, every man thinking it was on their individual efforts the result of the match depended. I shall never forget the shout our players gave when [George] Lohmann bowled the last man (Fred Spofforth) out and the groan of disappointment that arose from the spectators. I am sorry to say that some of the players did not take their defeat as gracefully as we should have liked, saying that our umpire [Rawlinson of Yorkshire, an old experienced umpire] had given two bad decisions. I won't enter into what further was said, but should wish that colonial teams could bear a licking with the same graceful manner as they can a win.

Set 111 to win the first Test in Sydney – having bowled England for just 45 on the first morning – Australia was dismissed for 97 with England's Billy Bates taking six for 28 and breaking his wrist immediately afterwards attempting to punch Australia's captain Percy McDonnell. He struck the wall and so injured his fist that he was unable to play until the end of the tour.

Give Me Arthur: A Biography of Arthur Shrewsbury,
Peter Wynne-Thomas (Arthur Barker Ltd., London, 1985)

Twelve Classic Commentaries

'Bowled Shane.'
— If he said it once, he said it dozens of times, each and every
  innings ... wicketkeeper Ian Healy on the bowling of the sultan
  of spin, Shane Warne throughout the 1990s

'Oh! ... He's got him. Has he caught him? Yes he has. He's got him.
It's a hat-trick. Yes, he's gone ... what a catch by David Boon.'
— Channel Nine's Tony Greig describes Shane Warne's hat-trick,
  day 5, Melbourne, 1994–95

'Bowled 'im! Last ball of the day! Can you believe that?!'
— Channel Nine's Bill Lawry when Merv Hughes bowls Mike
  Gatting with the final ball, day 4, Manchester, 1993

'In comes Edmonds, and he [Merv Hughes] swings it, it is a good
sweep, but he is going to be caught! And England has won the
Ashes.'
— The BBC's Christopher Martin-Jenkins, day 3, Melbourne,
  1986–87

'He's ... got him! Second time. Tavaré knocked it up and it was
taken by Miller. So close. England win by three runs.'
— Channel Nine's Richie Benaud, day 5, Melbourne, 1982–83

'That's it. That's a half volley, through mid-on for 4. The bat is
in the air, the England players come out to applaud a moment
that has got to be a main one in cricket history. Geoffrey Boycott,

100 hundreds and what a place to get it: in a Test match, against Australia, in front of his 'ome crowd.'
— BBC Television's Jim Laker, day 1, Leeds, 1977

'Here's the last ball of the day's play. He's hit it! It could be 4! Magnificent shot! It's out to the boundary! A six was it? A six! A six! Walters 103. What a fantastic finish.'
— ABC Television's Norman May as Doug Walters completes his century and 100 runs in a session, day 2, Perth, 1974—75

'Mackay and Burge got together in a fine farting partnership.'
— The ABC's Lindsay Hassett, who had meant to say 'fine fighting partnership'

'Bob Massie having a dream of a Test match debut. Eight wickets in the first innings and now at tea two more for 8 runs, bowling now to Tony Greig … (Pause) And he's gone! Caught at first slip by the captain Ian Chappell. What a match Bob Massie is having.'
— BBC Television's Peter West, day 3, Lord's, 1972

'I don't anticipate that [Peter] May is going to lob one into the outfield yet, if he does at all. But he has had a go at that! Has he been bowled around his legs? Must have been. Bowled for zero around his legs.'
— BBC Radio's Rex Alston as Richie Benaud inspires an unexpected Ashes victory, day 5, Manchester, 1961

'[Eric] Hollies pitches the ball up slowly and … he's bowled … Bradman bowled Hollies nought … bowled Hollies nought … and what do you say under those circumstances?'
— BBC Radio's John Arlott describing Don Bradman's final dismissal in Test cricket, day 1, The Oval, 1948

'Here's Fleetwood-Smith again. Ah, there we are. There's the record, round the corner and it's going for 4 down here. I don't think Hassett can possibly cut it off. Ah well, that's gone for 4. And that is the record. The highest score ever made by an individual in any kind of Test match. Bradman's record is beaten.'
— BBC Radio's Howard Marshall describes the shot from which Len Hutton surpassed Don Bradman's Ashes-high 334, The Oval, 1938

Twelve Songs with Ashes References

'Ashes Victory Song, We So Outplayed the Aussies' (2011)
— A gentle ode celebrating England's Down Under dominance in the 2010–11 series, by Paddy Wex.

'Ode to Shane Warne' (2007)
— Paul Kelly wrote this song based upon a great old Calypso song 'London's the Place for Me', by Lord Kitchener.

'Jerusalem' (2005)
— A version of 'Jerusalem' by crossover soprano Keedie Babb, with the final verse supplied by the victorious 2005 Ashes English team.

'The England Eleven' (1994)
— From Greg Champion's *Everybody Loves to Watch the Cricket,* an entertaining summary of the incoming English team including Atherton, Stewart, Hick, Gooch, Gatting and Tufnell.

'Bradman' (1986)
— Paul Kelly's tribute to the Don includes details of the first years of his career including his inaugural Ashes series home and away.

'Ian Botham's Wild West Cricket Show' (1981)
— A great song about listening to Ian Botham's 149 not out to turn around the Headingley Test in 1981 by the Fingerstyle Guitar Man. The innings stopped the stockmarket and captured the imagination of Britain as 'Botham slew the Aussie foe'.

'Der Rhythmische Lauf' (1981)
— German-based English songwriter Colin Wilkie wrote this song in German about Jim Laker's epic 19 wicket haul in 1956, the finest Test bowling performance in Ashes history.

'Lillian Thomson' (1975)
— Richard Stilgoe's ditty highlighting Dennis Lillee and Jeff Thomson's demolition of England in 1974–75. It made Britain's Top 40 charts.

'Cricket' (1973)
— A popular tribute to the 'Britishness' of cricket by Ray Davies, frontman for the Kinks in which the Demon Bowler, Fred Spofforth, is referenced; taken from a popular English choir song.

'Here Come the Aussies' (1972)
— The song sung by Ian Chappell's 1972 tourists previewing and publicising their Ashes tour. One of the lines declared: 'And we'll play on through the English rain.'

'Ashes Song' (1971)
— The English cricket team's song celebrating the winning of the Ashes in Australia in 1970–71.

'Our Don Bradman' (1931)
— Iconic tune by Jack O'Hagan regaling the Don's early Ashes exploits.

Twelve Cricket Knights

Australia
Sir Donald Bradman (knighted 1949)

England
Sir G. O. B. 'Gubby' Allen (1986)
Sir Alec Bedser (1996)
Sir Ian Botham (2007)
Sir J. F. Neville Cardus (1967)
Sir Colin Cowdrey (1992)
Sir J. B. 'Jack' Hobbs (1953)
Sir Leonard Hutton (1956)
Sir Francis E. Lacey (1926)
Sir H. D. G. 'Shrimp' Leveson-Gower (1953)
Sir Frederick C. Toone (1929)
Sir P. F. 'Plum' Warner (1937)

Twenty 'Firsts' and 'Lasts'

First ever Ashes Test played outside England or Australia: first Test, Cardiff, Wales, July 2009.

Last ever sixth Test of a series: the Oval, August 1993.

First Ashes Test where two New Zealand-born players debuted: Brendon Julian (Australia) and Andy Caddick (England), first Test, Manchester, 1993.

First dismissal that contained three rhyming names: Lillee c. Willey b. Dilley 19, first Test, Perth, 1979−80.

First Test abandoned due to vandalism: third Test, Leeds, August 1975.

Last Ashes Test to be played on a rain-affected wicket: first Test, Birmingham, 1975.

First and last Test where the wicket was ruined by the obscure grass killing fungus fusarium: fourth Test, Leeds, 1972.

First and last ever seventh Test in a series: Sydney, February 1971.

First Test televised in its entirety, ball-by-ball, to every capital city in Australia by the ABC: first Test, Brisbane, 1970−71.

First deliberately mid-match watered Test pitch: third Test, Melbourne, January 1955.

Last Test in Australia to be played on a rain affected uncovered pitch: first Test, Brisbane, December 1950.

First draw in Australia for 63 years: third Test, Melbourne, January 1947.

First Test to be televised: second Test, Lord's, June 1938 [to only a few thousand Londoners wealthy enough to own TV sets − ed.].

First and last Ashes Test to be played over eight days: fifth Test, Melbourne, 1928−29.

First and last series where one side selected 30 players during the five Test matches: England in England, 1921.

First and last time a bowler sent down two consecutive overs in a Test: Warwick Armstrong in the fourth Test, Old Trafford, 1921.

First and last Test ever at Sheffield: third Test, Bramall Lane, July 1902.

First ever abandoned Test: third Test, Manchester, August 1890.

First double century in an Ashes, or any Test: 211 by Billy Murdoch for Australia, third Test, the Oval, 1884.

First and last Test where all 11 fielders bowled: England, third Test, the Oval, 1884.

Twenty-five Player Superstitions

Australia

Terry Alderman: Always taped his left ankle before bowling.

Allan Border: Wouldn't shave during a match.

Michael Clarke: Listens to loud music through headphones before batting.

Rick Darling: If not out overnight, would wear the same clothing as the day before.

Matthew Hayden: Noted for signing a 'cross' on his chest upon reaching 100.

Andrew Hilditch: Had an unwashed lucky jockstrap.

Merv Hughes: Liked to be last to leave the changing rooms.

Dean Jones: Lucky jockstrap.

Ken Mackay: Hated everything to do with the number 13. Refused to have a chapter 13 in his autobiography *Slasher Opens Up*.

Norman O'Neill: Liked to wear a thin pair of 'lucky' lemon socks under his normal cricketing socks.

SUPERSTITIOUS: Ken Mackay (left), Norm O'Neill, Steve Waugh and Dirk Wellham.

Michael Slater: Was the first to kiss the coat of arms on his
    helmet upon reaching three figures.
Steve Waugh: Liked to carry a red handkerchief when batting.
Dirk Wellham: Wore a 'lucky' gold chain.
Kepler Wessels: Another to sign a cross on his chest upon
    reaching 100.
Mike Whitney: Kissed the ball before his first delivery.
Tim Zoehrer: Always kept a one dollar note in his pocket.

England

Mike Atherton: Would not give interviews when not out
    overnight.
Ken Barrington: Kept a lucky half crown in his blazer pocket;
    a present from Peter May during his first Test. Also had a
    favourite telegram from his wife which he carried in the back
    pocket of his flannels during every Test.
Geoff Boycott: Fastidiously laid out his gear neatly so it would
    dry quickly.
Denis Compton: Kept a lucky silver four leaf clover in his pocket.
Len Hutton: Carried a five shilling coin in his pocket, a gift from
    one of his grandfather's friends. In the deciding Test at the
    Oval in 1953, he wore his faded record-breaking '364' cap from
    1938 and scored a match-high 82 and 17 in England's eight
    wicket win.
Alan Knott: Insisted on having part of a white handkerchief
    protruding from his left trouser pocket.
Phil Mead: Was renowned for his elaborate shuffle around the
    crease before the bowler was allowed to come in at him.
    Cricket historian David Frith says many bowlers had to stop
    and go back to their mark before Mead finally settled.
Jack Russell: One of the most superstitious of all; would use all
    his gear, from towelling hats to gloves until they were simply
    no longer useable. Each morning he'd soak his Weetbix in milk
    for exactly 12 minutes. He also hated the numbers 37 and 87.
Arthur Shrewsbury: Would ask the Trent Bridge room attendant
    to bring him a cup of tea just before he was walking out to bat.

Thirty Household Names

The Big Ship: Warwick Armstrong

The Champion/The Doctor/The Grand Old Man of Cricket: W. G. Grace

The Count: Ian Meckiff

The Croucher: Gilbert Jessop

The Demon: Fred Spofforth

The Don/The Knight/The Boy Wonder: Don Bradman

The 'Errol Flynn' of Cricket: Keith Miller

The Fiend: Jack Ferris

Gelignite Jack: Jack Gregory

The Giant/The Colonial Hercules: George Bonnor

The Governor-General: Charlie Macartney

The Guardsman: 'Chuck' Fleetwood-Smith

Guy the Gorilla: Ian Botham

Johnny Won't Hit Today: J. W. H. T. Douglas

The King (of Collingwood): Jack Ryder

Lillian Thomson: Dennis Lillee and Jeff Thomson

The Little Dasher: Harry Graham

The Little Fave: Johnny Martin

Lord Ted: Ted Dexter

The Master: Jack Hobbs

Mr Cricket: Mike Hussey

Mr Smith: K. S. Duleepsinhji

Mutt & Jeff: Bill Ponsford and Bill Woodfull

The Prince of Wicketkeepers: John Blackham

Stodge & Plodge: Colin McDonald and George Thoms

The Tamworth Twister: John Gleeson

The Terror: Charlie Turner

The Twins: Denis Compton and Bill Edrich

W.G.: Dr W. G. Grace

The W. G. Grace of Australia: George Giffen

187 Nicknames

Australia

A.B.: Allan Border
Alfie: Justin Langer
Babs: David Boon
Bacchus: Rod Marsh
Bagga: Sid Barnes
Barlow: William Carkeek
Baz: Graeme Wood
Beatle: Graeme Watson
Bertie: Ian Chappell
Big Bill: Bill Johnston
Billy: Craig McDermott
Bing: Brett Lee
Bish: Rick McCosker
Bomber: Jeff Hammond
Boof: Darren Lehmann
Braddles: Don Bradman
Bull: Harry Alexander
C.C.: Colin McDonald
China: Shaun Young
Chip: Adam Dale
Chook: Bruce Reid
Chopper: Kepler Wessels
Chuck: L. O'B. Fleetwood-
  Smith
Clag: Kim Hughes
Claw: Alan Davidson
Clem: Terry Alderman
Cracka: Trevor Hohns
Dainty: Bert Ironmonger
Deafy: Don Tallon
Digger: Andrew Hilditch

Dizzy: Jason Gillespie
Ernie: E. R. Mayne
Fat Cat: Greg Ritchie
Ferg: Bob Massie
Fitteran: Alan Turner
Flip: Wayne Phillips
FOT: Dennis Lillee
Freddie/Bikkie/Hanoi:
  Doug Walters
Fritz: Eric Freeman
Froggie: Alan Thomson
Frosty: Michael Beer
Funky: Colin Miller
Garth: Graham McKenzie
Gaz: Nathan Lyon
Gladdy: Jim Higgs
Griz: Wally Grout
Grum/Scarl: Clarrie Grimmett
Henry: Geoff Lawson
Herb: Matthew Elliott, Brian
  Taber
Hollywood: Shane Warne
Ima: Grahame Corling
Jaff: Gary Cosier
Jonah: Ernie Jones
June: Mark Waugh
Kasper: Michael Kasprowicz
Kat: Simon Katich
Larry: Trevor Laughlin
Mad-dog: Laurie Mayne,
  Ian Callen
Mad Mick: Sid Emery

FREDDIE: Funloving Doug Walters was known to his cricket mates as 'Bikkie' or 'Freddie' . . . his National Service mates called him 'Hanoi' – they reckoned he was bombed every night!

Mo: Greg Matthews, Leo O'Brien

Mocca: Carl Rackemann

Molly: Maurice Sievers

Monty: M. A. Noble

Mule: Bruce Francis

Musso: Jack Badcock

Napper: Stan McCabe

Ned: E. J. Gregory

Nin: Neil Harvey

Nip: C. E. Pellew

Noodles: Alan Fairfax

Nugget: Keith Miller

Perker: P. K. Lee

Phantom: Bill Lawry

Pigeon: Glenn McGrath

Pistol: Paul Reiffel

Pud: H. M. Thurlow

Puddin': Bill Ponsford

Punter: Ricky Ponting

Pup: Michael Clarke

Ranji: H. V. Hordern

Rock: Don Blackie

Roo: Bruce Yardley

Rowdy: Ashley Mallett

Roy: Andrew Symonds

Sam: J. B. Gannon

Sammy: H. Carter

Sarf: Stuart Clark

Skull: Kerry O'Keeffe

Slash: Ken Mackay

Slats: Michael Slater

Slip: Len Pascoe

Slox: Sam Loxton

Solo: Mick Malone

Sounda: Peter Sleep

Spotty: Ray Bright

Stumper: Steve Rixon

Stumpy: Bruce Laird

Snork: Marcus North

Spinner: Lindsay Kline

Stork: Hunter Hendry

Swampy: Geoff Marsh

Tang: Max Walker

Tibby: A. Cotter

Tiger: Bill O'Reilly

Tim: T. W. Wall

Timbers: Paul Sheahan

T.J.: Terry Jenner

Tubby: Mark Taylor

Tugga: Steve Waugh

Two-up: Jeff Thomson

Waggie: Mike Veletta

Wal: Bob Cowper, Graham Yallop

Wizard: Ian Davis

Wok: John Watkins

X: Xavier Doherty

Ziggy: Tim Zoehrer

England

Arkle/Rags: Derek Randall

Banger: Marcus Trescothick

Barney: Syd Barnes

Beau: Tony Lock

Beefy: Ian Botham

Beast: Nick Cook

Benny: Nasser Hussain

Boil: Trevor Bailey

Bumble: David Lloyd

Carl: Chris Lewis

Cat: Phil Tufnell

Chalky: Craig White
Chat: Bob Taylor
Chef: Alistair Cook
Cheese: Matt Prior
Chilli: Chris Old
Chub: Maurice Tate
Creepy: John Crawley
Crime: David Steele
Daffy: Phil DeFreitas
Dazzler: Darren Gough
Deadly: Derek Underwood
Des: Andy Caddick
Dolly: Basil D'Oliveira
Drewy: Andrew Stoddart
Dude: Devon Malcolm
Dusty: Geoff Miller
Ernie: John Emburey
Fat Gatt: Mike Gatting
Fiery: Geoff Boycott, Fred
    Trueman
Flash: Norman Cowans
Foxy: Graeme Fowler
Freddie: Andrew Flintoff
Frog: Dean Headley
Gaffer: Alec Stewart
George: Brian Statham
Gladdie: Gladstone Small
Gnome: Keith Fletcher
Goose: Bob Willis
Gubby: G. O. B. Allen
Harv: Neil Fairbrother

Henry: Phil Edmonds
Horse: Geoff Arnold
Jack: R. C. Russell
Jake: John Lever
Judge: Robin Smith
K.P.: Kevin Pietersen
Kipper: Colin Cowdrey
Lol: Harold Larwood
Legger: Allan Lamb
Lubo: David Gower
Monkey: A. N. Hornby
Ned: Wayne Larkins
Ollie: Colin Milburn
Patsy: E. H. Hendren
P.B.H.: Peter Barker Howard
    May
Percy: Pat Pocock
Picca: Graham Dilley
Plum: P. F. Warner
Shagger: Graham Thorpe
Sherminator: Ian Bell
Shrek: Matthew Hoggard
Skid: Vic Marks
Splash: Ashley Giles
Tiger: E. J. Smith
Typhoon: Frank Tyson
Virgil: Michael Vaughan
Walter: Chris Broad
Westlife: Stuart Broad
Wingnut: Bill Athey
Zap: Graham Gooch

155 Occupations

Australia

Warwick Armstrong: Manager whisky business

Alick Bannerman: NSW Government Printing Office

Charles Bannerman: Umpire

John Barrett: Doctor

Richie Benaud: Journalist

David Boon: Bank officer

Harry Boyle: Sports store proprietor

Don Bradman: Stockbroker

Bill Brown: Sports store proprietor

'Sammy' Carter: Undertaker

Herbie 'Horseshoe' Collins: Bookmaker

Arthur Coningham: Shopkeeper, bookmaker

Bob Cowper: Stockbroker

Ian Craig: Pharmacist

John Dyson: Schoolteacher

Jack Edwards: Bank clerk

Jack Ferris: Bank clerk

George Giffen: Postal worker

Clarrie Grimmett: Signwriter

Wally Grout: Cigarette salesman

Andrew Hilditch: Solicitor

Clem Hill: Racing handicapper and steward

Brad Hogg: Farmer

Rodney Hogg: Milkman, greengrocer, after-dinner speaker

Tommy Horan: Journalist

'Ranji' Hordern: Dentist

Mike Hussey: Schoolteacher

John Inverarity: School headmaster

Bert Ironmonger: Hotelier, shopkeeper, lawnmowing man

Barry Jarman: Sports store proprietor

Affie Jarvis: Sports store proprietor

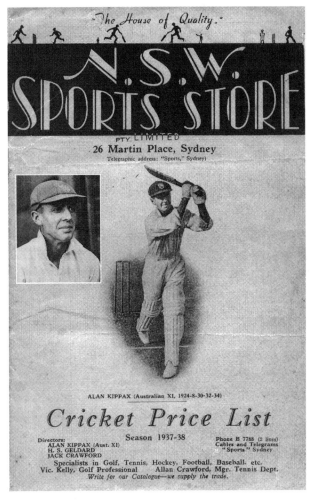

BUSINESSMAN: Alan Kippax was co-director of the NSW Sports Store in Martin Place, Sydney for years.

Terry Jenner: Sports store proprietor, blinds salesman, car
    salesman, coach, after-dinner speaker
Ian Johnson: Secretary, Melbourne Cricket Club
Bill Johnston: Sales representative at Dunlop Rubber
Dean Jones: Public servant
Alan Kippax: Sports store proprietor
Geoff Lawson: Optometrist
Bill Lawry: Plumber, pigeon breeder

Dennis Lillee: Bank clerk
Ray Lindwall: Florist
Martin Love: Physiotherapist
Sam Loxton: Parliamentarian
Jack Lyons: Stockbroker
Arthur Mailey: Cartoonist
Geoff Marsh: Farmer
Ernie McCormick: Jeweller
Percy McDonnell: Bank clerk
Keith Miller: Soccerpools promotions officer
Roy Minnett: Doctor
Arthur Morris: Tenpin bowling proprietor
Billy Murdoch: Solicitor
'Monty' Noble: Dentist
Otto Nothling: Dermatologist
Leo O'Brien: Taxation clerk
Kerry O'Keeffe: Life insurance salesman, after-dinner speaker,
    broadcaster
Bert Oldfield: Sports store proprietor
Norman O'Neill: Cigarette salesman, broadcaster
Bill O'Reilly: Schoolteacher, journalist
Roy Park: Doctor
Roland Pope: Doctor
Vernon Ransford: Secretary, Melbourne Cricket Club
Ian Redpath: Antique shop owner
Greg Ritchie: Travel agent, after-dinner speaker
Ray Robinson: Slaughterman
'Tup' Scott: Doctor
Craig Serjeant: Pharmacist
Paul Sheahan: School headmaster
Johnnie Taylor: Dentist
Peter Taylor: Farmer
George Thoms: Gynaecologist
Charlie Turner: Bank clerk
Harry Trott: Postman
Hugh Trumble: Secretary, Melbourne Cricket Club

Bill Woodfull: Schoolteacher, Headmaster
Sammy Woods: Cricket administration (in the UK)
Jack Worrall: Journalist ('J. W.' of the *Australasian*)

England

Bobby Abel: Bat and ball manufacturer, sports outfitter
Bob Appleyard: Engineer
Trevor Bailey: Essex CCC secretary, broadcaster and author
Richard Barlow: Sports store proprietor
Charlie Barnett: Poultry wholesaler
Kim Barnett: Bank clerk
Alec Bedser: Office equipment business
Ian Botham: Pantomime performer, author and commentator
Bill Bowes: Journalist
Geoff Boycott: Civil servant, commentator
Mike Brearley: Psychoanalyst, author
Johnny Briggs: Sports store proprietor
Chris Broad: Furniture importer
Norman Cowans: Glassblower
Ken Cranston: Dentist
Graham Dilley: Diamond setter
Alfred Dipper: Umpire
George Duckworth: Hotelier, farmer, pigeon breeder, writer and
    broadcaster
K. S. Duleepsinhji: Indian Foreign Service (became India's High
    Commissioner in Australia)
George Emmett: Club secretary and groundsman
Godfrey Evans: Bookmaker's representative
Percy Fender: Wine and spirits
Wilfred Flowers: Framework knitter
Neil Foster: PE teacher
C. B. Fry: Writer and broadcaster. Also represented India at the
    League of Nations.
Mike Gatting: Plumber
Paul Gibb: Bus driver
W. G. Grace: Doctor

Darren Gough: Motorway maintenance worker
David Gower: Commentator
Tony Greig: Insurance, commentary
John Gunn: Curator
William Gunn: Sports store proprietor and manufacturer
John Hampshire: Umpire
Lord Harris: Governor of Bombay
Jack Hearne: Sports shop proprietor
F. S. Jackson: Governor of Bengal
Walter Keeton: Sports shop proprietor
Albert Knight: Methodist lay preacher
Jim Laker: Commentator
Harold Larwood: Coalminer, sweet shop proprietor
Alfred Lyttelton: Parliamentarian
Peter May: Insurance broker
Martin McCague: Electrician
Geoff Miller: Calligrapher, after-dinner speaker
Arthur Milton: Postman
Peter Parfitt: Hotelier
Jim Parks: Brewery representative
Eddie Paynter: Umpire
Ian Peebles: Wine trade, writer
Richard Pilling: Sports store proprietor
Derek Pringle: Journalist
Geoff Pullar: Jeweller, fish and chip shop proprietor
K. S. Ranjitsinhji: Prince
Tom Richardson: Publican
Fred Rumsey: Travel agent
Jack Russell: Artist
Phil Sharpe: Amateur opera singer
Alfred Shaw: Sports store proprietor
David Sheppard: Bishop of Liverpool
Mordi Sherwin: Hotelier
Arthur Shrewsbury: Sports store proprietor
Reg Simpson: Managing director Gunn & Moore
Reg Sinfield: Church warden

Herbert Strudwick: Scorer

Raman Subba Row: Cricket administration

Maurice Tate: Hotel owner

Fred Titmus: Post office manager

Fred Trueman: Commentator, after-dinner speaker

Frank Tyson: Schoolteacher, Victorian Cricket Association
director of coaching, broadcaster and author

Derek Underwood: PE teacher

Bill Voce: Coalminer

Cyril Walters: Wine merchant

Albert Ward: Sports store proprietor

Jack White: Farmer

Peter Willey: Umpire

Bob Woolmer: Sports store proprietor

8

Truly Unforgettable

The Greatest Test
Andrew Flintoff

Sunday, 7 August 2005 was one of the most
momentous days in Ashes history, Australia clawing
back into an unforgettable match against all odds.

Everybody was saying we had already won, but we knew we must not get ahead of ourselves. [Shane] Warne had scored runs in the past and [Brett] Lee is also no mug with the bat. They needed 107 to win next morning and we arrived at the ground determined we weren't going to be complacent about it. The really worrying thing was the rate at which they were scoring during the early stages. Warne is a tricky batsman to bowl at because he squirts it here and there and he was scoring really quickly. I tried to push him back by bowling a few bouncers at him. I could see he was getting back close to his stumps and I went for a leg-stump yorker. I know he trod on his stumps, but I'm going to take some credit for it! When we got him out with Australia still needing a further 62 to win, we all thought that was it. I reckoned I had [Michael] Kasprowicz leg-before at one point and he also skied one down to third man, but Simon Jones missed a difficult chance. When they got down to needing less than 20, we started thinking to ourselves:

STARTING WITH A BANG: Don Bradman's 1948 Invincibles were rarely challenged from the opening match at Worcester where the Don and Arthur Morris both scored centuries and combined in a second wicket stand of 186.

'Surely not!' By the time they needed less than 10 there was almost a feeling among us that this could not be happening! I remember standing next to Marcus Trescothick at slip with both of us saying: 'They can't get this, can they?' We kept smiling nervously at each other. The one thing we were clinging onto was the hope that pressure would get to them. When tailenders are chasing a total and they need around 30 they can play how they want, but by the time they get into single figures they are suddenly expected to win and they try and play a lot tighter, rather than relying on the method that got them there in the first place. But with only 3 runs needed by the Aussies, Steve Harmison came up with the goods with a short ball into Kasprowicz's ribs which he nicked down the leg side for Geraint Jones to take the catch and earn us all an amazing victory. It is incredible to think that just one shot edged past the field would have done it for them and one ball did it for us. To win by only 2 runs after almost giving it up for dead at one point was incredible. I don't think any of us could believe what had happened. It had been a bizarre game from start to finish and it will probably go down as the most exciting cliffhanger of a Test match ever.

Everyone started celebrating all around the place. In the stands, on the field, everywhere. I went straight over to Brett Lee because I really felt for him. He had tried everything to get Australia over the line, and to hit an unbeaten 43 in those circumstances was unbelievable. I remembered what it felt like to lose against the West Indies in the ICC [International Cricket Council] Trophy final and how, when we went to shake hands with them at the end, there wasn't one of them anywhere to be seen because they had all set off on their lap of honour. I told Brett that he should be proud of the way he had played because he was absolutely brilliant, and then I went over and said the same to Kasprowicz who had sunk to his knees after being given out.

A lot was made of my conversation with Brett Lee out on the pitch because of the battle we had had, but I thought he was tremendous that day. In every Test series there are always a few personal battles going on and there was certainly a duel developing between Brett and me. It was great to be involved, particularly with

SUPERMAN: Andrew Flintoff again dominated the newspaper headlines throughout July and August as he inspired England's 2009 Ashes series victory.

PERPETUAL SMILE: Brett Lee loved playing for Australia and remains one of an elite group to take 300 Test wickets.

someone like that. I like the way he plays his cricket, with a smile on his face, but still giving everything for his team. I also like him off the pitch. He's a really nice lad. But when you get out there in the middle he will give you everything. He has the odd smile at you and has a word from time to time, but he goes about his cricket the way it should be played.

The good thing about this series was the way the two teams had a drink with each other after each Test and, despite the tense circumstances, this was no different. The Aussies quickly joined up with us for a beer and every one of us was proud to be involved in such a match. I certainly was. Getting the man-of-the-match award in a fantastic Test like that has to rank as a major highlight.

Set 282 to win at Edgbaston, Australia slumped to 7-140 and 8-175 before a gallant revival led by tailenders Shane Warne, Brett Lee and Michael Kasprowicz lifted the Australians to within a boundary of victory on the gripping final morning. With 68, 73 and seven wickets for the game, Andrew Flintoff was truly 'InFredible' – one English newspaper portraying him on its front page in a Superman suit.

Being Freddie: My Story So Far, Andrew Flintoff
(Hodder & Stoughton, London, 2006)

Shades of Albert Trott
Christian Ryan

Only one player, Albert Trott, has ever cleared the Lord's Pavilion, but several others have gone close, including Kim Hughes in the 1980 Centenary Test.

Now [Chris] Old was galumphing in. Right line. Short of a length. Dangerous ball. Kim [Hughes] took one small step forward, then one large skip, bat rising behind him. His back foot pivoted. A puff of dust stirred. Freeze-framed, it was like a full-colour replica of George Beldam's famous photo of Trumper stepping out to drive. The ball nearly burst. The cameras lost it. Umpire Dickie Bird swivelled round. Non-striker Greg Chappell clapped his bat. Mike Gatting on the leg side laughed. Voices cracked in the ABC commentary box.

'Down the ground again,' said Norman May. 'What a shot. That's 6.'

Beside him, Keith Miller murmured indiscernibly. Miller had been marvelling at Kim's timing all game. May continued: 'We'll nearly catch that. A magnificent hit. That almost finished in our broadcast box. Keith, have you ever seen a better hit at Lord's than that one?'

That Miller happened to be on air was a lucky break. It was like asking Jack if he had ever climbed a beanstalk so tall. 'Well,' said Miller, 'I hit a couple up there myself Norman, oddly enough. But not many have. That is one of the biggest hits I've seen for many, many a year. [It's] On top of the balcony.'

Those in the vicinity maintain the ball was rising still as it struck the top deck of the Pavilion. Distance travelled was calculated at 125 metres; a couple more and it would have hurdled the roof. Only one man had done that, Albert Trott, putting a hand to his forehead and gawping at the ball's steepling trajectory after middling one in 1899.

Miller did indeed go close, landing one on the top tier and another

TEN EPIC 'ASHES' HITS

Kevin Pietersen (England) – The Oval, London, fifth Test, 2005

On his way to an Ashes-saving 158 on the final day of the grandest modern day series of all, Kevin Pietersen smashes seven 6s, most from the bowling of Australian Brett Lee in the general direction of the old gasometer outside the ground.

Brett Lee (Australia) – Trent Bridge, Nottingham, fourth Test, 2005

Brett Lee's soaring mid-wicket lift against England fast bowler Steve Harmison sails out of the Trent Bridge ground.

Andrew Flintoff (England) – Edgbaston, second Test, 2005

In smiting nine 6s for the game, to go alongside his seven wickets, in-form all-rounder Andrew Flintoff assumes Superman status; he reaches his second half-century of the game in the English second innings, and one of his 6s against Brett Lee soars straight over the R. V. Ryder Stand and out of the ground.

Matthew Hayden (Australia) – Melbourne, fourth Test, 2002–03

During his imperious Boxing Day century, Matthew Hayden twice lifts England's pace bowler Craig White over wide mid-on 20 rows back onto the concourse of the Great Southern Stand. Both hits are enormous.

Adam Gilchrist (Australia) – Edgbaston, Birmingham, first Test, 2001

Adam Gilchrist helps himself to an Ashes record 22 from an over from the little-used Mark Butcher, his thumping leg-side hits including three 6s, one of which is as high as it is long, threatening low-flying aircraft.

Devon Malcolm (England) – Sydney, third Test, 1994–95

No. 11 in any team, anywhere, anytime, Devon Malcolm amazes teammates when he twice lifts England's tormentor Shane Warne into the outer reaches of the Sydney Cricket Ground members.

Ian Botham (England) – Edgbaston, Birmingham, fifth Test, 1985

An imperious straight drive for 6 from Ian Botham from the very first ball he faced from Australia's Craig McDermott was repeated two balls later. McDermott's over: 4W6064.

Doug Walters (Australia) – WACA Ground, Perth, second Test, 1974–75

Doug Walters hooks the ball for 6 from England's Bob Willis to reach his century in a session from the final ball of the day. Expecting a tumultuous reception from teammates, Walters instead finds an empty room, the players having hid in the showers!

A **ONE-OFF**: Modern day players opt for ice baths after a day's play. Dougie Walters preferred a beer and a cigarette.

Ken Barrington (England) – Melbourne, fifth Test, 1965–66

Dropped previously during his momentous career for slow scoring, Ken Barrington races to a second hundred in a row from just 122 balls with a towering 6 over mid-on from Australian off-spinner Tom Veivers. Even keeper Wally Grout is surprised: 'Where did that one come from Kenny?' he exclaims as the ball disappears over the pickets into the Melbourne Cricket Club members.

Freddie Trueman (England) – Sydney, third Test, 1958–59

England's Freddie Trueman swats Richie Benaud over the leg side into the Sydney Cricket Ground Ladies Stand. Of the 11,291 deliveries in the series, it is the only one hit for 6.

TEN CLASSIC ASHES CATCHES

Andrew Strauss (England) – Nottingham, fourth Test, 2005

Strauss executes a trapeze-like horizontal left-handed grab at second slip which removes Adam Gilchrist, off Andrew Flintoff – one of the signature images from the greatest Ashes series of the modern era.

Glenn McGrath (Australia) – Adelaide, second Test, 2002–03

The 198 cm (6 ft 6 in) fast bowler sprints and launches himself at the ball on the deep mid wicket boundary to take a spectacular diving one-hander in front of the Adelaide members. England's No. 1 batsman Michael Vaughan is out and Shane Warne has yet another Ashes wicket as Australia cruise to another comfortable win.

Mark Ramprakash (England) – Melbourne, fourth Test, 1998–99

A match-changing, one-handed catch at square leg after Australia is comfortably placed at 2-103, chasing just 175 for victory. Ramprakash flings himself to his right and holds a full-blooded pull shot by Justin Langer from the bowling of Alan Mullally. That catch and some irresistible reverse swing from Dean Headley sees England win in a cliffhanger.

Mark Waugh (Australia) – Leeds, fourth Test, 1993

Alec Stewart's edged cut against Paul Reiffel is going down when Waugh at second slip takes a remarkable one-hander, diving to his right. So fast is the ball going that Waugh takes the catch almost behind him. It is a screamer and removes Australia's last major obstacle to an Ashes securing victory.

Greg Chappell (Australia) – Sydney, fifth Test, 1982–83

Chappell is the sole slipsman as paceman Geoff Lawson begins the final over before lunch on day 3 to David Gower when Gower, looking to drive, edges to where a second slip would have been. The ball is going low and wide of Chappell before he triumphantly emerges with the ball, having dived full length to his left, catching the ball spectacularly in his outstretched left hand. It is a miraculous interception.

Ian Botham (England) – Manchester, fifth Test, 1981

A stunning 'leaping like a salmon' high slips catch from England's greatest all-rounder, as Dennis Lillee looks to guide Paul Allott high over the catching cordon. Many regard it as Botham's best ever. It effectively ends Australia's brave and unlikely fight towards 506.

Bob Simpson (Australia) – Manchester, fourth Test, 1961

As leg-spinning captain Richie Benaud sweeps through the England middle-order on the way to a famous come-from-behind Ashes securing victory, slips master Simpson dives low and to his left to spectacularly hold a David Allen edge that Benaud himself rates the best catch he has ever seen.

Don Tallon (Australia) – The Oval, fifth Test, 1948

Perhaps the finest wicketkeeper's catch ever taken at Ashes level. Having anticipated a Len Hutton leg glance, Tallon dives full length to his left to take the catch of his career from the bowling of expressman Ray Lindwall. Hutton 30, Lindwall six for 20, England all out 52.

Percy Chapman (England) – Brisbane's Exhibition Ground, first Test, 1928–29

A brilliant reflex catch at gully sees Bill Woodfull's dismissal for a duck in Harold Larwood's opening over, after the English started with 521. In his first full Test series as England's captain, Chapman successfully defends the Ashes 4-1.

Clem Hill (Australia) – Manchester, fourth Test, 1902

One of the most celebrated boundary-riding catches of them all. Hill sprints flat out across the Old Trafford outfield and takes the catch in his outstretched left hand to dismiss England's wicketkeeper Dick Lilley from the bowling of Hugh Trumble in front of the pavilion. England had needed eight to win before Hill's heroics, the Australians eventually securing a famous victory by 3 runs.

A SPECIAL: Bobby Simpson's reflex catch to dismiss David Allen was Richie Benaud's all-time favourite.

SPECTACULAR: Don Tallon was almost at leg slip when he took the finest catch of his career to dismiss Len Hutton.

on the commentary box when the Dominions played England. But old England captain 'Gubby' Allen could recall no straight hit more remarkable than Kim's. Several festive fellow old-timers missed it — or spied a glimmer in the mirror of the Q Stand bar. The Board's David Richards was one who picked the right second to turn and look: 'Oh yeah, there's Hughesy, he's batting alright.' Then *clunk*.

Kim had batted on all five days and swiped 6s on four of them.

In an era of slimline bats, Kim Hughes' 125 metre straight hit onto the top deck of the Lord's Pavilion, having advanced at England's Chris Old like he was a slow bowler, was phenomenal. Hughes was in a rare zone during the 1980 Centenary Test, scoring 117 and 84, becoming the first Australian to bat on all five days of an England–Australia Test match.

Golden Boy: Kim Hughes and the Bad Old Days of Australian Cricket, Christian Ryan (Allen & Unwin, Sydney, 2009)

One Hit Wonder
Robin Marlar

No-one has captivated as incredibly as swing specialist Bob Massie on his debut at Lord's in 1972.

Leading a group of Australian supporters from the spectacular city of Perth at this (1997) Ashes Test, the pinnacle of the cricketing calendar for the next few years, is a modest 50-year-old, a cheerful fellow, his frame not much thicker than it was when he made history a quarter of a century ago.

In the space of four of the most startling days ever played at Lord's, Robert Arnold Lockyer Massie bowled England out twice, destroying them. Operating mostly from the nursery end, he took eight for 84 in the first innings and even more crucially, eight for 53 in the second. No mean side, England conceded a lead of 36 runs but were so utterly discomforted on the Saturday, day 3, that Australia needed only 81 to win the match. They had eight wickets and more than nine hours to spare.

No Australian bowler had ever before taken 16 wickets in a Test match and none has done so since. Only two bowlers, the Englishmen Jim Laker and Sydney Barnes, had ever taken more and the only man to better Massie's figures since, and by only one run, was the Indian Hirwani. Nor was this a stunning performance in mere figures. Watching him then and there was to realise what could happen to a cricketer touched by unprecedented, unimaginable magic. Looking back at Massie's career, which was short and never again as successful, we can understand how much luckier is the cricketer who blazes once rather than not at all. Fame, even for 15 minutes, lasts a lifetime.

Never much more than medium-paced, Massie had found favour in Western Australia as a bowler who could operate into the wind and could swing the ball even when the Fremantle Doctor was blowing hard up the Swan River. Invited over to Sydney for the Test against the Rest of the World team substituting for South Africa, Massie took seven wickets and thereby won his place in the team to tour England in 1972.

He was not going to be short of mates from his state side. No fewer than six WA players were chosen, amongst them Dennis Lillee who had already been blooded against England as a 21-year-old, and was pawing the ground in his eagerness to hurl yet more thunderbolts at England's best batsmen. Another key member of the squad was also from Perth, Rodney Marsh, the wicketkeeper they were starting to call 'Iron Gloves', but who was nonetheless good enough to catch five of those 16 wickets. More importantly, it was the left-handed Marsh who stayed with the game's only century maker, Greg Chappell, to establish a lead. Marsh hit 50 runs in an hour and a quarter, including two 6s and six 4s. It may still be known as 'Massie's Match', but cricket is a game for 11 players and under Ian Chappell's leadership these Australians were becoming formidable, even if, eventually, they had to share this series, 2-2 and leave the Ashes in England's possession.

Massie had taken six wickets in the opening match against

Worcester, but he had not been fit to play in the first Test at Manchester which England won well. David Colley had shared the new ball with Lillee and had taken four wickets in the match. What clinched Massie's selection as opening bowler was the overcast heavy atmosphere which eventually gave way to a breeze from the northwest coming in over the Warner Stand. The Lord's pitch was hard and so conditions must have reminded Massie of home.

Massie clean bowled Geoff Boycott, and Lillee removed John Edrich and Brian Luckhurst, whereupon Massie slowly worked through the rest of the order, taking England's last wicket with the penultimate ball of his 33rd over. England's strong middle order – Alan Knott was at 7 and Ray Illingworth, the skipper at a lowly 8 – all reached 30 but only Tony Greig got as far as a half-century. Spectators could see that the batsmen were never wholly in control.

John Snow had led England's bowling in Australia when the Ashes were splendidly regained, but although he took five wickets, these conditions suited him no better than Lillee. The young Australian speed merchant managed to remove Boycott quickly a second time, the batsman offering no stroke to a ball which hit him and dropped unluckily on the stumps. Again Luckhurst fell to pace, and once again Massie proceeded to work his way through the rest of the order. England batted as if they were thoroughly demoralised. Resistance was distressingly feeble, with the sole exception of Mike Smith. Six catches were picked up in the thickly populated slip cordon and a record crowd of 31,000 went home in a grisly mood.

How on earth had Massie done such damage? He had made a cricket ball swing as if he was a conjuror, first this way and then the other. Unable to believe what I thought I was seeing, I went round to the gap at the nursery end on both the first and third day, just to see what Massie was doing. Mainly he swung the ball away from the right-hander, but his inswinger was wickedly late and apparently impossible for the England batsmen to pick. As for the outer, that seemed to dip at the end of its flight, like a well-pitched baseball, and then scuttle away off the pitch at an even sharper angle, like a fast leg-break. Above all, Massie pitched the ball up to

DREAM START: Bob Massie's unforgettable first Test wicket at Lord's in 1972: Geoff Boycott bowled for 11. *Patrick Eagar*

the batsman, just short of half-volley length and kept it in the air long enough for it to swerve. Furthermore, although he played the demon he never gave way to excess. There was no pressing need for results, no sudden surges of speed with consequent loss of accuracy, no temptation to be clever, no need for further variation. It was as if the God of Bowlers had borrowed this young banker for the weekend just to confirm that He was still capable of miracles. Then He went away again.

Massie took five more wickets in the remaining Tests of that series and played twice more against Pakistan. He played a few seasons for Western Australia but never took five wickets in an innings in the Sheffield Shield and thereafter retired, having somehow lost his signature outswinger. His mantle was eventually donned by Terry Alderman whose command of both swing and movement off the pitch proved more durable.

Massie still comments on cricket as part of the Australian Broadcasting Corporation's radio team. He has made his working career with the Commonwealth Bank, where he now works in the investment department. There are times, perhaps when he may seem wistful, as if he would have liked more sustained success. Perhaps that would have been asking too much. For those few days, Bob Massie was just too beautiful for words.

It has become fashionable for the cricketing cognoscenti to look slightly askance at Massie's amazing achievement. Some refer to the freakish weather conditions, as if in those nuclear days of heavy water the bowler had found some heavy air. Others will tell you that all his wickets were taken at the other end, that batsmen were thoroughly shaken up at the other end by Lillee's speed and hostility. Thus when they came to face the gentler pace of Massie, they lost both their heads and their wickets.

That is not how it struck me at the time. The weather, particularly on the Saturday when Massie was at his decisive best, was warm with a lot of fleecy clouds bowling along in the blue sky above Lord's. As for Lillee, he came to Lord's as a bright new star and did not disappoint. Now he stands at the top of the Australian Test wicket-takers, with 355, his only challenger Shane Warne and then not until the millennium. In no fewer than seven Tests did Lillee take 10 or more wickets, the true mark of a matchwinner. Wonderfully, both Dennis Lillee and Jeff Thomson, his long-term partner and yet another possessed of a dramatic fast bowler's action, will also be at this splendid Test match. Watch out for them. Don't expect them to look as they did in action photos long ago. Lillee still has his dark moustache but like many of us baldness has cleaned up his pate. As for Thomson, the long, blond locks are greying now. Never doubt that this pair have done wonders for the continuing popularity of cricket in Australia.

For the first time in half a century we shall not see their predecessors among Australian fast bowling partnerships, Keith Miller and Ray Lindwall, another pair who put the wind up all but the bravest England batsmen. Miller ran half the distance of many a bowler half his pace. So natural, so smooth, so strong was his

TEN MORE SHORT ASHES CAREERS

Shaun Young (Australia)

From the Tasmanian northwest coastal town of Burnie, Young was in the UK representing Gloucester when called into the Australian touring squad late in the 1977 summer as a reinforcement. He played a county match and was selected ahead of Shane Lee, Brett's brother, for the final Test at the Oval, Australia beaten in under three days, Young making 0 and 4 not out, from No. 8 and bowling eight overs in two innings. It was to be his only international.

Jack Iverson (Australia)

Thirty-five-year-old debutant, 'mystery' spinner Iverson amassed 21 wickets in his solo Ashes series against Freddie Brown's Englishmen in 1950–51, only to soon disappear back into the anonymity of Melbourne sub-district ranks, a victim of self-esteem issues. In Sydney, 'Big Jake' had claimed a Test-best six for 27, the Englishmen having no idea of which way he was turning the ball from his bent finger grip.

GIANTKILLER: Jack Iverson disappeared as quickly as he arrived.

Colin McCool (Australia)

World War Two delayed leg spinning all-rounder McCool's entry into Ashes cricket until he was 30. In his one and only series in 1946–47, he averaged almost 55 with the bat and 27 with the ball. He was selected for the 1948 tour of England, but didn't play a Test.

Reg Sinfield (England)

He played only one Test, the opening match of the 1938 summer at Trent Bridge, making 6 and taking one wicket for 51. It was a big wicket though: Don Bradman.

Archie Jackson (Australia)

Jackson was every cricket-loving boy's hero in the late 1920s after making 164 as a 19-year-old on his enchanting Ashes debut against Harold Larwood and Co. in Adelaide. On the eve of the tour of England in 1930 he was made – by the Cricket Board of Control – to have his tonsils taken out as he had complained of a sore throat. Bill Ponsford had suffered from acute tonsillitis on the previous tour and the Board was reluctant to take another player with a sore throat in case it developed into something more serious. Surgery in those days was quite primitive and it was only a matter of weeks before Jackson was on the ship to England. There was little time to recover and he under-achieved. This tour was to be his last for Australia, although he did play against Jack Grant's 1930–31 West Indians on his return home. Just two years later, he was to die from tuberculosis, having averaged almost 60 in his four Ashes Tests.

Roy Park (Australia)

Harry Howell's first ball bowled Park in Melbourne, 1920–21. It was to be the Melbourne doctor's only Test. It is said that Park's wife bent down to pick up her knitting and missed her husband's entire Test career.

Jack Crawford (England)

Repton all-rounder J. N. Crawford amassed 30 wickets in his only five Ashes Tests Down Under in 1907–08, before a dispute with the Surrey committee saw him quit English cricket and immigrate to Adelaide where he lifted South Australia to two Sheffield Shield titles. His only two 'home Tests' were in 1907 against South Africa.

'Tip' Foster (England)

Champion all-sportsman R. E. Foster was the most talented of seven brothers to represent Malvern and Worcestershire. On his Ashes debut in Sydney in 1903–04 he made a Test-high 287 on his way to almost 500 runs at 60. It was to be his only Ashes series and he refused the captaincy of the 1907–08 team because of his stockbroking interests. He died young, at 36 years of age, from diabetes.

Fred Tate (England)

Fred Tate, Maurice's father, had just three days as an international cricketer, dropping Australia's topscorer Joe Darling in the Australian second innings and being bowled with only four runs needed for a series-squaring victory at Old Trafford in 1902. Australia won by just three runs and Tate was not selected again. Asked later how he felt about his misfortune, he said: 'I have a little lad at home who will make up for that.'

Fred Grace (England)

The youngest of five cricketing brothers, Fred Grace made a pair in his only appearance in the one-off Test at the Oval in 1880. He did, however, accept one of the remarkable high catches of them all, George Bonnor turning for a third run when the catch finally was taken. He died just two weeks later, from congestion of the lungs.

rocking action at delivery that he needed only a dozen yards of run-up, his hair flying, the ball likely to deviate all over the place, his intent unknown, his menace momentary, his friendship immortal.

A night-fighter pilot with the Australian Air Force, Miller was the charismatic star of the Victory Tests at Lord's in 1945. The crowds were almost as large and enthusiastic as today and much closer to the action because they were squatting many deep on the grass around the boundary.

One of Miller's favourite stories is about the first match in that series over the Whitsun holiday. Pilot Officer K. R. Miller was on his way to a century in 'elegant, emphatic style' when down the Pavilion steps came Warrant Officer R. G. Williams on his way to one of the most extraordinary 50s ever seen on the ground. Forty-eight hours before the match, Williams had been freed from a Prisoner of War camp in Silesia. That day the crowd let him know that he was home and free. We must never forget. As for the game, Australia won at seven o'clock on the third day off the fourth ball of the last over with England fieldsmen scurrying to give them the chance. Times change. More than 1100 runs were scored.

As for Ray Lindwall, whom we mourn alongside Denis Compton, I was one of the fortunate few who watched him kill off a famous cricketing experiment in the nets at the nursery end. They were pitched that day close to the path leading to the North Gate. There was a theory that the game would be better if the size and weight of the ball could be reduced. Balls half an inch smaller were duly manufactured. The greatest living fast bowler was then invited to test them. As the assembled big-wigs watched from the back of the net, marshalled by Sir 'Gubby' Allen, Lindwall nominated which way he would swing the ball. Pitching each and every one on a perfect length for his purpose, he sent three outswingers boomeranging into the net pole on the right side of the stumps and the other three swung in and crashed into the opposite corner. Swerve? No-one had ever seen such mastery. Smaller balls were not the silliest idea devised in the '50s, but none of the others were killed off quite so quickly, by five minutes of bowling genius.

That exhibition, that need to experiment, brings us neatly back to Bob Massie. All through his Test match, and especially on the Saturday, he found the ball sometimes swinging too much for his purpose, missing everything as it dipped and moved off the pitch. From my vantage point at the nursery end, I watched, fascinated, as the bowler tried outswingers round the wicket to right-handers. Then from the same angle he would make an inswinger duck into the batsmen. It was the equivalent to an off spinner bowling round the wicket on a turning pitch, always a question of angles; Massie had to keep control of the ball and himself. You can imagine how much advice he was getting from his fired-up colleagues. And to think, all this was done in his very first Test match. This was, in truth, a unique performance. If you are fortunate enough to meet him this weekend, please stand in awe. We shall never see anything like it again.

Bob Massie was to play only five more Tests for Australia, taking 15 wickets.

ECB Second Cornhill Test Match Souvenir Program (Lord's, 1997)

The Headingley Epic of '48
The Cricketer

It was the most stunning victory of all for Don Bradman
and his 1948 Invincibles and the only time Australia
has chased 400 on the final day to win an Ashes Test.

I — A glorious match which will be remembered by all who saw it.

II — To have any chance of saving the rubber we (England) had to win this match. If we had won it, the fifth Test at the Oval would have been played out and we might have made the score level at two all.

III — Our batting was so good that we could certainly have drawn the game, but quite rightly we forced the game on Monday afternoon and some wickets were lost.

IV — [Len] Hutton and [Cyril] Washbrook were splendid in each innings. Perhaps Washbrook batted even better than his partner. His first innings was the best of all the good innings on our side. He only got out from exhaustion in the last over of the day.

V — [Bill] Edrich's first innings was of great value, but he was often in difficulties and found runs hard to get. His second innings was fine free cricket and put us on terms with the clock.

VI — [Denis] Compton had to wait with his pads on while 423 runs were made. Admirably though [Alec] Bedser batted, it was probably a mistake to alter the batting order and send him in for Compton on the first night. On the second morning Edrich and Bedser made only 23 runs in the first hour, Compton, after his long wait, was not in form. In his second innings he made some grand strokes but did not reach his best.

VII — Bedser hit with great power after lunch. He and Edrich put on 155 runs and both were out to splendid catches. After their departure the Australians bowled and fielded like a winning team and we were out for 496 after being 423 for two. [Ray] Lindwall showed remarkable stamina, and [Bill] Johnston was always bowling well and making the ball run away from the batsmen. [Norman] Yardley alone looked like settling down and he was last out forcing the game. There can be nothing but admiration for the way in which Australia fought on at a time when a score of 600 seemed probable.

VIII – The Australian fielding was up to their own highest standard. The only mistake one remembers was a nasty catch off [Sam] Loxton to [Lindsay] Hassett, at short leg, given by Hutton when 26. The slow bowling was not as good as the fast.

IX – [Don] Bradman and Hassett, who had tided Australia over a nasty period at the end of the second day, were both out in [Dick] Pollard's first over on Saturday. There had been an hour's rain at Leeds at 7 a.m. and Hassett was out to a ball that got up straight and we hoped for more, but the wicket soon dried.

X – [Keith] Miller and [Neil] Harvey came together at a critical moment but both hit with the greatest freedom and added 100 in under an hour and a half. Miller was at his best. One low straight drive off [Jim] Laker would have been worth nine if run out, and Harvey, on debut, made all sorts of beautiful strokes on the off side. No cricketer in the whole series can have scored a finer century on his first appearance. We can only remember two balls which he played at and missed. He opened with remarkable confidence for a boy of 19. Possibly a slow or medium-paced bowler bowling at his leg stump with six men on the on side might keep him quiet. His catch, which ended the second Hutton–Washbrook first wicket stand, was truly remarkable. Nobody but a very fast runner could have got to the ball and he caught it just above his boots. It can be compared with Clem Hill's great catch at Manchester in 1902.

XI – Loxton carried on the good work. He had fielded here splendidly on the boundary and bowled well. As a batsman he does not look so safe as Miller, but he is a fine hitter and drove five 6s.

XII — Even after his innings, eight wickets were down for 355 at tea time. Lindwall gave a wonderful display of batting for a fast bowler. He seemed master of the situation. Johnston was nearly out again and again but lasted until 403 and then to the disappointment of the crowd the lame [Ernie] Toshack with a runner stayed until the close of play, Lindwall not out 76. The crowd were strangely silent during Lindwall's rapid scoring.

XIII — Our faster bowlers were steady and stuck to their work well. [Jim] Laker looked easy to hit. He does not seem to flight the ball. Yardley should have bowled more. Our fielding was not discreditable but seemed slow in comparison with that of the Australians. Some old cricketers wished that Yardley had set a defensive field for Lindwall.

XIV — [Ron] Saggers kept wicket so well that [Don] Tallon was not missed. [Godfrey] Evans was good in the first innings.

XV — The Australians were much handicapped in the second innings by the loss of Toshack, especially as Miller was not bowling his full pace. The ball did not rise at Leeds as it did at Lord's.

XVI — Tuesday, 27 July 1948, was probably the most disappointing day from an English point of view in all the long history of matches between England and Australia and the great crowd at Leeds which previously had so keenly and impartially applauded both sides, were so stunned and disappointed that there was only some perfunctory clapping as Bradman and Harvey returned to the pavilion at 6.18 p.m. It was not that they did not appreciate the fact that Australia had won a great victory with only 12 minutes to spare, but that one and all felt that the match had been thrown away by indifferent leadership and bad fielding. The England XI, as the cricket correspondent of the Manchester *Guardian* put it, 'looked an ill-assorted shambles, and had it not been for the beauty of Washbrook's fielding on the boundary it would have been hard to find a thing of undisputed Test Match standard in it.' These are hard words, but which scarcely deserve contradiction, though we would add the names of Edrich and Compton to that of Washbrook as two others who kept up a high standard of keenness and alacrity in the field.

XVII — Australia were set to make 404 runs in a little less than five hours and three-quarters — an average rate of slightly more than 70 runs an hour on a very fast outfield. When Hassett was splendidly caught and bowled by Compton low down with the left hand, Australia were behind the clock, the ball could be made occasionally to turn, and neither Bradman nor Morris looked exactly comfortable early. Morris when 32, and the total 54, should have been stumped off Compton, but the ball came to Evans chest high and could not be called an easy chance. Bradman did not appear to spot Compton's googly and at 22 was missed at slip by [Jack] Crapp, the ball coming straight to him chest high.

Now Compton bowls a difficult ball, but his length is most uncertain and runs were bound to come freely off him. It was therefore, imperative to hold one end tight. Yardley now called on Hutton to bowl. What passage of thought, what evil genius, induced him to do so is hard to imagine. Hutton used to bowl leg breaks of moderate quality but he is not a bowler for a Test match. He did not bowl against India in 1946, on the MCC tour in Australia in 1946–47 he sent down three overs and against South Africa in 1947 he bowled just four, very expensive, overs. There was, therefore, no previous performance from him to justify his being asked to bowl at this period and, incidentally, to Bradman of all people. Off four overs, which included five full tosses, all of which were hit for 4, 30 runs were scored, the Australians were ahead of the clock and the whole atmosphere and tempo of the game had changed. 'We must take the current when it serves or lose our ventures.' After lunch, two overs of Compton's produced 29 runs, the need for a strong 'outpost line' to save the 4s being neglected.

XVIII — It is not pleasant to criticise a captain. One would infinitely prefer to praise, but to do so in this case would be foreign to anything like an accurate account of the play. Yardley has over and over again proved himself a most valuable change bowler — he heads the English bowling averages in Test matches with nine wickets for 21 runs each but he did not put himself on until after tea on the last day and he obtained his usual wicket.

XIX — Towards the end of the Australians' first innings we were in a strong position with eight men out for 355 in face of an English total of 496, and only Johnston and Toshack to bat. It would have been sound policy ... indeed the *only* policy to cut off the 4s from Lindwall's bat and to bowl dead on the stumps to Johnston and Toshack, in fact to bowl 'tight'. But this was not done and Australia found themselves only 38 runs behind on the first innings.

XX — England has a side of distinct possibilities — though the bowling is not of a high standard and in some respects not markedly inferior to the Australians, but it lacks punch and needs electric treatment to stimulate and galvanise it. Can a man be found to supply this? One with a sense of a tactical situation who can inspire and enthuse his team and with that quality of leadership which inspires others to do what they otherwise would not... it is essential that English cricket should find such a leader and at once.

XXI — Australia has now won three of the four Test matches played and we must not overlook the fact that in each match they had been handicapped. Lindwall was unable to bowl for most of the first Test match, Miller could not bowl in the second and third, [Sid] Barnes was badly injured while fielding at Old Trafford, and at Leeds Toshack could not bowl in England's second innings owing to a strain. Moreover, Tallon was unfit for the fourth Test. That these accidents have been overcome emphasises Australia's great strength.

Don Bradman's Australians won the fifth and final Test a fortnight later by an innings and finished their 34-game tour undefeated.

The Cricketer (W. H. Hillman & Co., London, 7 August 1948)

The Holy of Holies
Robert Menzies

Few loved cricket or an Ashes battle like Bob Menzies who as Australia's long-time Prime Minister made a habit of being in London in July … at the time of the Lord's Test.

As the [1948] Australians are in England, it's topical to tell you something of that very famous ground known all over the English speaking world as Lord's.

It has a longer history than any other cricket ground in England and for that reason is venerated.

Though my anecdotes may seem flippant, I join in this veneration. As a lover of the greatest of games, I have never entered Lord's without the keenest and most pleasurable emotion and pride.

I had an experience there which epitomised much of what the ground means. It happened, in 1935, when there was a very good team of South Africans in England, and the English standard was unimpressive.

I had gone to Lord's, and was sitting in what is called a 'box'. The only other occupant was an elderly gentleman with a white moustache, who sat bolt upright, looking very stern, watching the rout of the English batsmen.

The South African slow bowler was [X. C.] Balaskas. I thought his bowling rather indifferent and not at all in the class of [Arthur] Mailey or [Clarrie] Grimmett, but he was certainly getting the English wickets. Knowing 'the rules', I did not say a word for an hour. But at the end of that time, about three wickets had fallen, and while we were waiting for a new batsman to come in, I turned around and said: 'I hope you'll excuse me, sir, addressing a remark to you, but how do you explain this frightful collapse?'

He turned round, looked me up and down, and said: 'It's perfectly simple, sir. There are not enough gentlemen in the team!'

There are several extraordinary things about that ground. The pitch runs between the Pavilion and what is called the 'nursery end'. There is a slight slope across the ground and one side of the pitch is actually a couple of inches or so higher than the other side.

Why not regrade it, you say?

The answer is that this would be blasphemy, so well understood is it that the pitch has always sloped down from one side to the other.

This slope, of course, means that a straight up and down bowler, bowling from the nursery end, will come in from leg and if bowling from the Pavilion end will turn the ball back from the off.

In addition, there is the business of the sightboard. We are all familiar with sightboards at each end of the major grounds, so that a batsman can see the bowler's arm and hand coming over. But there is no sightboard at the Pavilion end of Lord's, because one would interrupt the clear view of the play from the famous Long Room in the Pavilion. As there is a glass door opening from the Long Room into the front of the Pavilion, many a batsman before today has been troubled by the flash of light from the glass.

During the second Test in 1938, a wicket had fallen and [Stan] McCabe went into bat, and took strike at the nursery end. To a batsman standing at the nursery end of the pitch, there is a hotel directly to square leg. It opens onto the street, and also into the cricket ground.

I believe [Ken] Farnes was bowling. He was a beautiful bowler, fast and accurate. He whipped one in, his first to McCabe, and, assisted by the slope, it pitched on the off stump and went away towards leg.

McCabe hardly moved his feet at all. He did not swing his arms, but just turned his body a fraction, while with a flick of his wrist he hit the ball out of the ground, in among the tankards in the hotel!

I was in ecstasies until I suddenly realised that I had witnessed what was practically a violation of all tradition. No man should ever hit a 6 first ball at Lord's!

The best story I have heard about Lord's is one told to me by Neville Cardus. It illustrates how the celebrated British phlegm is reflected perfectly in the Pavilion at Lord's.

Two or three days before war broke out in 1939 there was a cricket match going on at Lord's. Cardus was sitting in the Long Room and at a discreet distance from him was one of the veteran inhabitants of the room.

A British workman walked into the room with a sack, stepped across to the bust of Dr W. G. Grace, lifted it from its pedestal, put it into the sack, swung it over his shoulder, and walked out.

Cardus followed these proceedings with immense interest. Thereupon the old gentleman, who had also watched them closely, turned to Cardus and said: 'Do you know what that means, sir?'

'No,' said Cardus.

'Sir,' said the old gentleman, 'that means war!'

And, having spoken, resumed his unruffled contemplation of the game.

The famous ground did not even have a properly informative scoreboard; for many years someone had held the right to print scorecards and after the fall of each wicket the boys went around selling the cards for a few pence.

Another memory is of a visit to Lord's in 1936, I went out to see the Eton and Harrow match, and having read *The Hill* when I was very young, I decided I was a supporter of Harrow and wore a cornflower in my buttonhole.

To my astonishment, no-one seemed particularly interested

in the game, except a few people near the Pavilion. Carriages were drawn up all round the ropes, with parties on top. Red-faced, white-moustached, retired British colonels were there, surrounded by their families, and with hampers tactically disposed, with gold-foiled bottles protruding from them. A few ladies strolled around in summer frocks, carrying parasols.

I went and sat with some fine old boys near the Pavilion. We seemed to be the only people watching the play. I remember it well, because young P. M. Studd, a good cricketing name, was off-driving with great violence. This really intrigued the experts with whom I was sitting, because nobody had been seen off-driving like that for years.

I've seen matches on other grounds in England, too, and here are a couple of stories of the Nottingham Test of 1938 I'd like to share.

It was in that match that I had the luck to watch what I always regard as the greatest innings I have ever seen. I have Don Bradman's authority for saying that it was quite possibly the greatest innings ever played.

It was an innings by Stan McCabe. Two or three wickets had fallen fairly cheaply in the Australian innings on the previous afternoon. The dust was a little inclined to 'pop' on a wicket, which had originally been dead and the wicket was at last 'doing something'.

McCabe, who was never able to cultivate a dour outlook on cricket, batted as if he had had the good fortune to run into the picnic match against the jockeys and trainers.

Farnes was bowling extremely well, and so was Douglas Wright. Yet McCabe made his own length of every ball.

If it was short on the off side, he square cut it to the boundary ... if it was short on the on side, he belted it past square leg ... if it was well pitched up, he drove it violently past the bowler ... if it was a bit shorter than that, he lifted it to the outfield, so that it went over the ropes on the first hop ... if it was fast, and outside the off stump, he leaned back in the most incredible fashion and late cut it to the boundary.

He made over 200 in as many minutes. In London they were reading in the evening papers that at a certain stage McCabe was 202 not out and they all thought it was a misprint for 102 not out, the pace was so tremendous.

It was really the most complete exhibition of batting that I can imagine. I found myself wishing that the cricketing world had engaged slow-motion cinematographers to reproduce it all, because I am sure that, if it had been recorded, it would have been better coaching material than anything else one can contemplate. [Bradman later told McCabe he would have been proud to have played an innings like that. − ed.]

I have another story about that Nottingham match. Australia's slow bowlers in that match were Bill 'Tiger' O'Reilly and 'Chuck' Fleetwood-Smith and they could not succeed in turning the ball half an inch.

At the tea adjournment I went down from where I had been sitting with 'Plum' Warner and a few other MCC people, and greeted the Tiger with friendly derision.

'Tiger,' I said, 'I always understood you were a spin bowler.'

Tiger drew himself up, looked at me for a moment and said: 'Spin bowler! Do you know what that wicket is like? It's just as if somebody had dug a trench, put in three feet of cow dung and laid two feather mattresses on top of it.'

I have had a good deal of experience in dealing with crowds and of excitement of one kind and another. But really, I think the most dramatic moment, for any man who loves cricket is that one which just falls as a Test match opens.

Picture it to yourself. Imagine that you are sitting there on the morning of the opening day of a vital Test against England. The players have finished their practice hits and have left the ground. The captains have tossed, the fielding side has come out and the two opening batsmen have walked out and taken their places.

Silence falls over perhaps 80,000 people in the 20 seconds that elapse between the setting of the field, the slow walk back of the opening fast bowler and the delivery of the first ball. Then there is a universal sigh as that first ball is played back along the middle of the pitch. That is a great moment, because it is full of suspense. And I have always believed there can be no dramatic quality without suspense!

Robert Menzies was Australia's longest-running Prime Minister. Stan McCabe's epic 232, one of the most celebrated of all Ashes knocks, included a 6 from the bowling of Ken Farnes, but he was on 62, rather than 0 at the time. However, he did hit it from the first ball of an over after a wicket (Jack Badcock) had fallen in the previous over, which may have confused the cricket-loving Menzies – given he was writing 10 years after the event.

Sporting Life (Associated Newspapers, Sydney, 1948)

The Fiercest of Battles
Jack Ryder

From the time he witnessed England's famous one-wicket win at
Melbourne in the New Year Test of 1908, future captain-to-be
Jack Ryder was gripped by the atmosphere of Ashes combat.

The first time Victor Trumper batted for Australia in 1899 he made a duck. Don Bradman was only marginally more successful in his debut in 1928 but, as with champions in all walks of life, they soon made up for the disappointment.

Both made centuries against England in their second Tests: Trumper at Lord's, Bradman at Melbourne. What better introductory theme to the battles between England and Australia than to highlight the pair who, for me, are the greatest Australian batsmen to pull on a green cap.

England and Australia. Other cricketing countries should take no offence if these matches for the Ashes take precedence in our minds over any others. I, and Australian cricket followers, do not say West Indies, India, South Africa, Pakistan and New Zealand provide any less excitement but something extra is always tugging at an Australian's heartstrings when it is England as the foe.

Sixty-four years ago I played in a match, a Victor Trumper benefit game, with all the great names of Australian cricket present. In the previous seven Tests between England and Australia, rain had produced draws in two and England had won the other five.

'Monty' Noble was captain of one of these teams, Clem Hill skipper of the other – five years earlier I had seen that pair together with Trumper, [Warwick] Armstrong, [Charlie] Macartney and others lose by one wicket, one of the most exciting matches of all time, in Melbourne. England, needing 282 to win, had a great start from [Fred] Fane and Hobbs but, even so, when the last wicket pair came together England still needed 39. Of all people, that great bowler S. F. Barnes, who averaged eight with the bat in his career, hit a best ever 38 not out, despite Monty Noble's bowling changes and field placings.

From that moment England and Australia was the fierce battle, fierce and fair on the field, and friendly off the arena. It has always been a keen atmosphere, nerve-wracking at times.

Having watched Jack Hobbs in that earlier game, I later came to respect him as England's finest player of all in every type of conditions. Superb on uncovered pitches, he made more than 500 runs in my first Test series (in 1920) … and that in a five-match rubber where England did not win a match! It was a tragedy that he couldn't play an innings against us in 1921 in England but he was back again in magnificent form in the 1924–25, 1926 and 1928–29 series, averaging more than 50 an innings each summer.

Herbert Sutcliffe was a very good partner for him, a fine player in his own right, and it must have been most comforting for him to have Jack Hobbs at the other end.

The best off-side player I have ever seen was Wally Hammond. In the end we used to try and tie him down on the leg side but he was such a great player that he could overcome any tactical ploys of this kind. The one demerit mark with Wally was his captaincy which I always thought to be no better than ordinary.

Players like the Gilligan's [Arthur and Harold], Bob Wyatt and Percy Chapman were the most charming of men whilst being hard

THE KING OF COLLINGWOOD: Jack Ryder (centre) with fellow 1926 tourists Jack Gregory and Arthur Richardson (no relation to Vic).

competitors on the field and Frank Woolley was one of the best all-rounders ever: useful bowler, hardhitting batsman and brilliant slip. Of the left-hand orthodox bowlers, I must give the accolade to Wilfred Rhodes. He was a wonderful bowler with great control and possessed of more spin, in my opinion, than either Hedley Verity or [Jack] 'Farmer' White.

Of the Australians who graced the cricket fields from the turn of the century, Bradman and Trumper are at the top of my list, with Macartney and [Stan] McCabe joining them in the top four. Bradman and Trumper were different types, Trumper like a nice smooth piece of machinery, Bradman magnificent in his strokeplay and a delight to watch for thousands upon thousands he pulled through the turnstiles, Don was the finest captain I watched in the pre-war period.

There will always be comparisons between Warwick Armstrong and Don as captains — Warwick was a hard man, a bit too hard at times with both administrators and players. Both countries have had some fine bowling combinations — for Australia [Clarrie] Grimmett and [Bill] O'Reilly were a wonderful pair of differing types, though each had pinpoint control. Arthur Mailey was completely different in style — the last of the real spinners, with the ball fairly buzzing out of his fingers ... and what a great and lovable character he was! English cricket followers may disagree, but to me, their greatest ever bowling combination to come to Australia was Barnes and [Frank] Foster. Everyone has their golden era of cricket and their own ideas on the game and its stars. We all share the same love of the game and the England and Australian players taking part in this 1977 Jubilee Series will share the same heartbreaks and triumphs as others over the hundred years of friendly cricketing warfare.

Seventeen of Jack Ryder's 20 Tests were at Ashes level where he averaged 44 with the bat and 48 with the ball. He captained Australia in the 1928–29 Ashes summer and was the oldest living Australian Test cricketer, at 87, at the 1977 Centenary Test in his hometown Melbourne.

Cricket '77 (Test & County Cricket Board, London, 1977)

True Grit Down Under
Frank R. Foster

One of England's foremost amateurs before the Great
War explains what it's like to first visit the Antipodes.

We played many times in temperatures of 108 [42°C] in the shade. An Englishman gains a lot of good things in Australia. For instance, he gains the Australians' brogue, the power to kill — and the power to perspire.

When I opened the hotel door one bright and sunny (Melbourne) morn, the heat knocked me back into the hotel bar. The following morning I again opened the hotel door, but, as I have a strong will, I went through the bar as a passenger, and out of the buffet entrance.

FAREWELL: Frank Foster on the eve of the 1911–12 tour, which he and his new ball partner Sydney Barnes were to dominate.

The heat outside was not so bad as the heat of the hotel bar, but before I had gone many yards I had finished perspiring.

There is a limit to one's perspiration, and after you have been in Australia for a few days you soon discover the limit and you feel as fit as a racehorse trained to the minute.

The dry heat of Australia is perfectly exquisite when you get used to it … the hot weather at home in 1911 paved the way for my appreciation of the hot climate of Australia.

There is one thing which is *dead certain*. The Australian understands the full meaning of the word 'grit'. To see you, my dear Australian cricketers, fighting like blazes with your backs to the wall, is the sight of a lifetime. To see you fighting against tremendous odds, as you did in that third Test match at Adelaide, in 1912, is wonderful. I take off my hat, every time, to each man who assisted the Australian cricket eleven to amass that magnificent total of 476 in the second innings.

You were facing a first-innings deficit of 368, you were handicapped by an accident to [Vernon] Ransford (the writer being the unfortunate cause); you were further handicapped by [Victor] Trumper's injured knee (the writer *not* being the cause) and you were handicapped further still by the England bowlers having their tails 'well in the air' and yet you glued your noble backs to the wall and you fought the finest battle it has ever been my good fortune to see on any cricket ground.

At one period of your second innings, we, the English XI (it is no secret) were beginning to get the 'wind-up'. If Clem Hill had not been caught by a wonderful catch (by Bill Hitch), when that great batsman had made 98, we (England) would most certainly have lost more than three wickets in gathering the runs required to win.

The Australian is rather similar to the American. When he, the Australian, is talking to you he yawns and drawls, but between each yawn and drawl he has 'got you', searched you, summed you up and 'placed you'. If he yawns for long at you — he has picked your brains as well.

His 'power of suggestion' is great, too great for the average Englander. Stop him drawling, stop him yawning, and eliminate that society 'small chat'. Do that, and you have laid the foundation for a lifelong friendship.

One of the most outstanding in England's 4-1 Ashes victory in 1911–12, all-rounder Frank Foster excelled with 32 wickets with his left-arm in-swingers. He formed one of the great combinations of all with the masterly Sydney Barnes. In the keenly contested third Test in Adelaide, he took six wickets for the game, including five for 33 in Australia's first innings and scored 71, batting at No. 6.

Cricketing Memories, Frank R. Foster (The London Publishing Co., London, 1930)

HE LOVED CRICKET: Sir Robert Menzies with Sir Donald Bradman and Ted Dexter at the 1962-63 P.M's match at Manuka.

9
Warnie

Warnitude
Gideon Haigh

He possessed the best pause cricket has ever known
and the most ripping leg break of them all ...

For Shane Warne, the walk back was a social occasion. If it wasn't the umpire, it was the captain, a fielder or an opponent. Anything to add a little spice to the contest, a little theatre to the event, to enhance the sense of ease, command and imminent opportunity. All the while, Warne would also be unconsciously rolling the ball from his right hand into his left, savouring the physical sensations of imparting and experiencing spin, the muscle and metacarpal memory. Most spinners do something similar.

Muthiah Muralidaran whizzes the ball inside a cupped hand, as though to give nothing away; Daniel Vettori gives the ball an almost neurotically tiny twist, like he is winding it up; Stuart MacGill's trademark is an obsessive gimballing of the wrist, as if to ensure the joint's looseness. Warne rotated the ball from hand to hand languidly, voluptuously, like somebody feeling warm sand run through their fingers. It was as amiable and intimate as a friendly handshake.

BRAVE: Shane Warne never made a Test century, but he played some magnificent down-the-list hands, none better than at Edgbaston when he all but triggered one of the great comeback Ashes victories of all with a gutsy 42 on Sunday, 7 August 2005. *Patrick Eagar/Australian Cricket Summer Guide*

As Warne rounded his disc, his demeanour began to change. He did not switch on – Warne was always 'on'. No, he switched the rest of the game off, brought all the activity on the field into himself. There was a pause. It was the best pause cricket has ever known: pregnant, predatory. It was this pause that Fanny Rush chose to capture for Warne's portrait in the Long Room at Lord's. Warne looks keenly out of the painting – down the wicket, as it were, straight back into the observer's eyes. The gaze is rock-steady. The body is a study in relaxed readiness. The ball is hovering, preparatory to dropping back into his hand. You begin to wonder. What's going on in there? What's next? Most bowlers at the top of their run are thinking about what they might bowl. Warne's pause was as much about letting you wonder what he might bowl. To quote one of his best bowling mottos: 'Part of the art of bowling spin is to make the batsman think something special is happening when it isn't.'

More than any other game, cricket involves a kind of catechism – a proposition and a reply. There is the ball the bowler lets go; there is the ball the batsman receives. The same ball to two different batsmen can draw profoundly different responses and consequences; the same ball released from different hands at different stages of a game likewise. Warne let us see this maybe more clearly than any other bowler. There was a leg break, *then* there was a leg break from Shane Warne. To all obvious intents and measurements they might be identical – spin, arc, deviation. But one was simply a delivery, the other increasingly invested with what we might call Warnitude: a cognisance of the science, skill, lore and legend surrounding the bowler.

I am exaggerating here, because nobody has been capable of bowling a leg break like Warne. But what I wish to convey is that the delivery – and indeed the whole introductory choreography – were invested with an additional dimension by the identity of the bowler.

On Warne, Gideon Haigh (Simon & Schuster, London, 2012)

A Flaming Genius
David Lloyd

It was back to spin school for Shane Warne in 2009
as part of a feature for Sky Sports in England.

To Shane the art of leg spin came so ridiculously naturally that he makes a mockery of his competition. When, during his initial summer with Sky in 2009, he did a spin-bowling demonstration at a break in the Oval Test, he did so after borrowing a pair of shorts and shoes from Michael Clarke. He must have had five fags before he went out into the middle, chain-smoking one after another. 'I 'ope it goes okay,' he said. 'Don't wanna mess it up.'

He hadn't bowled anywhere since last Pancake Tuesday at the IPL [Indian Premier League] and was accompanied for the feature by two of our young English leg spinners, Will Beer, of Sussex and Somerset's Max Waller, their limbs loose towards the end of their seasons.

When Warne chats away as he does, the camera is his own; he has as much presence as a commentator as he did as an international performer. He knows when to look and when to look away, when to make his point and when to keep quiet.

And just as in the middle, he knows how to milk the big moments, with that inherent sense of timing. This particular afternoon Nasser [Hussain], who was hosting the live feature, threw him the ball in real Nasser style, as if throwing down the gauntlet to an old nemesis for the final time. 'C'mon then, show us one,' he said, abruptly, not long after he had warned the TV audience that this Aussie, fast approaching 40, had not bowled for several months.

Well, blow me if Warne didn't rip this flippin' leg spinner three feet. With no warm-up, no practice deliveries, his very first ball produced that trademark fizzing sound through the air.

'Ah, pretty good that,' Warne said. 'Don't think I'll bother with another.'

The jaws on these two young kids just dropped. They are two

nice young leg spinners, who can both give the ball a pleasant little spin, but Warnie absolutely tore his one ball. That was enough to confirm to anyone what we already knew — he's a flaming genius.

The World According to Bumble: Start the Car,
David Lloyd (HarperCollins, London, 2010)

Strutting Rarefied Air
Mike Atherton

No-one was more tormenting or intimidating
than Shane Keith Warne … especially if an
Englishman happened to be 22 yards away.

Shane Warne revitalised the art of leg spin when it was in danger of dying and then he mastered it. Often you would see him go through his repertoire in a single over, gradually varying the amount of side and over-spin on the ball, before throwing in a flipper and a googly for good measure. Warne had the full armoury; it always amazed me, in contrast, that after a career as a professional leg spinner, Ian Salisbury never added a flipper to his repertoire. It was like being a fast bowler without a bouncer. Apart from [Muthiah] Muralidaran, Warne was also the biggest spinner of the ball, and the most accurate; it was a deadly combination.

On top of his ability, he was by far the smartest bowler that I played against. His close catchers — Ian Healy, Mark Taylor and Mark Waugh — were his extra eyes and ears, but he could usually work out a batsman's weakness without much help. In the second innings at Lord's, for example, in 2001, I took guard on middle stump. Warne quickly worked out that I had exposed my leg stump and he attacked me behind my legs, eventually bowling me. In the next match, at Trent Bridge, I took a leg-stump guard to protect against that line of attack and Warne quickly switched to bowling outside off stump, making me reach for the ball. He soon spun one past my outside edge and I was adjudged caught behind.

He knew instinctively which batsmen to goad. I never saw him say much to Sachin Tendulkar, the only batsman who made him look ordinary, but he was always ready with some choice words to batsmen whom he suspected he could rattle. In the second innings at Trent Bridge in 2001, Warne constantly baited Mark Ramprakash who looked eager to attack him. 'Come on Ramps, you know you want to.'

'That's the way Ramps, keep coming down the wicket!'

Ramprakash fretted, caught between the desire to attack and waiting to see out the day. Eventually, just before the close, he ran down the wicket, had a mighty heave and Warne had his man.

Warne's variations were easier to pick than, say, Mushtaq Ahmed's, but he was more difficult to play. I liked to use my feet against the spinners, but I found Warne the hardest to come down the wicket to because of the amount of drift he used to get in the air. As a result, when I came down the wicket to him, I felt unbalanced, as though my head was too far to the off side of the ball. Of course, being marooned in your crease was a short cut to disaster as well. Leg spinners had occasionally attacked around the wicket [Richie Benaud memorably against England in 1961 – ed.] but nobody had bowled a leg-stump line so often before or used the rough outside the right-hander's leg stump as successfully as Warne did.

It was hard enough for good players, so imagine the tangle tailenders got into. Phil Tufnell was constantly in a flap. For a start, Warne spun the ball twice as far as Tufnell, who often looked innocuous in comparison. 'That bloke's making me look crap! He's ruining my career,' Tufnell constantly complained.

To add insult to injury, Warne would have some fun when Tufnell came in to bat. At Melbourne in 1995, Warne continually bowled around the wicket at him, creating such confusion that Tufnell decided the only answer was to sit on the ball as it pitched, which he did, and then he lost his balance and crumpled backwards in a heap. Even the inscrutable David Boon at short leg cracked a smile.

Having witnessed Warne's control, craftiness and competitiveness over a decade or more, having seen him embarrass us on numerous occasions and having watched him raise his game when the stakes were highest, there is no doubt in my mind that he must be one of the greatest bowlers to have played the game. His golden period was 1993–97, before his shoulder gave way. Like Tufnell, I bemoaned the fact that it coincided exactly with the period of my captaincy.

Opening Up, Mike Atherton (Hodder & Stoughton, London, 2003)

'Show Me What You've Got Son'
Ken Piesse

Shane Warne's ability to implement fresh skills within days of having been shown them was extraordinary.

Shane Warne's first indoor practice session at the Adelaide Oval was as important as any in his lifetime in the headlines. 'Show me what you've got son,' said the Cricket Academy's head coach, ex-Ashes tourist Jack Potter. Gripping an old four-piecer, the roly-poly teenager bowled a big leg break, then another and another. Each of them had a hint of curl before ripping sideways and imprinting Potter's hands.

Potter had been told that the new kid with the ready smile and genuine handshake could spin it. But he had no idea how much. Here was a natural who could play for Australia for years.

Every now and again Potter would amble down the wicket to make a subtle suggestion or two. He noted that Warne telegraphed his googly, but it still spun and sharply.

After 15 minutes or so, Potter said: 'That's enough for now, Shane,' and the two chatted expansively, Potter saying how much he liked Warne's leg break. It bounced. It spun. And it also curved.

'But Shane,' Potter said, 'it's also predictable. The best players are going to wait for the bad one and simply pick you off. You need to have something else … an lbw ball. Something which is straighter and quicker … something that will slide. Maybe a toppie, or a flipper … Richie Benaud used to bowl one …'

Potter showed him the flipper, the under-spinning faster ball squeezed from the hand like an orange pip. It had been handed down from generation to generation, Benaud, Bruce Dooland and Clarrie Grimmett three of the beneficiaries. While Potter was a batting specialist, he'd been having fun with the delivery in the nets for years — well before becoming a career coach.

Warne listened with growing fascination at Potter's colourful lingo. Much of it was new to him: flippers, toppies, sliders, back-spinners. He'd hardly heard of any of them. 'They are all deliveries, Shane which can be both attacking and defensive,' Potter said. 'You need to be able to defend yourself, mix things up. Keep 'em guessing.' Warne had missed all the elite junior cricket squads as a teenager. If anything, he was keener on football than cricket. But Potter was unveiling new mysteries which were genuinely compelling and exciting.

The pair had many sessions in the following weeks, Warne frustrated at his initial failure to master the new delivery. His first attempts had seen his flippers rebound against the side of the net, the roof, everything. Exasperated, he told Potter that he doubted if he would ever be able to master it.

But he continued to work assiduously and within days his flipper was landing and zipping through at pace. 'Such is the Warne genius,' said Potter. 'He had the happy knack of being able to absorb the lessons and implement the new skills, far quicker than anyone else I've ever coached. He had such a beautiful personality, too. Still has. He was always the life of the party. I told him once: "Shane don't ever let me catch you smoking."

'Quick as a flash came back his reply, "Jack, you will *never* catch me smoking!"

'And I didn't. Not sure what I would have done if I had. Coaches always have to give themselves a get out clause! Especially with a player like Warnie; you can't afford to say two strikes and you're out. He could have had 10 strikes!' [Ironically shortly after Potter's departure from the Academy, Warne was to be suspended for improper conduct after a trip to Darwin. He headed back to Melbourne and landed almost immediately in Victoria's Sheffield

Shield team, beginning his fast tracking which saw him play Test cricket within 12 months. — *ed.*]

In the months ahead, working with another former Australian, Terry Jenner, Warne was to refine and develop his deadly flipper and truly understand its mechanics.

Warne remains firmly in his debt, however, having introduced a challenging fresh dimension to his game which Warne instinctively knew could make him stand out in any crowd.

Soon Warne was to become the 'Flipperman', mixing his signature leg break from heaven with a faster, flatter one which zeroed onto their stumps while unsuspecting batsmen still had their bat at the top of the downswing.

Shane Warne's career-defining moment came in his old hometown on the final day of the 1992 Christmas Test. And unsurprisingly it was the flipper which sparked the greatest of all bowling careers.

Walking down to the ground from the Hilton hotel that morning — still uncertain of his standing within the team — Warne told wicketkeeper Ian Healy how apprehensive he was about the day ahead. The newspapers were highlighting his unflattering career analysis, saying to survive he simply had to improve, especially bowling on a wearing, fifth day wicket. All his mates were coming to the game. He didn't want to embarrass himself. He realised he was still very much an apprentice. Just 12 months earlier on his Test debut in Sydney he'd been too frightened to even try his googly in case it bounced twice.

The world champion West Indies had made a bold start at a target of 300-plus. Warne was well into his first spell and while he'd been tidy, he was 'one-paced'. Every time he dropped short, Richie Richardson and Phil Simmons would put him away.

Lunch loomed and many in the old Melbourne Cricket Club cigar stand opted to make their way into the Long Room for the roast of the day. As the crowd acknowledged Richardson's half-century, Warne decided it was now or never. He had to do something different. Pausing ever so slightly at the top of his mark, he went through his normal routine, walking several paces before bowling. Instead of another leg break, this one was flatter, a little quicker and full. Richardson sensed the danger and shuffled into line, only for the ball to scuttle past his dead bat and zero into the off stump. There was a pause and then a whoop of delight from Healy. Shane Warne had castled Richie Richardson, the best batsman in the world. The commentators initially called it as a wrong-un, but [Jack] Potter, [Terry] Jenner and Co. knew exactly what had happened. Richardson had been flipped out. It may not have been the Ball of the Century, but it was as important as any wicket in the Warne CV.

More than a decade on and 500 Test wickets later, Warne's signature flipper is now back in his kitbag, reserved only for special occasions. He prefers a slider, another front-of-the-hand delivery, which also curves in and if it hits the seam, sometimes goes the other way like a quick wrong-un.

It's not that he can't bowl the flipper. As weapons go, it's still destructive, but his slider is more economical — and less stressful on his battle-scarred shoulder. It also enables him to build pressure, with fewer 'hit-me' balls.

In Sri Lanka in March [2004], having only just returned to the game after an enforced 12-month absence, Warne amazed even his closest mates by taking 26 wickets in three Tests, including his 500th in the first Test in Sri Lanka's southern citadel of Galle.

He'd told David Hookes during one winter-time practice session indoors with the Victorian squad that it would take him just 20 or so balls to be back to his best after a lay-off. Hookes shook his head in wonderment and that night on his radio show talked about the sheer genius of the man.

In the return short-series against the Sri Lankans in Cairns, Warne was still making the ball rear and spit well into his 36th over, just as he had all those years before during his impromptu first session with his old Academy coach.

Watching from his television easy chair, Potter marvelled at his control and his sheer zest for the game. 'But then again, Shane was something special,' he said, 'always has been … always will be.'

Sunday Mail (Brisbane, October 2004) & Cricket Victoria's
website (www.cricketvictoria.com.au, December 2012)

'Temperamentally Unsuitable'
Ken Piesse

Alongside Keith Miller, Shane Warne remains the best cricketer
never to captain Australia in Tests. Was he a victim of arch
conservatism? Did non-cricket issues ruin his chances?

Shane Warne's running battle with his failing marriage made him
temperamentally unsuitable to captain Australia, according to
Australia's coach John Buchanan.

Warne may have been the matchwinner of his generation but his
stormy off-field relationships often left him sulky and withdrawn
and not the ideal leader of men.

Speaking at the Australian Cricket Society's 2007 annual dinner
in Melbourne on Friday night, Buchanan said Warne could be a good
captain from session to session, but his focus tended to lapse and
he could be almost childlike in the dressing rooms.

'No, I don't think he should have been Test captain,' Buchanan
said. 'He could do it for a session or a couple of sessions, but not
every day, five days in a row. Sometimes he would have stayed up
until 4 a.m. talking through things with [ex-wife] Simone. Once
he felt that was all sorted and he could relax, he was able to then
compartmentalise his game and be the cricketer he was.

'No-one can deny though what a fantastic player and terrific
team man he was.'

Buchanan's volatile relationship with another leg spinner Stuart
MacGill is also to be outlined in his summer release autobiography,
If Better is Possible.

Both Warne and MacGill were among the most vocal against
Buchanan's controversial 'boot camp' outside Brisbane at the start
of last summer. At one stage during a night-time drill, MacGill fell

down a hole and twisted his ankle. When Buchanan enquired if he was all right, MacGill said: 'I'll see you in court.'

With a record of 40 wins and just two losses in Test matches in Australia, Buchanan built a reputation as the outstanding cricket coach in the world.

Buchanan said he was disappointed by constant barbs from detractors like Ian Chappell who steadfastly refused to give Buchanan credit for Australia's world championship ways.

Cricket had moved to another level in recent years and what may have worked 30 years ago in the Chappell era were not always appropriate now.

He said the loss of the Ashes in 2005 may have been averted had fast bowling coach Troy Cooley been assisting Australia's speedsters and not England, 'but many events conspired against us'.

He omitted Michael Clarke from the best Test XI of his seven-year reign, preferring Andrew Symonds at No. 6 and relegating Mike Hussey to 12th man.

John Buchanan's best Test XI:

1. Matthew Hayden
2. Justin Langer
3. Ricky Ponting
4. Mark Waugh
5. Steve Waugh
6. Andrew Symonds
7. Adam Gilchrist
8. Shane Warne
9. Brett Lee
10. Jason Gillespie
11. Glenn McGrath
12th man: Mike Hussey

Sunday Herald-Sun (Melbourne, July 2007)

Taking His Chance
Ken Piesse

Few have given cricket the kiss of life as Shane Warne.

Shane Warne was hosting a party at his million-dollar Brighton Beach property for some old St Kilda teammates when one saw his red Ferrari and said: 'Mate, you've done all right for a fella who used to cart beds!'

Warne stared, suddenly serious. 'I've taken my chance and run with it,' he said. 'Everyone gets a chance at some time. It's a matter of taking it when it comes.'

No longer was Warne the happy-go-lucky, social butterfly who treated cricket as a diversion. He may have been the Chosen One, fast-tracked like no-one before or since and enjoying more than his share of life's luxuries, but he'd deserved it and was grateful. For all his extroverted ways, over-exuberance and good fortune, his commitment, focus and hard work ethic had been absolute.

He may have been blessed with the ability to rip prodigious leg spinners with a flick of a wrist, but it could all have ended prematurely years ago, when thumped on debut by the Indians in Sydney, or more recently after career-threatening operations.

For a roly-poly, hesitant rookie played ahead of his time, Warne's advancement has been as extraordinary as his start. In Auckland earlier this year, he became Australia's all-time Test wicket record-holder, surpassing the feats of his childhood idol Dennis Lillee.

He has made mistakes and has genuine regrets, but few have so consistently exerted such a matchwinning influence or so rejuvenated what seemed to be a lost art.

Challenging convention with his dyed blond hair and liking for custom jewellery, Warne has enlivened cricket with his flamboyance and personality.

He has also showed great courage to bowl and keep bowling, despite the deleterious effect it was having on his body.

Win at all costs it might have been, but had his first captain,

Allan Border, not bowled him into the ground so often, Warne's very best years would surely have extended longer.

For all the warts, millions of cricket fans around the world are privileged to have seen Warne bowl. Without his ability to demoralise, Australia would not today be the reigning World Cup champions.

No-one, not even Dennis Lillee, has intimidated or so consistently confounded opposing batsmen. Like kangaroos dazzled by headlights, opposing batsmen have been powerless to stop his momentum.

A spinner with a fast bowler's psyche, Warne's genius in perfecting a series of menacing, mysterious deliveries like the flipper and the zooter and the spitting leg break others can only dream about has led to a rare celebrity status and levels of adulation unparalleled since the Bradman era.

Before he finishes, body withstanding, he may even become the first to take 500 Test wickets, one of world cricket's previously unobtainable records. Maybe by then even the non-believers will have been converted.

Warne may not be everybody's idea of a national treasure, but without him over the last decade, the game would never have been as irresistible or diverting. Like a young Don Bradman who lifted spirits during the Depression with his fabulous runmaking feats, Warne has given cricket a kiss of life likely to endure for years.

Warne took his 500th wicket in Galle, Sri Lanka in 2004.

The Complete Shane Warne, Ken Piesse (Penguin Viking, Melbourne, 2000)

Below the Belt
Adam Gilchrist

Not everyone appreciated Shane Warne's on-field persona.

Imade two centuries that [1998–99] season, including a very satisfying 125 against New South Wales at the Sydney Cricket Ground and an equally satisfying 55 against a Victorian team for which Warnie was bowling. He was nowhere near his best but I treated every ball as if it was a hand grenade.

I was on the receiving end of more than just tough bowling from the Victorians. It was a tight game, and after an early collapse [Michael] Hussey, [Simon] Katich and I put together some partnerships. Warnie and [wicketkeeper] Darren Berry were absolutely giving it to me, verbally.

That was not unexpected, but the nature of what they said was extremely hurtful. They were saying, 'Arse-licker, you've only got where you are because you're an arse-licker.' It was playground stuff, but I thought, 'If they're going to sledge me, fine, but why do they have to say that?' I felt it had a lot to do with me being above Chuck [Berry] in the pecking order behind [Ian] Healy. Chuck might have envied me because of that and Warnie was Chuck's best friend. But considering I'd played some [one day] cricket with Warnie now for Australia, it was below the belt.

Later, I fronted Warnie about it. He laughed it off: 'We were only trying to unsettle you.' And I do believe that. The thing about Warnie was he said a lot of things on the field that were consistent with what he saw as legitimate gamesmanship – none of it was personal and he wouldn't hold onto things. But I don't skate across the surface like that and the wound they inflicted took a long time to heal. On reflection, maybe I was over complicating things. Maybe they had no hidden agenda in their verbal barrage and it *was* a tactic to get under my skin and dismiss me cheaply.

Warnie and I would talk about it years later, when we knew there was no residual problem; but at the time it killed me.

True Colours, Adam Gilchrist (Pan Macmillan Australia, Sydney, 2008)

Tough Words at Campbelltown
Terry Jenner

It was a career-turning lecture for a young Shane Warne after his first two Tests produced the unflattering analysis of one for 228.

At the end of that first [Test] season [for Warne], the Australian Cricket Board ran what was called Camp April. Shane came over and stayed with me for a few days. We worked in the nets, talked and then worked again. Shane was such a natural. But everything had come relatively easy to him. He hadn't been forced to make too many sacrifices. Like most kids in their early 20s, he enjoyed a drink and a smoke and the company of his mates.

I felt he needed to lose some weight, get leaner and meaner, which would show his detractors he was serious about his cricket. It would also repay those who had shown a lot of faith in him. I'd decided to give him the big talk before he went back to Melbourne.

He came in with a slab of beer under one arm and with a bottle of Limestone Ridge red and a bottle of St George's red under the other. He asked which bottle I'd prefer. He intended giving the other to Rodney [Marsh] as a token of his appreciation for Rod's efforts. (Rod drank his when Shane took seven-for against the Windies in Melbourne in 1992–93. I've still got mine.)

The carton of beer remained unopened in my little place in Campbelltown and Shane said: 'Are we going to have a beer?'

'No, we're not going to have a beer.'

'What's wrong?'

I said, 'I'm angry Shane,' and launched into my speech, telling him how he hadn't made the necessary sacrifices to be playing for Australia. I didn't want him to make the mistakes that I had. There wasn't a decent wrist spinner, under 35, good enough to be playing.

I wanted him to go home, put his head down and really see how good his best was. He knew that I understood exactly what he was going through. We were so alike in so many ways. Needing to be liked was high on the list.

He looked thoughtful and said: 'You wouldn't want me to lie to you would you?'

'No, I wouldn't, Shane.'

'Well, I can't promise I'm going to go home and do something about it.'

'If you don't, Shane, you might lose some support. A lot of people have faith in you.'

Next morning in the car heading to the airport, not much was being said. 'Do you mind if I light up a cigarette?' he asked.

'Why do you ask, Shane? You've never asked before. You've just lit it up.'

'I won't have one if you don't want me to.'

'Shane, if you want to have a cigarette at eight o'clock in the morning, that's your choice. I'd rather you had some breakfast — not because that's what I do, but because it's better for you.'

There I was being a pain in the arse again.

He had his cigarette and there was silence again until we hopped out. He thanked me and caught his plane.

Two weeks later there was a phone call from Brigitte, Shane's Mum, in Melbourne. 'I don't know what you said, Terry, but it's working,' she said. 'He is running every morning bar Tuesday when he goes to golf. He has already lost four kilograms.'

I thanked her for calling and said we'd have to see how long his fitness regime lasted. He had Merv Hughes' wedding coming up. That would be a challenge. But he was to have only one beer and otherwise drank nothing but water.

He trained with a football mate of his, Craig Devonport from St Kilda and went from strength to strength. It was no coincidence that his bowling grew in stature every day as he became fitter and stronger. He got more 'body' into his action and in a very short time, went from being a very good leg-spin bowler to a great leg-spin bowler.

Terry Jenner was mentor and mate to Shane Warne, who always insisted there was 'daylight' between T. J. and everyone else when it came to the world's finest leg-spin coaches. Jenner also triggered the rise of Bryce McGain into Australia's Test team in 2009.

T. J. Over the Top: Cricket, Prison & Warnie, Terry Jenner with Ken Piesse (Information Australia, Melbourne, 1999)

Spooking the Poms
Ian Healy

It was the ball of the century, Shane Warne's
first in Ashes cricket, at Old Trafford in 1993.

The big plus we had in '93 that we hadn't had four years before was Shane Warne. When we arrived, the Poms were bracing themselves for an assault from [Craig] McDermott and [Merv] Hughes, but dismissed Warnie on the basis that he was young and blond and leg spinners don't succeed in England anyway. When he struggled in our opening first-class game, after Graeme Hick smashed a big hundred for Worcestershire, the wise old cricket heads around England sat back and nodded as one — Warne wouldn't be a factor. Then Shane came on in his first Ashes Test and knocked over Mike Gatting immediately with one of the best leg breaks ever seen in Test cricket anywhere and everything changed.

As Gatting stumbled off, a stunned buzz enveloped Old Trafford. Into our huddle from wide mid-on came Merv Hughes, who from his angle couldn't see what the delivery had done. He had no idea what all the fuss was about.

'What'd it do?' he asked.

'Pitched off and hit off,' I replied, poker-faced.

'Oh, is that all,' he said, but soon he was back, having been told a very different story elsewhere.

'Heals, it might have done a bit,' he said.

'Merv, it pitched off the wicket and hit the off stump!' Which is about what it did, but only after starting on the off-stump line and then drifting viciously so it pitched around six inches outside the leg stump. Then it buzzed back to take the off bail.

Warnie hadn't played in the Texaco Trophy matches which preceded the Test series, which we won 3-0, not because there was any grand strategy to leave him out, but simply because at that stage in his career he wasn't a regular in our one-day team. We still knew he was going to be a threat in the Test matches. However, the way Gatting reacted when he was bowled, as if he'd seen some sort of ghost, built up a sudden mystique that Shane didn't let diminish for the rest of the series; he thus became a very, very lethal weapon. The Poms were spooked.

Hands and Heals, the Autobiography, Ian Healy with Robert Craddock (HarperSports, Sydney, 2000)

Enter Hulk Hogan
Ken Piesse

Shane Warne was expecting an immediate
promotion after a successful summer of
League cricket in England in 1989.

Keith Warne barely recognised his son on arrival at Tullamarine airport in early September. Warne's indulgences overseas had seen his weight balloon by 12 kilograms, most of it, his father thought, to his face. His mates at St Kilda were equally amazed. 'I thought he was Hulk Hogan the wrestler and someone had brought him out here for a PR exercise to wrestle a few of us in the bar,' said Warren Whiteside. 'He was huge, like a beached whale,' said Laurie Harper. 'He had all this blond hair and was simply very, very fat. I thought, "Who the hell is this bloke?" Graffy [coach Shaun Graf] wouldn't let him train until he'd run two laps of the [Albert Park] Lake.'

'It was normal to do the Lake once,' said his club and UK team-mate Rick Gough, 'but anyone who'd played up or according to Graffy needed disciplining, had to do two. Warnie had stacked on the weight in our time away, probably a couple of stone, especially in the face area. It was unbelievable.'

'He hadn't exactly been on a tremendous diet while he was over there,' said David Johnstone, 'but at the same time I've never seen a guy come back from England, whether batting or bowling, such an improved player.'

Buoyed by his success in England, Warne had told Gough on the plane home how keen he was to do well in the new season. 'I want to play ones,' he said. It was a particularly wet autumn and only two weeks remained before the first selection. The new-look Warne had hardly had a bowl, other than in a lighthearted practice game on the malthoid at Seaford, a game in which he lifted ex-Saints spinner, 52-year-old Graham Smith, out of the park and over the nearby railway line.

He hoped that six maiden second XI games earlier in the year combined with his efforts in England, would be taken into account. Come the Thursday night before the first game, he was relaxing with teammates when selection chairman Geoff Tamblyn read out the sides. He wasn't in the ones. And he wasn't in the twos, either.

As the third XI was announced, he was in a daze and hardly heard his name. He was stunned. Frankston's Shaun Walker, one of the newcomers to the thirds, was sitting next to Warne at the time: 'Graffy told everyone to go into team meetings. The firsts went upstairs, the seconds into their group and the thirds somewhere else. Warnie couldn't believe he was in the thirds. Graffy pulled him aside and said unfortunately we haven't got room for a leg spinner in the seconds. I don't think it made him feel any better. Having just come back from a season in England, he was devastated.'

Years later, Graf conceded it was more of a disciplinary move to help motivate Warne to become more tunnel-visioned and professional about his cricket — and to encourage him to lose a truckload of weight.

The St Kilda thirds were drawn to play miles away, against

Ringwood at Jubilee Park No. 2. The thought of playing back with his old schoolboy mates at East Sandringham seemed a more pleasurable option. 'Graffy probably didn't realise what Shane had done in England,' said Gough, who was named in the seconds.

'Shane thought he was better than that. He'd expected to at least have started in the seconds.'

Warne never got to play in the thirds as the opening two rounds were washed out. When the season officially started on 21 October, St Kilda had re-selected its sides and Warne was in the seconds, under the captaincy of Stephen Maddocks.

'In one game against University, we had been beaten and had to go out and bowl again,' said Maddocks. 'It was a bitterly cold day and Shane was complaining about how he couldn't feel the ball in the fingers. I just said, "If you haven't got the $#&%ing ball in the hand, you're not going to get any wickets!" That was it, he never again as far as I know complained about the cold again!'

Maddocks said Warne was 'no different' to any other 18 or 19-year-old. 'He dipped his head in a jar of peroxide and was a bit of a lair, but he was easy to captain and really wanted to learn ... he also had a fierce [competitive] streak. One night training had been washed out. We'd run the Lake and Peter Chambers and I were doing some extra work on the main oval, jogging the ends and striding out on the straights. Shane joined us. It was a muggy night and he was hating it. We said to him how he needed to improve his fitness. It was a fairly solid session and he moaned and groaned but we stuck with it and he was still there at the end. He didn't drop off. He just kept going. It showed a deal of mental toughness. It was a good sign that he wanted to go on and really do it.'

Several weeks later, after the Saint's No. 1 leg spinner James Handscomb injured his hand, Warne was named for his senior debut, against Northcote at Westgarth St.

'He'd improved so dramatically over just six months,' said Saints and ex-Sheffield Shield opener David Robinson. 'All of a sudden, you couldn't hit him. He had the flight right, the trajectory, the line and length and from there just worked on his variety. I walked out of the nets one night and said to someone: "Gee, I can't get to him."

You'd go to drive and the ball wouldn't quite be there. He was really zipping the ball around.'

Wicketkeeper Jason Jacoby says Warne's rise from thirds to firsts in just eight weeks may have been fortuitous, but as one of the keenest at training, he demanded and deserved an opportunity. 'When he came back from England, he'd had a pretty good time,' Jacoby said. 'He'd seen the improvement in his game. Maybe it was a bit of a kick going down to the thirds. He may have thought, "What am I doing here?" Perhaps a little bit of the surfie was coming out in him. He didn't have much money as well. He was a little bit lost.

'I remember him thinking about giving the game away and going back to East Sandy because he wasn't getting anywhere. He thought Graffy would play only one slowie in the firsts. But Jimmy Handscomb did his tendons in his finger and Warnie took full advantage of his chance.'

Jacoby said Warne had always been able to turn the ball sharply, without having the necessary variations. 'It really was just the leg spinner and maybe a toppie that he wasn't too sure why it didn't in fact turn. But when he went to England he was bowling all the time. He came back and his accuracy was still there and he'd worked out his toppie and his leg spinner. It made an unbelievable difference. He went from being just a second XI player to a very good first XI player. He was always as keen as mustard. He couldn't wait to get down to the ground.'

According to Johnstone, Warne was a '200 per cent better bowler' and while he had only one over on his senior debut against Northcote, he made an immediate impression in his second match, against Rodney Hogg's Waverley-Dandenong, taking 3-31, from 13,1 overs in a Saturday-Sunday game at Shepley Reserve.

'We could see he had heaps of ability,' said Graf, 'but we didn't really know how good he could be until one day at Dandenong, when he really spun it and with good control. We had them in a bit of trouble and Hoggy had just come in. Warnie beat him three times in a row with big-spinning leg breaks which pitched on leg and went outside off. Hoggy turned around to me (at slip) and said,

"Why isn't this bloke in the Test side? He's already a better bowler than Sleepy [Peter Sleep]!"'

That week, writing in the Melbourne *Truth*, Hogg said he'd just seen a kid who could take 500 Test wickets. The *Truth* sacked him on the spot for being ridiculous. Hogg was 208 wickets out – Warne ended his Test career with 708 wickets, not a mere 500!

Warne, Sultan of Spin, Ken Piesse (Modern Publishing Group, Baxter, 1995)

What They Said About Warnie

'You will never see the like of him again in terms of his character and ability. He was a complete and utter one-off.' — David Lloyd, 2009

'Durability is a trait that has made Shane what he is. Physically he has suffered a number of injuries. Emotionally he has been put through the wringer many times. He has played under four captains without being given the chance to lead his country. He has had three Australian coaches who have all had different approaches. Yet throughout his long service, he has constantly sought ways to improve his unique skills.' — John Buchanan, 2008

'They weren't too keen on the idea of each other, much as a lair at the back of the class and the head prefect can't quite reach mutual approval. Warne was often too self-indulgent and undisciplined for Gilchrist's taste; Gilchrist too clean cut and conformist for the man he replaced as vice-captain.' — Malcolm Knox, 2009

'Warnie is so unpredictable. When you think he'll be cold he's warm and sometimes viceaversa. But when he's with you as he was with me that week, he's truly with you and can lift you up and make you feel like a million bucks.' — Adam Gilchrist on the week of his Test debut, 1999

'Shane spun the ball prodigiously and because of the revolutions on it, he managed to get it to dip in to your pads quite alarmingly at times. No-one did that as much as him.' — Mark Ramprakash, 2009

'Shane was bowling to [NZ's] Andrew Jones at the Basin Reserve in a Test in 1993. The ball was short and Jones went back onto his stumps and pulled it for 4. Warne got the ball back, walked past me and said very quietly: "He thinks he can pick me." He bowled a couple of orthodox leggies and then he said, "This is it." Sure enough, he bowled a top spinner, Jones went back onto his stumps but this time the ball shot through about a yard faster, the bat was nowhere near and Jones was out lbw, hit below the knee-roll. It was brilliant bowling by a master spinner.' — umpire Steve Dunne, 1995

'To drop Shane Warne from the Test side was the toughest decision I have ever had to make.' — Australian coach Geoff Marsh, 1999

'Warnie is one of the best bowlers I have faced. His aggression is one thing which makes him so successful. He's willing to try different things even if he gets hit for the odd 4 or 6. He's always thinking and is always at you. You can never feel as if you're completely on top of him.' — Mark Waugh, 2004

'I have seen a lot of people come out against him with a plan and when it doesn't work they are gone. The South Africans the other day were like kangaroos caught in the headlights. They didn't know what to do.' – Ian Healy, 1997–98

'Warne fizzed them off the pitch, spun them out of footmarks, tortured the batsmen by bowling around the wicket and into the rough. Each ball was a test in itself, a battle for survival. Warne wheeled down 42 overs for the innings and took three for 64, not spectacular figures. Yet his greatness was evident.' – Martin Blake in the Melbourne *Age,* 1997

'Shane Warne has made a goose of himself. Again. Swaying on the [Trent Bridge] balcony outside the players' rooms, waving a stump high above his head. He then appeared to give the crowd the thumb as he left. His provocative and immature actions have sullied a great victory.' – Patrick Smith in the Melbourne *Age,* 1997

'I had no problem with it [Warne's behaviour at Trent Bridge]. It was just exuberance.' – Australia's captain Mark Taylor, 1997

'I had to make up a bit of ground, but I made it with one finger hanging on underneath. I must admit, I did "erupt" off the turf, both arms pumping the air in absolute jubilation. And I reckon Shane ran the fastest he has ever run to congratulate a teammate on taking a catch off his bowling.' – David Boon on his spectacular, diving one-hander at short leg which clinched Warne's memorable hometown hat-trick in 1994–95

'To his mates at the Australian Institute of Sport in Adelaide in 1990, Shane Warne was the life and soul of the party, a champion bloke, a lovable larrikin who lives life to the full. Those who ran the Cricket Academy there were not so taken. Some of them found the 21-year-old leg spinner a pain and a problem. He was overweight, he gambled, he partied too late, he drank too much beer, he smoked like a chimney, he didn't train hard enough and he had an attitude problem.' – author Paul Barry, 2008

'He had a gift from God and I felt if his talents could be harnessed, he could be anything.' – Terry Jenner, 1999

MENTOR: Terry Jenner with his star protégé Shane Warne.

10
You Can Quote Me

'Give your hand to cricket and it will take you on the most fantastic journey, a lifetime journey both on and off the field.' — Tony Greig, 2012

'I find it difficult to describe just how pissed off I felt at the end of that day. I don't ever remember feelings as bad after a cricket match in the whole of my career.' — Matthew Hoggard after England's infamous second innings collapse in Adelaide, 2006—07

'At one point Justin Langer [the substitute fieldsman] sledged me. "Look," I said, "I don't mind this lot chirping me, but you've just come on. You're just the fucking bus driver of this team, so you get back on the bus and get ready to drive it back to the hotel tonight." Even Mark Waugh gave me a little smile after that one. I think he found it amusing.' — a pumped-up Nasser Hussain on his way to an Ashes-best 207 at Edgbaston, 1997

'Geoff Lawson was about the only player I didn't get on with. He was a good bowler but on the field as a bloke … well, perhaps that's better left unsaid.' — Graham Gooch, 1996

SHEER TALENT: Andrew Symonds was a once-in-a-lifetime entertainer and frontline member of an all-star team in the 2000s, his fielding sublime and batting always belligerent. *Patrick Eagar*

'It was an amazing ball. Long after we have all retired, that one delivery will be etched in the memory of everyone who witnessed it.' – Steve Waugh on Shane Warne's 'Ball of the Century', 1993

'I played seven Ashes series against Australia and lost all seven but before every one of them I always went in with the attitude that "we can win this".' – Alec Stewart, 2004

'I never read newspapers, except cricket results.' – The Rolling Stones drummer Charlie Watts, 2001

'Warnie's idea of a balanced diet is a cheeseburger in each hand.' – Ian Healy, 1999

'Wickets are more important than waistline.' – Merv Hughes, 1993

'No, I'm no Pom mate. I'm a fair dinkum Aussie.' – Andrew Symonds, 2006

'Apart from Sir Donald himself, Steve [Waugh] would have to be the most respected and admired cricketer in our history.' – Bill Brown, 2002

'The one who really got up my nose was Steve Waugh who spent the entire series giving out verbals — a bit of a joke really when he was the one bloke wetting himself against the quick bowlers.' — Mike Atherton on the eve of the 1994–95 series

'They are traitors.' — Shane Warne on Anglo-Aussies and fellow graduates of the Australian Cricket Academy Martin McCague and Craig White, 1994

'Not bad for the worst team ever to leave England.' — Mike Gatting on winning the Ashes in Australia in 1986–87

'They can't bat, they can't bowl and they can't field.' — journalist Martin Johnson on the prowess of the 1986–87 touring team shortly before the opening Test in Brisbane, a team which was to win the Ashes!

'I don't care what money I get man — it's the buzz of playing for Australia that's got me.' — Greg Matthews on his debut in 1983

'It will be remembered in 100 years — unfortunately.' — Australian captain Kim Hughes on the 1981 Ashes series

'It was my lot to be an Australian selector during the period of Brian Booth's Test career. In stark contrast to many other players was his expressed appreciation on being given an opportunity to serve his country. But even more impressive was his written acknowledgement, on being dropped from the side, that his omission was expected and justified. What a difference between his attitude and that of another Test player [Jack Fingleton], who after being left out of a touring team [in 1934], spent the rest of his life blaming me and conducting a vendetta against me in his writings. The irony of it was that I wasn't even a member of the selection committee which omitted him.' – Sir Donald Bradman, 1982

'Goochie hadn't used it much and I thought there were a few runs left in it.' – Ian Botham who borrowed teammate Graham Gooch's bat for his miraculous Headingley onslaught in 1981

'Put five [pounds] on for me too mate.' – Rod Marsh at Headingley after his mate Dennis Lillee had put 10 pounds on an *English* win at 500-1 in 1981

'Cricket needs brightening up a bit. My solution is to let the players drink at the beginning of the game, not after. It always works in our picnic matches.' – comedian Paul Hogan, 1982

'Playing against a team with Ian Chappell as captain turns a cricket match into gang warfare.' – Mike Brearley, 1977

'Who's this then? Father Bloody Christmas.' – Jeff Thomson as silver-haired David Steele emerged on his English debut at Lord's in 1975

'Dear Mum, things are looking up. Today I got a half volley in the nets.' – David Lloyd in a letter home during the high-octane 1974–75 tour Down Under

'Thommo was by far the quickest bowler I've ever seen or opposed. Thommo didn't go to any Academy, he just grabbed the ball and wanted to kill some prick. That was as scientific as Thommo got. Before he got injured, we reckoned he was closer to 170 km/h, not 160. He was as far ahead of any other bowler for sheer speed as what Bradman was ahead of all the others for runs.' – Kim Hughes, 2012

'There was quite a deal of money riding on the series from the sponsorship of Benson and Hedges. This led to a serious embarrassment for Ian Chappell during the sixth Test. Ian was approached by [Mike] Denness after the first Test to see if the Australians would split the incentive money, as was the habit in England. Ian put the matter to the vote with the Australian players and it was a unanimous "no" because we wanted to play for keeps. The trouble was Ian didn't get back to Denness and when he was approached by the England captain for his decision as late as the sixth Test, it was a ticklish situation [given Australia's 4-1 lead – ed.]. In a way it was fortunate the tourists had won the last Test [in Melbourne], which meant they had picked up $2000 of the "win" money. This saved Ian a bit of face when he had to say to Denness, "Look, I'm sorry I didn't come back to you, Mike, but our fellows decided they wouldn't split the money." It is highly likely that some of the English players feel a bit cheated about this, but I can assure them our decision was "no splitting" and we would have adhered to that even if we had lost the last five Tests.' – Rod Marsh, 1974–75

'The selectors blundered for sure. If they had been frantic to tie the [1970–71] series they should have played [Bill] Lawry, because with him we would have won the last Test at Sydney.' – Keith Stackpole, 1974

'I've seen people hit by bottles and it makes a bloody mess of them.' – Ray Illingworth on why he led the walk-off in Sydney in 1970–71

'A really good "blue" got under way among the crowd and what with the yelling crowd and the concentrated roar when Jeff Jones began his run up, Australian cricket crowds – for the first time – reminded me of those in India. Jones' odd habit of bowing like a judo wrestler before he starts his approach tickled the fancy of Australian crowds. And they roared approval. It was not unlike the roar of Indian spectators trying to upset a bowler on his approach when a home-side batsman is in the nineties. I hope the Australians did not have similar intentions. When police finally broke up the fight they were roundly booed for spoiling the fun so the MCG crowd at this time resembled more an audience for the Beatles.' – Ken 'Slasher' Mackay, 1965–66

'It's like standing in the middle of a darts match.' – Jim Laker on the 'actions' of several of the Australian bowlers, 1958–59

'The aim of English Test cricket is, in fact, mainly to beat Australia.' – Jim Laker, 1961

'I don't think we'll ever see a better fielding side. Eight of your team ran like stags and threw like bombs.' – Peter May on the 1954–55 Australians

'Remember lad, one day we'll have a fast bowler — and I hope that day isn't too far off.' — Len Hutton to expressman Ray Lindwall during the 1950–51 tour

'England was just out of the war [in 1948] and people were breaking their necks to have fun and forget what had gone past and turn on whatever hospitality they could. Tucker [food] was still rationed over there. England really was in a mood to appreciate a tour by Australia and it made the trip a lot happier for everyone.' — Lindsay Hassett, 1996

'Had every chance he gave been accepted, Bradman's Test average would have been 74.79 rather than 99.94.' — author B. J. Wakley, 1959

'Where's the groundsman's hut? If I had a rifle I'd shoot him now.' — Bill 'Tiger' O'Reilly during England's massive 7-903 at the Oval, 1938

'None of us likes fast bowling, but some of us don't let on.' — Maurice Leyland, 1938

'But [Bill] Woodfull belonged to the old school of captain who played the game by his own principles and refused to have any part of what he considered unfair tactics. If only he'd had a rush of blood to the head and said to his bowlers, "Go give 'em hell," 1932–33 might be remembered as nothing more than just another controversial series. After all, Englishmen weren't so keen on the (short) stuff when [Learie] Constantine bowled it for the West Indies a little while later (in 1933).' — Colin McCool, 1961

'He [Jardine] spoke to me once or twice when I was fielding up at short leg. But the crowd didn't worry him. He got hit on the upper thigh by Bull Alexander [in Sydney] and I've never heard such an outburst of raspberries, catcalls and blurts.' — Leo O'Brien, discussing the final Test of 1932–33

'He is a queer fellow. When he sees a cricket ground with an Australian on it, he goes mad.' — 'Plum' Warner on England's Bodyline captain Douglas Jardine, 1936

'Don't give the bastard a drink — let him die of thirst.' — a Sydney barracker taunts Douglas Jardine, 1932–33

'I felt sorry for the umpire standing at square leg. I stood on his toes a lot; Bill Woodfull told me not to get hit under any circumstances.' — Bill O'Reilly on his method of playing the Bodyliners, 1992

'All Australians are an uneducated and unruly mob.' — Douglas Jardine, 1934

'If I happen to get hit out there Dad, keep Mum from jumping the fence and laying into those Pommy bowlers.' — Stan McCabe on resuming his innings of 187 in the opening Test of the Bodyline series, 1994

'We had to use club bats. We didn't have our own bats. It was Depression days and you couldn't afford to buy a bat. Then you had to break it in. I said to Harold [Larwood]: "Any chance of getting a bat from you when you finish [the 1932–33 tour]? I'll buy a couple from you." "I'll fix it up," he said. And after the last game against Victoria, George Duckworth — he was a good fellow, George — said he wanted to see me in the English room. I went in and he said, "Here's a bat, Leo. Harold said to give it to you. He's not playing today." I said, "How much is it?" He said, "No, you can have it." So we sat down and talked to him. "You know George", I said, "this bodyline can't bloody well last." And he said, "You're right but listen we didn't come 14,000 miles in a boat to give this little bastard a hand. In a fortnight he would have made 500." Don was the one they were after. In England they reckoned that every time he hit a 4, he turned around and grinned at them.' — Leo O'Brien, 1993

'It's always a good idea to aim the first ball right here at the bowler's head. They don't like it. It rattles 'em.' — Charlie Macartney, 1930

'He got 'em on good-uns, he got 'em on bad-uns, he got 'em on sticky-uns … he got 'em all over t'world.' — Wilfred Rhodes on the 'Master', Jack Hobbs, 1955

'Hill overbalanced and I had the bails off sharpish. The square leg umpire Bob Crockett said, "Good God Clem, you're out!" and I replied, "Ay and by a long way."' — E. J. 'Tiger' Smith on stumping Clem Hill in Adelaide, 1911–12

'Sydney Barnes from Staffordshire was the greatest bowler on all wickets this world has ever seen.' — Frank R. Foster, 1930

'They are capital winners out here, but I am afraid that I cannot apply the same adjective to them as losers.' — Lord Harris on Australians, 1888

'Sorry, sir.'

'Don't be sorry Barnes ... you're coming to Australia with us.' — an exchange in 1901 in the Old Trafford nets between a young Sydney Barnes and Archie MacLaren after Barnes had accidentally struck England's captain in the head

'I have met cricketers who maintained that C. T. B. [Charlie] Turner was the best bowler who ever lived. Without quite subscribing to this judgment, I agree that he had few equals and no superior ... he bowled with a most delightful easy swing and run-up to the wicket. His length was impeccable and he would suddenly produce, on the truest wicket, a ball that would break back very quickly ... he always impressed me as a bowler who could be depended upon to do absolutely the right thing at the right moment, and on a sticky wicket I should doubt if he ever made a mistake.' — Archie MacLaren on 'Terror' Turner, 1925

'Bury me 22 yards away from Arthur so I can send him down a ball every now and again.' — Alfred Shaw's last request to be buried beside his old teammate Arthur Shrewsbury, 1902

Bibliography

Annuals

Denis Compton's Annual 1952 (Stanley Paul & Co., London, 1952)

The Cricketer Spring Annual 1940 (W. H. Hillman & Co., London)

The Sporting Globe Cricket Book: Records of the Tests, International & Interstate Games and Players, edited by Ernie Baillie (Herald & Weekly Times, Melbourne)

Wisden Cricketers' Almanac, various years

Books

Atherton, Mike, *Opening Up* (Hodder & Stoughton, London, 2003)

Barry, Paul, *Spun Out: The Shane Warne Story* (Bantam Books, Sydney, 2006)

Booth, Brian & White, Paul, *Booth to Bat: An Autobiography* (Anzea Publishers, Homebush West, 1983)

Border, Allan et al., *Ashes Battles and Bellylaughs* (Swan Publishing, Byron Bay, 1990)

Border, Allan et al., *The Laugh's On Us: Cricket's Finest Tell Their Funniest* (Swan Publishing, Byron Bay, 1989)

Brearley, Mike, *Phoenix from the Ashes: The Story of the England– Australia Series 1981* (Hodder and Stoughton, London, 1982)

Buchanan, John, *If Better is Possible: The Winning Strategies from the Coach of Australia's Most Successful Cricket Team* (Hardie Grant Books, Melbourne, 2007)

Cardus, Neville, *Australian Summer* (Jonathan Cape, London, 1937)

Carr, A. W., *Cricket with the Lid Off* (Hutchinson & Co., London, 1935)

Chalke, Stephen, *At the Heart of English Cricket: The Life and Memories of Geoffrey Howard* (Fairfield Books, Bath, 2001)

D'Oliveira, Basil, *Time to Declare, an Autobiography* (J. M. Dent & Sons, London, 1980)

Denness, Mike, *I Declare* (Arthur Barker Ltd., London, 1977)

Dunne, Steve with Brent Edwards, *Alone in the Middle, an Umpire's Story* (Penguin Books, Auckland, 2003)

Fender, P. G. H., *The Tests of 1930, 17th Australian Team to England* (Faber & Faber, London, 1930)

Fingleton, Jack, *Brightly Fades the Don* (Collins, London, 1949)

Flintoff, Andrew, *Being Freddie: My Story So Far* (Hodder & Stoughton, London, 2006)

Foster, Frank R., *Cricketing Memories* (The London Publishing Co., London, 1930)

Fraser, Angus, *My Tour Diaries, the Real Story of Life on Tour with England* (Headline Book Publishing, London, 1999)

Gilchrist, Adam, *True Colours* (Pan Macmillan Australia, Sydney, 2008)

Gooch, Graham with Frank Keating, *Gooch: My Autobiography* (CollinsWillow, London, 1995)

Haigh, Gideon, *On Warne* (Simon & Schuster, London, 2012)

Harvey, Neil, *My World of Cricket* (Hodder & Stoughton, London, 1963)

Healy, Ian, with Robert Craddock, *Hands and Heals, the Autobiography* (HarperSports, Sydney, 2000)

Hendren, Patsy, *Big Cricket* (Hodder & Stoughton, London, 1934)

Hoggard, Matthew, *Hoggy: Welcome To My World* (HarperSport, London, 2009)

Hussain, Nasser, *Playing with Fire: The Autobiography* (Michael Joseph, an imprint of Penguin Group, London, 2004)

Jenner, Terry with Ken Piesse, *T. J. Over the Top: Cricket, Prison & Warnie* (Information Australia, Melbourne, 1999)

Kippax, Alan with Eric Barbour, *Anti Body-line* (The Sydney & Melbourne Publishing Company, Sydney, 1933)

Knight, James, *Mark Waugh: The Biography* (HarperSports, Sydney, 2002)

Knox, Malcolm, *The Greatest: The Players, the Moments, the Matches 1993–2008* (Hardie Grant Books, Prahran, 2009)

Lemmon, David, *Johnny Won't Hit Today: A Cricketing Biography of J. W. H. T. Douglas* (George Allen & Unwin, London, 1983)

Lloyd, David, *G'day Ya Pommie B ...! And Other Cricket Memories* (The Orion Publishing Group, London, 1992)

Lloyd, David, *The World According to Bumble: Start the Car* (HarperCollins, London, 2010)

Mailey, Arthur, *And Then Came Larwood* (The Bodley Head, Sydney, 1933)

Mallett, Ashley, *Clarrie Grimmett: The Bradman of Spin* (University of Queensland Press, Brisbane, 1993)

Mallett, Ashley, *Rowdy* (Lynton Publications, Blackwood, Adelaide, 1973)

Mallett, Ashley, *Thommo Speaks Out: The Authorised Biography of Jeff Thomson* (Allen & Unwin, Sydney, 2009)

Martin-Jenkins, Christopher, *The Top 100 Cricketers of All Time* (Corinthian Books, London, 2009)

Mason, Ronald, *Warwick Armstrong's Australians* (Epworth Press, London, 1971)

McDonald, Colin, *C.C., the Colin McDonald Story* (Australian Scholarly Publications, Melbourne, 2009)

McFarline, Peter, *A Testing Time* (Hutchinson Group Australia, Melbourne, 1979)

Peel, Mark, *The Last Roman: A Biography of Colin Cowdrey* (Andre Deutsch, London, 1999)

Piesse, Ken & Davis, Charles, *Encyclopaedia of Australian Cricket Players* (New Holland Publishing, Sydney 2012)

Piesse, Ken, *Our Don Bradman* (ABC Books, Sydney, 2008)

Piesse, Ken, *The Complete Shane Warne* (Penguin Viking, Melbourne, 2000)

Piesse, Ken, *Warne, Sultan of Spin* (Modern Publishing Group, Baxter, 1995)

Ramprakash, Mark with Mark Baldwin, *Strictly Me: My Life Under the Spotlight* (Mainstream Publishing, Edinburgh, 2009)

Robinson, Ray, *On Top Down Under: Australia's Cricket Captains* (Cassell Australia, Stanmore, Sydney, 1975)

Rogerson, Sydney, *Wilfred Rhodes, Professional and Gentleman* (Hollis & Carter, London, 1960)

Ryan, Christian, *Golden Boy: Kim Hughes and the Bad Old Days of Australian Cricket* (Allen & Unwin, Sydney, 2009)

Sissons, Ric, *The Terror, Charlie Turner, Australia's Greatest Bowler* (www.cricketbooks.com.au, Mt. Eliza, 2012)

Smith, Terry, *Bedside Book of Cricket Centuries* (Angus & Robertson, Sydney, 1991)

Steele, David with John Morris, *Come in Number 3* (Pelham Books, London, 1977)

Tyson, Frank, *In the Eye of the Typhoon: Recollections of the Marylebone Cricket Club Tour of Australia, 1954–55* (The Parrs Wood Press, Manchester, 2004)

Warner, P. F. 'Plum', *How We Recovered the Ashes* (Chapman & Hall, London, 1904)

Washbrook, Cyril, *Cricket: The Silver Lining* (Sportsguide Publications, London, 1950)

Watson, Willie, *Double International* (Stanley Paul & Co., London, 1956)

Waugh, Steve, *Out of my Comfort Zone: The Autobiography* (Viking, Melbourne, 2005)

Wellings, E. M., *No Ashes for England, the Story of the Australian Tour, 1950–51* (Evans Brothers Ltd., London, 1951)

Wooldridge, Ian, *Travelling Reserve* (Collins, London, 1982)

Wright, Wally, *It's Your Wally Grout, a Grandson's Tale* (www.cricketbooks.com.au, Mt. Eliza, Melbourne, 2011)

Wynne-Thomas, Peter, *Give Me Arthur: A Biography of Arthur Shrewsbury* (Arthur Barker Ltd., London 1985)

Wynne-Thomas, Peter, *Trent Bridge, a History of the Ground to Commemorate the 150th Anniversary (1838–1988)* (Nottinghamshire County Council, Trent Bridge, 1988)

Brochures

World Tour Souvenir Brochure (Australian Cricket Society, Sydney, June 1979)

Cricket '77 (Test & County Cricket Board, London, 1977)

ECB Second Cornhill Test Match Souvenir Program (Lord's, 1997)

Magazines

Australian Cricket (Mason Stewart Publishing, Sydney)

Australian Cricket Tour Guide, edited by Ken Piesse (Emap Australia, Sydney)

Cricketer (Newspress Pty. Ltd., Melbourne)

Pavilion, edited by Ken Piesse (Australian Cricket Society, Melbourne)

The Cricketer (W. H. Hillman & Co., London)

Sporting Life (Associated Newspapers, Sydney)

Newspapers

The Age (Melbourne)

Smith's Weekly (Sydney)

Sunday Herald Sun (Melbourne)

The Sunday Mail (Brisbane)

The Times (London)

Unpublished Interviews

Bob Coleman with Ernie McCormick (1990), held by www.cricketbooks.com.au

Websites

Cricket Victoria (www.cricketvictoria.com.au)

ESPN cricinfo (www.espncricinfo.com)

Ken Piesse Football & Cricket Books (www.cricketbooks.com.au)

Acknowledgements

Having access to a most magnificent picture library lovingly collected over 50 years by my old friend Gordon Vidler has added an eye-catching extra dimension to this book. The majority of the photographs, many I'd never seen before, are from the Vidler Collection, courtesy of Gordon's son Bob and wife Sue.

Other photographs have been provided by the Melbourne Cricket Club's David Studham, Patrick Eagar, David Frith, Peter Bull, Michael Saunders and John Hart.

The extra research provided by Mark Browning, Charles Davis, Stephen Gibbs, Ric Sissons, Colin Clowes, Peter Rhodes, Patrick Skene and others was again wholehearted and considerable while David Frith's encouragement, expertise and advice was, as always, greatly appreciated.

Greg Chappell kindly provided the Foreword, flashing back to his most memorable Ashes Test at Lord's when he made a century on debut at the grand old ground. Another ex-Australian captain Ian Craig added never-before-published first-hand memories of Jim Laker's Test, one in which his Ashes-best 38 was spread over three days and 21 hours! Brian Booth agreed to the publication of his 'thanks but no thanks' letter from Sir Donald Bradman on his omission from the Test team in 1966. Master coach Jack Potter spoke of his first sessions with Ashes-hero-to-be Shane Warne in Adelaide.

My daughter Jessie's production skills, keen eye and command of Photoshop ensured that the very best photographs have been used. It's lovely to share them with you, in this, my 48th cricket book.

Thanks, too, to my lifelong friend Geoff Poulter for his editing skills and advice and the expert team at Five Mile especially Julia, Kyla and Shaun for their unwavering belief in this my fourth book with The Five Mile Press.

— KEN PIESSE

About the Author

It was the Australia Day long weekend and we were staying at Rupertswood, the majestic gold-rush mansion where the Ashes originated way back in 1882. The wonderfully opulent gardens and old cricket ground have long disappeared, but the ambience and vibe of the cricketing mansion is still considerable with its spectacular stained glass entry wall and special 'Ashes' rooms.

Walk into the larger of the two dining rooms with its high ceilings and main table with room for two cricket teams side by side and it's like stepping back in time. The turret is still negotiable by 48 tiny stairs and once there you look out on all of Sunbury with its rolling hills which must have so captivated Ivo Bligh and his visiting Englishmen when they spent Christmas week with Sir William and Lady Clarke.

Rupertswood is now a must-see cricketing treasure for Anglo-Australian cricket lovers. It was fortuitous, I told our hosts, that we were staying overnight for a mate's wedding as this latest Ashes book of mine was nearing completion. It would be a further chance to embrace the direct history of sport's greatest symbol, how an impromptu pick-up game was played and how in the very same dining room in which we sat, Lady Clarke, Melbourne's leading socialite, had one of her staff burn a bail from the game and enclosing it in a tiny clay urn, presented it to the Hon. Ivo Bligh as a memento of the game and their stay.

Months earlier Australia had defeated England in a one-off Test, the London *Sporting Times* running a mock obituary stating that the body of English cricket would be cremated and the ashes taken to Australia.

AT HOME: Author Ken Piesse at historic Rupertswood, 45 minutes north of Melbourne, where Lady Clarke presented MCC captain the Hon. Ivo Bligh with the Ashes urn in 1882.

Rupertswood was always a special place for Sir Ivo and he was to marry Florence Morphy, Lady Clarke's governess, the Ashes urn remaining on the mantelpiece at their country house in Kent until Sir Ivo's death in 1926.

My lovely wife Susan only vaguely knew the story of the Ashes and how important Rupertswood is to the Ashes legend. She laughed as we entered when she saw all the Ashes memorabilia adorning the walls. She had thought she was just going to a wedding.

'There has to be a cricket angle in everything doesn't there,' she said. 'Greg Chappell is right. You are a cricket nuffie.'

Yes, I am.

Journalist, commentator and master storyteller KEN PIESSE is Australian sports most published living author with a rare passion for cricket and football. Ken has written 67 books and edited more than 500 magazines from cricket to football and boating to business.

President of the Australian Cricket Society since 2006 and a member of the Melbourne Cricket Club's Media Hall of Fame, Ken has written a number of books with leading sportsmen from cricketers Max Walker, Terry Jenner and Brad Hodge through to footballers Dermott Brereton, Jason Dunstall and Tony Lockett.

His most recent cricket book for Five Mile Press is *Dynamic Duos: Cricket's Finest Pairs and Partnerships* in which Matthew Hayden in his foreword commented: 'Ken Piesse's service to cricket is truly remarkable. He knows and loves the game like few I know.'

Ken and Susan live on the Mornington Peninsula and have five grown-up children, two pups, two cats and innumerable goldfish. They conduct Ashes tours to England every four years.

Ken can be contacted at kenpiesse@ozemail.com.au or via his website www.cricketbooks.com.au.

Index

Boxes

EST AT LORDS—Acknowledging the cheers when he reached 200 on the way to his record score of 254

THIRD TEST (July 12, 1930)—Running to pavilion at close of play after scoring 334—a world's record for a Test match.

THIRD TEST—Hitting a boundary off Tate while making his world record score in Test Cricket—334 runs.

BRADMAN, record-breaker, in characteristic action.

Bowral, his home town, welcomes its hero on his return from his many triumphs in England.

Going out to bat in Third Test at Leeds. In this match he made the world's record Test match score of 334.

Miss Wendy Palmer congratulates Don on his decision to stay in Australia.

We've kept

Play that amazed England.

Knocking up score of 252 out again rsey.